HEROES, ROGUES AND ECCENTRICS

A Biographical Journey Through Scarborough's Past

by

JACK BINNS

BLACKTHORN PRESS

Blackthorn Press, Blackthorn House
Middleton Rd, Pickering YO18 8AL
United Kingdom

www.blackthornpress.com

ISBN 0 9540535 5 9

© Jack Binns 2002

All rights reserved. No part of this publication may be reproduced, stored in a retrieval system or transmitted, in any form or by any means, electronic, mechanical, photocopying, recording, or otherwise, without the prior permission of the Blackthorn Press.

The cover photograph is of Richard III by an unknown artist and is reproduced by permission of The Royal Collection © 2002 Her Majesty Queen Elizabeth II.

Printed and bound by Antony Rowe Ltd, Eastbourne

PREFACE

"Scarborough has given birth to no person of particular celebrity" was the confident but ill-informed assertion of S R Clarke, author of *The New Yorkshire Gazetteer or Topographical Dictionary* published in 1828; and if Clarke was already wrong then, the list of Scarborough's native celebrities has grown much longer since his time.

William Lacey, the seventeenth-century Jesuit theologian, began his life as William Wolfe, the son of a Scarborough tanner. Sir John Lawson, Admiral of the Red, Dicky Dickinson, the first self-styled governor of the Spa, Thomas Hinderwell, the town's first distinguished historian, and Sir George Cayley, one of the world's most inventive scientific geniuses, were all born in Scarborough long before 1828. Consequently, Lacey, Lawson and Hinderwell were all included in the *Dictionary of National Biography* more than a century ago; Cayley did not appear as one of that dictionary's *Missing Persons* until as late as 1993; but Dickinson is still waiting for appreciative recognition.

Since 1828 many resident Scarborough families with names such as Rowntree, Tindall, Harland Whittaker, Denison, Woodall, Sitwell, Laughton, Plaxton, Boyes and Pindar have produced men and women of outstanding merit, who have made their good influence felt well beyond the boundaries of their home town and county. For example, Sir Edward Harland, who was born at 11 Newborough, which is now part of the site of Marks and Spencer, eventually joined Gustav Wolff to form one of the world's most famous shipbuilding partnerships. Lady Edith Sitwell and her younger brother Sir Sacheverell were both born in the town, Edith at the main family home Wood End, Sacheverell at 5 Belvoir Terrace. Though Charles Laughton is most commonly associated with Hollywood film-making and became an American citizen, he began life in Scarborough's Victoria Hotel in 1899.

Because Scarborough was involved in almost every major episode in English history since 1066, it has been temporary residence and sometimes home for a long succession of monarchs, barons, physicians, engineers, architects, hoteliers, artists, entertainers, invalids, propagandists and charlatans.

Harald Hardrada, king of Norway, was a brief but destructive visitor in September 1066. William le Gros, count of Aumale, was the first to build a fortress on the coastal headland, but it was Henry II who paid for the great keep which 850 years later remains Scarborough's most familiar landscape feature. His son, king John, stayed in his castle at Scarborough no fewer than four times and kept his galley-ships in its harbour; Edward I twice held his court and council at the castle; and the town's best royal patron, Richard III, provisioned and directed his war fleet from there in the summer of 1484.

During seven centuries of military use and occupation Scarborough's formidable royal fortress had many notable governors. Piers Gaveston, Ralph

Eure, Henry Gates and Hugh Cholmley, all included in this collection, represent the worst, the best and the bravest of them all. Of the castle's involuntary inmates, George Fox was probably the most honourable and courageous.

If the castle was the strongest magnet during much of Scarborough's distant past and its harbour was greatly favoured by North Sea fishermen and colliers, the town's more recent role as a health and pleasure resort drew a rich variety of visitors, some of whom made it their permanent residence. Robert Wittie, William Simpson, William Travis, William Harland, John Taylor and Stanley Linton were just a few of the many outstanding doctors who practised medicine in Scarborough. Anne Bronte is perhaps Scarborough's best known invalid visitor and her grave in St Mary's churchyard the most sought after, but Mrs Alice Thornton has been chosen to represent the many thousands of ladies who drank the Spa waters to cure their ailments.

Scarborough has benefited handsomely from the professional skill of gifted architects and civil engineers, both outsiders and home-bred. Joseph Paxton, of Crystal-Palace fame, designed the Spa Grand Hall and planned the Weaponness park estate below Oliver's Mount. Cuthbert Brodrick was responsible for Scarborough's "Wagnerian extravaganza", the monumental Grand Hotel, as well as his other masterpieces at Leeds, the Town Hall and Corn Exchange. South Cliff's St Martin's church was the work of George Bodley, the prolific Gothic stylist. And last but not least in creativity, Thomas Edwin Cooper was another Fellow of the Royal Institute of British Architects who had a hand in the design of the Municipal School, Scarborough College and the Spa bandstand and cafe. He was born in Scarborough's Nelson Street in 1874, the son of a cab proprietor.

Of the great civil engineers who planned and supervised the construction of Scarborough's superb harbour defences, three stand out above the others: William Vincent, who built the spur to the old middle pier on which the lighthouse was placed later; John Smeaton, designer of the colossal east pier as well as the Eddystone lighthouse; and William Chapman, architect of the harbour's final form. However, since there is room here for only one engineer, preference has been given to Harry Smith, who completed the Marine Drive and created most of Scarborough's modern gardens, parks and lakes.

Scarborough's scenic splendours have been inspiration and subject for many talented painters and artists. Though none of them was born in the borough, Francis Place, Francis Nicholson, J M W Turner, Paul Marny, H B Carter, Atkinson Grimshaw and Frank Mason all felt compelled to draw and paint the town's dramatic sea and landscape. Their omission from this collection is argument only that their works are more important and revealing than their biographies. Scarborough's only one famous native artist, Frederic, Lord Leighton, who was born in Brunswick Terrace, left the town at the age of ten and never returned.

Of the multitude of criminal cheats who came to Scarborough to prey on the rich and gullible none achieved greater infamy than the bigamist, forger and impersonator, John Hatfield. His prolonged stay in Newborough gaol qualifies him for a place in this collection. At the opposite extreme, of the well-intentioned men who first came to the town with a moral purpose, none had a greater, long-term influence than Thomas Whittaker. He failed to convert Scarborians to total abstinence but he founded their only surviving daily newspaper in 1882.

The old *Dictionary of National Biography*, published for the most part more than a century ago, was notoriously neglectful of female achievement. Lady Margaret Hoby of Hackness did not finally win recognition as a "missing person" until 1993, more than 350 years after her death. But the other dead ladies in this assembly - all heroines - Thomasin Farrer, Elizabeth Cholmley and Alice Thornton, have yet to receive due recognition in national history. Some might say that Edith Sitwell has already had more literary attention than she deserves, and for this reason her father, Sir George, has been preferred as an outstanding eccentric.

In the context of this lengthy catalogue of Scarborough celebrities, readers might well regard my selection as arbitrary, miserly and even bizarre. Not everyone will agree that my heroes and heroines were truly heroic, my rogues sufficiently villainous, or my eccentrics as odd as others known to them. However, I rejected many candidates because their lives are already well reported in extended biographies and autobiographies or they lived too recently. All of them here are very dead even if in some cases their works are still evident. On the other hand, a positive choice was made only when enough could be found about a life to make it real and interesting. Above all, my purpose was to show that history is about individual people however they spent or misspent their lives.

CONTENTS

1	Kormak and Thorgils	p 1
2	Tostig and Hardrada	p 7
3	Albemarle and Anjou	p 14
4	Lionheart and Lackland	p 21
5	Third Henry and First Edward	p 27
6	The Second Edward and Piers Gaveston	p 35
7	Carters, Accloms, Percys and Sages	p 41
8	The Third Richard	p 50
9	Sir Ralph Eure the Younger	p 58
10	The Gates of Seamer	p 65
11	The Hobys of Hackness	p 74
12	Mr and Mrs Farrer	p 85
13	Sir Hugh and Lady Cholmley	p 93
14	Admiral Lawson	p104
15	George Fox, Peter Hodgson and Scarborough's Quakers	p115
16	Robert Wittie and the doctors	p126
17	Mrs Alice Thornton	p135
18	Dicky Dickinson	p142
19	Thomas Hinderwell	p150
20	John Hatfield	p159
21	Sir George Cayley	p165
22	Thomas Whittaker	p175
23	Baron Albert and the Denisons	p183
24	Sir George Sitwell	p190
25	Joshua Rowntree	p200
26	Harry W Smith	p209
Glossary		p220
Bibliography		p221

1. Kormak and Thorgils:

Founding Fathers or Legendary Pirates?

Until the twentieth century all those who had previously written learnedly about the history of Scarborough, principally Thomas Hinderwell and Joseph Brogden Baker, assumed that its name was English in origin and that it described a fortification on or near a rocky hill. Even as late as 1923 the author of the Scarborough entry in the *Victoria County History of the North Riding of Yorkshire* accepted this traditional, unchallenged explanation; and about the same time the discovery of the remains of a Roman signal station on the headland cliff seemed to add weight to a Saxon origin and meaning of the town's name. However, an alternative explanation of Scarborough's name had already been advanced in 1910 by Professor Moorman of Leeds University in *The Place-Names of the West Riding of Yorkshire*. There the professor of English Language and Literature argued that Scarcroft near Leeds meant 'the field (croft) of Skarthi or Hare-lip', and that Scarborough similarly was 'the fortified place or manor house (burgh, borg, borough) of Skarthi'.

During the 1920s Moorman's hypothesis received scholarly endorsement. In 1925 Professor E.V. Gordon wrote a brief paper in *Acta Philologica Scandinavica*, published in Copenhagen, on the derivation of Flamborough and Scarborough. The origin of both place-names was to be found, he argued, in the nicknames of two tenth-century Icelandic vikings, Kormak and his brother Thorgils Skarthi: Flamborough was Fleinn's stronghold and Scarborough was Skarthi's. Three years later, Dr A.H.Smith, author of *The Place-Names of the North Riding of Yorkshire*, ignored the earlier work of Moorman, but accepted Gordon's proposition without question. Finally, in his introduction to Rowntree's *History of Scarborough* of 1931, M. Black, a distinguished geographer, merely quoted Dr Smith's confident conclusion on Scarborough's name without criticism or even comment. It now appeared indisputable that Scarborough was indeed 'Skarthi's fort' and that the name therefore dated from about 966 when the Icelandic brothers were thought to have been there.

Consequently, in 1966, Scarborough celebrated what was believed to be its one-thousand-year existence and the town's archaeological society published *Scarborough 966-1966*, a collection of essays by six different local authors covering the history of the borough during the previous millennium. In the book's opening chapter, A.L.Binns, then senior lecturer in English language at Hull University, conceded that 'the case for associating the name of Scarborough with Thorgils Skarthi' was 'quite a strong one', but argued that 'the assertion' that Thorgils and his brother Kormak had in fact first built the stronghold at Scarborough was inconclusive, though 'by no means ... unlikely'.

The 'assertion' that the name Scarborough originally derived from Skarthi's fort or stronghold rests on a single reference in the penultimate chapter of *Kormaks Saga*:

> Then the brothers [Kormak and Thorgils] harried in Ireland, Wales, England and Scotland and were thought to be formidable men. They were the first to set up a stronghold called Skardaborg. They raided in Scotland and performed many great deeds and had a great army...

Though Thorgils was not called by his nickname Skarthi in *Kormaks Saga*, in two of his brother's tenth-century poems he is addressed in this form, whereas the saga itself was written down about 1220 in Iceland.

Since 1966 more and more doubt has been cast on the historical veracity of Scandinavian sagas, particularly those composed centuries after the events they describe. Indeed, one *Times Literary Supplement* reviewer recently warned his readers that sagas were no longer cited as historical evidence except by writers who had 'failed to keep up with the scholarly times'. By 2001, he continued, Scandinavian sagas should be regarded as historical novels rather than histories and their authenticity continuously questioned. It was therefore only a matter of time before a contemporary scholar openly challenged the received orthodoxy concerning the origin of Scarborough's name.

Martin Arnold's chapter, 'The Legendary Origins of Scarborough', in the Yorkshire Archaeological Society's paper, *Medieval Scarborough*, was therefore expected, even overdue, when it was published in September 2001. However, it did more than pour cold water over an association between Thorgils Skarthi and Scarborough: it offered an entirely new (or very old) explanation of the town's name. According to Arnold's well-argued thesis, the word 'Scarborough' probably first described what were then perceived by the post-Roman Anglo-Saxon settlers as the principal topographical features of the headland: the element 'sceard' in old English meant gap or notch, and 'burgh' was their term for a fortified place or dwelling. The gap in question was the deep ravine later called the Castle Dykes, and the burgh was the abandoned but still then conspicuous Roman signal and watchtower near the sea cliff. Arnold contended that during the subsequent ninth and tenth centuries Scandinavian invaders adopted and adapted existing Anglo-Saxon place-names to their own language and pronunciation. The soft English 'ch' or 'c' became the hard, Old Norse 'k'. Centuries still later Icelandic writers confused a topographical description with the personal by-name of one of their folk heroes, Thorgils Skarthi. A scar on the landscape then became a cleft in the upper lip or palate of a viking. Finally, and perhaps conclusively, though Kormak certainly existed, there was no corroborative evidence of an historical brother called Thorgils: more than likely he was invented to fill 'the role of a teutonic Sancho Panza to [Kormak's] quixotic hero'.

Though most of *Kormaks Saga* is fictional romance and wishful heroic epic, there can be no doubt that Kormak the poet was historical. During the reign of King Erik of Norway (931-5), Kormak's father, Ogmund, had left his native land there and emigrated to Iceland where his son was born and brought up. After Ogmund's death Kormak left Iceland and served under Harald Greycloak, king of Norway from 961 until 965. In the latter year he took part in Greycloak's expedition to northern Russia. When the king died Kormak formed and led his own roving band of marauding vikings. Since Kormak died in 967 his raid on the Yorkshire coast and brief encampment there probably took place in the winter of 966-7.

It should be emphasized that *Kormaks Saga* described the foundation of a fortification or stronghold, not a settlement or a community, at Scarborough. This makes historical sense. Though archaeological evidence of it has yet to be uncovered, it would be astonishing if as late as 966 there had been no previous and permanent occupation of the headland or the sheltered shore to the south of it since Roman times. However, if there is little or no surviving or discovered trace of Anglo-Saxon dwelling at Scarborough, there is an abundance of Scandinavian place-names and artefacts in the locality.

As early as 876 a great Danish army under Halfdan had entered York unopposed and soon afterwards most of its warriors settled in the area as residential farmers and traders. The richness and variety of Scandinavian names of Danish origin recorded in the Domesday survey two centuries later indicate the density and extent of their colonisation of Yorkshire. The county's three ridings are so-called from the Old Norse word 'thrithing', meaning a third. As in other parts of the Danelaw, smaller administration units which raised local armed forces, levied taxes, and kept law and order were known by the Scandinavian name of wapentake because originally weapons were flourished at outdoor musters to signify consent and support. Scarborough lies near the point where the wapentake of Whitby Strand (shore) to the north met that of Pickering Lythe to the west. Weaponness, the old name for what later became Oliver's Mount, probably owes the first element in its name to such assemblies of local men. After the Danes came the Norwegian immigrants, though in far fewer numbers and this time from Ireland in the west rather than directly from across the North Sea. Of the 649 North Riding settlement names reported in Domesday Book, 223 were of Scandinavian origin and a further 66 Anglo-Scandinavian hybrids.

Not that a surviving English place-name necessarily proves the absence of Scandinavian influence: new viking settlers often left the existing old English names unchanged or modified them only slightly. If Scarborough itself was not originally a Scandinavian settlement, it was closely adjacent to several that certainly were. Scalby, Newby, Throxenby and Osgodby were once Danish farms and are now suburbs of the modern town. Moreover, an Ordnance Survey map of the vicinity of Scarborough reveals not only many Danish -by and -thorpe villages but also a rich concentration of Scandinavian becks, dales, kelds, meres, fosses, fells, gills, slacks and holmes.

Halfdan never settled in Yorkshire. He died in Ireland in 877 and was followed by a succession of self-styled kings at York, Danish and English, Christian and pagan, until the 'kingdom' was seized by Ragnald in 919. Ragnald was Norwegian with strong Irish connections and his reign at York began a period of about 35 years of association, political and commercial, between Dublin and Yorkshire. Finally, after 954, when the last Norwegian king at York, Erik Bloodaxe, was killed at the battle of Stainmore, Yorkshire became an English earldom.

It was during this short 'century' that Scarborough (whatever it might then have been called) could well have been an important link in a long chain of commerce and migration running from Oslo to Dublin via York. Scandinavian place-name endings *thorpe* and *by* run like a string of beads along the northern edge of the Wolds, which were then wooded, and the southern margin of the Vale of Pickering, which was largely marshland. From a group around Malton, with names such as Coneysthorpe and Scagglethorpe, this line stretches all the way to the sea coast at Gristhorpe, only five miles from Scarborough.

As well as place-names there are surviving Scandinavian

sculptures - stone crosses and hog-back tombstones - the distinctive work of Irish-Norse settlers and migrants of the tenth and early eleventh centuries. Again, their locations, notably at Stonegrave, Kirkdale, Kirkbymoorside and Middleton, form a pattern, a line curving northwards around the Howardian Hills, then eastwards towards Scarborough along the southern escarpment of the North Yorkshire moors. Irton, a village just two miles inland from Scarborough, has neither stone warrior cross nor hog-back gravestone, but its name probably means 'farmstead of the Irishman'.

If, therefore, Kormak and his putative brother, Thorgils Skarthi, had beached their longships in South Bay Scarborough in 966 they might have found there a port and a community already in decline. After 954 the trans-Pennine Norse corridor linking the North and Irish seas had been lost to the southern English. A formerly Scandinavian kingdom had been reduced to the status of an English earldom. No doubt there was still some traffic in goods and people between York and Scandinavia, but by 966 it must have diminished to a trickle.

Finally, to put the obvious question: why would the leaders of a sea-roving band of pillagers want to establish a permanent settlement or build even a temporary fort at a place like Scarborough? Why go to so much trouble to protect what could have been no more than a winter camp? Kormak and Thorgils were not potential immigrants. They had forsaken farming in Iceland for the itinerant life of mercenaries and freebooters. If they intended to stay ashore their purposes were only to repair their boats, replenish their provisions with local plunder, and wait for the weather to improve. They did not hope to become fishermen. Had they constructed a fort it would have been no more than a timber stockade and earth ditch close to their longships drawn up on the sands. Above them the headland afforded no shelter from winter winds; after 600 years the Roman signal station, now perilously near the seacliff edge, would have been no more than a pile of rubble.

The hill overlooking Scarborough from the south-west is now called Oliver's Mount. For centuries it was known as Weaponness, and its steep, wooded slopes and flat top, covering more than 400 acres, was the town's chief source of fuel and animal pasture. However, in 1770, a survey map of Yorkshire, engraved by Thomas Jeffrey, showed Weaponness as 'Oliver's Hill'. Subsequently, this new name, or variants of it, gradually displaced the old one. By 1811, in his second edition of *The History and Antiquities of Scarborough*, Thomas Hinderwell conceded that the modern name for what had been Weaponness was

'Mount-Oliver', but also declared loftily that the new description derived from 'a mistaken opinion that Cromwell erected batteries here against the Castle during the siege in 1644-5'. Though Oliver's Mount eventually won the day, as late as 1841 'Olive Mount', suggesting a different provenance from that assumed by Hinderwell, was still in use.

Of course, Hinderwell was right: Oliver Cromwell had never set foot in Scarborough, either in 1645 during the first Civil-War siege there, or in 1648, at the time of the second siege of the town and castle. Furthermore, no Parliamentarian commander would even have considered dragging cannon up the gradients of Weaponness, or expect artillery fire from there to reach even the town let alone the castle walls. Nevertheless, public ignorance and popular legend made sure that Weaponness gave way to Oliver Cromwell. Perhaps this also explains why a Civil-War earthwork on the north side of Peasholm Gap was labelled 'Oliver's Battery' on Scalby's enclosure map dated 1777. More than a century after his death it seems that the Lord Protector had become more mythological than historical: all Civil-War ruins were now his responsibility and every Civil-War fort his personal creation.

In the case of 'Skarthi's burg' a similar mistaken attribution might have taken place. That a well-known North Sea port was thought to have been named originally after an Icelandic pirate who had merely wintered there more than two hundred years earlier was probably the product of wishful fantasy. We do not know whether Thorgils Skarthi was particularly eccentric; his brother Kormak thought he was a hero; by our standards he was undoubtedly a rogue. Yet even if he was ever more than a fanciful fiction he did not deserve to have Scarborough named after him.

2. Tostig and Hardrada

Nearly every schoolboy and schoolgirl knows that King Harold of England lost his life at the battle of Hastings in 1066; far fewer of them know that three weeks earlier he had annihilated another invading army of Northmen at Stamford Bridge in Yorkshire; and probably none at all is aware that a fortnight before that those same Northmen had destroyed Scarborough and wiped out its population. The Northmen who burned Scarborough to ashes were led by the Norwegian king, Harald Sigurdsson, better remembered as Hardrada, the Ruthless, and his ally, Tostig Godwinsson, formerly the Earl of Northumbria, and younger brother of King Harold II of England.

Harald Sigurdsson was about 50-years-old by 1066 and had been sole king of Norway for the past 19 years. As a 15-year-old boy he had been forced to flee from his own country after his half-brother, King Olaf, was killed in a civil war. With his band of followers, Prince Harald sailed first to Novgorod, the city-state in Russia founded by vikings, and then from there eventually to Constantinople. Here the young Norwegian prince had taken mercenary service in the Varangian guard of the Empress Zoe. For the next ten years Harald built up a reputation second to none as a fearless, audacious and cunning military leader. Raiding deep into the Mediterranean he brought back mountains of booty from Italy, Sicily, Asia Minor and Palestine. According to his biographer, Snorri Sturluson, he captured no fewer than 80 towns, some by direct assault, others by clever deception. One walled town he is alleged to have set on fire by attaching lighted shavings of fir soaked in sulphur and wax to the feathers of sparrows; another stronghold fell to him after he had feigned death and the defenders foolishly allowed his empty coffin to be escorted through their gates; and a third fortress was literally undermined by a tunnel dug beneath its walls.

During his ten-year absence much had changed in Harald's homeland. His dead half-brother, once called Olaf the Thick, had become Olaf the Holy, since his corpse had refused to decompose and his hair and nails had to be cut regularly. Olaf's son, Magnus, had become king of Norway. On his way, collecting his great hoard of plunder, which he had been careful to store at Novgorod, Harold returned home to negotiate a treaty with his half-nephew. The two agreed to share equally Harald's treasure and Magnus's kingdom. When Magnus died in 1047, Harald was crowned sole king of Norway.

Not content with one kingdom, Harald continued to raid and

ravage neighbouring areas. Where once he had been the most feared warrior in the Mediterranean, now he became the most feared in northern Europe. Even his own subjects lived in terror of him: no one dare disagree with him. Norwegian farmers who failed to pay their taxes were maimed, killed or deprived of all their land and goods. Even by harsh viking standards, Harald was considered an exceptionally brutal and greedy tyrant. Only Icelanders were well treated by him.

When Harald failed to conquer Denmark or acquire it by treaty, every summer he descended on its people, killing, burning and pillaging without mercy. However, in January 1066, news of the death of the king of England, Edward the Confessor, diverted Harald's insatiable ambition in a new direction. Edward had no children and no natural successor. Harald's claim on the English throne was tenuous but no doubt sufficient for him to justify to himself if no one else. In 1038 or 1039 king Magnus of Norway had made a treaty with Harthacnut, King of Denmark and future king of England, that whoever lived longer would inherit the other's titles. Harthacnut died in 1042, leaving Magnus with a claim on England as well as Denmark. Through his dead half-nephew, Hardrada now staked his claim to the Confessor's crown.

Tostig was the third son of Godwin, Earl of Wessex, the most powerful lord in England after the king, and some said even more powerful than the king himself. Since the succession of Edward the Confessor in 1042, the house of Godwin had gradually tightened its control on the whole kingdom. Edith, the eldest daughter, was Edward's wife and queen. Sweyn, the eldest Godwinsson, had gone off to the Holy Land on pilgrimage and never returned, but Harold, second son and now heir, was made Earl of East Anglia, and in 1053, at the age of 31, succeeded his father as Earl of Wessex. Two years later, Tostig was appointed Earl of Northumbria.

Northumbria was notoriously feud-ridden and lawless. Tostig might be resented there as a Saxon outsider in a largely Scandinavian territory, but an internal choice might well have intensified vendettas and family rivalries. Besides, Tostig was much favoured by his sister Edith and Edward, his brother-in-law. Little is known for certain of Tostig as a person: all but one of the Scandinavian sagas depict him as honourable and courageous, whereas English sources either ignore or demonise him. The story of how he murdered some of his brother Harold's servants, pickled their parts, and then invited Harold to dine on them is almost definitely apocryphal, but it does illustrate the reputation for cruelty and malice he acquired.

There seems to be little doubt that Tostig was short-tempered and arrogant: on a visit to Rome he was said to have spoken impolitely to the Pope and threatened him with the stoppage of Peter's Pence from England. However, in the pursuit of criminals the earl was especially effective. According to a doubtless exaggerated account, whereas no traveller was safe from robbers in his predecessor's time, during Tostig's rule it was possible to cross the earldom from one end to the other with a bag of gold in perfect safety.

In 1064 Tostig went too far. Though they had come to him with the assurance of sworn promises of safe conduct, Gamel, son of Orm, and Ulf, son of Dolfin, were treacherously murdered in Tostig's own palace at York. At Christmas that year another Northumbrian thegn, Gospatrick, was killed on Tostig's orders at the earl's court. After the harvest of 1065, a rebellion against Tostig broke out in Yorkshire. Tostig was in the south, hunting with his brother-in-law. At a tumultuous gathering in York, Tostig was unanimously declared outlaw; his home there was attacked and ransacked; and two hundred of his guard and servants were butchered. Morcar, brother of Edwin, Earl of Mercia, was declared Tostig's successor. Determined to expel Tostig from England, not just Northumbria, the rebels advanced as far south as Northampton and even plundered his estate in Huntingdon.

The revolt against Tostig had split the kingdom in two. On one side, Morcar and Edwin controlled the earldoms of Northumbria and Mercia, and on the other Harold Godwinsson and Edward could count on the southern half of Wessex and East Anglia. However, the northerners had no quarrel with the King or Harold: all they demanded was Tostig's expulsion and the substitution of one of their own. Whatever their attitude to Tostig, Edward and Harold were given no real choice: Tostig had to go abroad or the kingdom would surely be torn apart by civil war. At Oxford, on 27 October 1065, the King's council confirmed Morcar's election and Tostig's outlawry. Angry and bitter, Tostig took his wife Judith and their children to find refuge with his father-in-law, Count Baldwin of Flanders. But he would not accept his fate: he was determined to take revenge on the brother who had betrayed him and the people who had rejected him.

If Tostig hoped that the death of the Confessor and the succession of his brother Harold would be followed by an invitation to return to England and his former estates there he was soon disappointed. Harold was crowned king and Morcar remained earl of Northumbria. Tostig now knew that he could never recover his lost power and possessions with the few followers he had taken into exile: he had to find allies. After first his father-in-law and then King Sweyn of Denmark had refused to help him, Tostig went to Oslo to see Hardrada. Together they came to a decision to invade England that summer. Tostig promised Harald that he could deliver the support of many of the English once the Norwegians had landed.

According to Snorri Sturluson, Hardrada recruited half the fighting men of his kingdom, and in more than 200 ships they crossed the sea to Orkney via Shetland. At Orkney they were joined by local men and warriors from Iceland, the Hebrides, Ireland and Scotland. Further south, at the mouth of the Tyne, they rendezvoused with Tostig. Now there were said to be close on 9,000 men in 300 ships - one of the most formidable armadas ever seen in northern Europe. Hardrada had left his queen and daughters behind in Orkney, but with him was his son Olaf and an enormous treasury of gold.

Blown by a strong northerly wind the fleet pressed southwards. To assert his dominance and blood his warriors Hardrada paused briefly to land in Cleveland and harry the people there. There was no resistance. Next they came to Scarborough. Again no resistance was expected. Tostig told the king that when Earl of Northumbria he had been lord in this vicinity, that it had strong Scandinavian connections, and that they were sure to be welcomed if they came ashore. Tostig was wrong: despite the odds, the men of Scarborough would not submit to the invaders. However, the town must have been well defended because, in the words of Sturluson, Hardrada was forced to resort to incendiary methods.

> He climbed up on to the rock that stands there, and had a huge bonfire built on top of it and set it alight. When the pyre was blazing they used long pitchforks to hurl the burning faggots into the town below. One after another the houses caught fire until the town was entirely destroyed. The Norwegians killed a great number of people there and seized all the booty they could lay their hands on. The English had no choice but to submit: if they wanted to stay alive they had to give in to King Harald. In this way wherever he went he subdued the country.

Against the record of Hardrada during the previous 35 years his treatment of Scarborough and its inhabitants was neither unexpected nor exceptional: he had already left a trail of terror and slaughter from Palestine to the Faeroes. Resistance to Harald was nearly always foolhardy and often fatal.

Four sagas refer to the destruction of Scarborough by fire, though only Snorri Sturluson's *Heimskringla* provides details of Hardrada's tactics. Still, whatever means used by the Norwegians, it seems fairly certain that the holocaust suffered by the town in September 1066 explains its absence from Domesday Book twenty years later. Though the coastal region of north Yorkshire suffered further plundering raids by the Scots in 1070 and the Danes in 1075, the devaluation and depopulation recorded in the Domesday census of 1086 were probably due mainly to Hardrada's unwelcome visit. Tostig's extensive manor of Falsgrave, which included 21 communities and farmsteads as far north as Staintondale, as far south as Filey, and as far west as Ruston, had once provided homes and livelihoods for more than 100 families of free men, but by 1086 it supported only half that number, and most of them were poor serfs and cottagers. In 1066 the manor of Falsgrave was worth £56 a year in taxable income; by 1086 William the Conqueror could not expect to raise more than 30 shillings from it.

Continuing southwards down the Yorkshire coast, Hardrada next came ashore in Holderness where he defeated a local force raised to do battle with him. From there the great armada rounded Spurn Head and sailed up the Humber and then up the river Ouse as far as Riccall, three miles south of its junction with the Wharfe and ten miles below the city of York. Leaving part of his army under Prince Olaf to guard the ships, Hardrada disembarked and advanced on York. The earls Morcar of Northumbria and his brother Edwin of Mercia came out of the city to meet the Norwegian host and a ferocious battle then occurred at Fulford Gate. There, just two miles south of York, on Wednesday, 20 September, the Vigil of St Matthew, a great slaughter took place. Both sides suffered grievous losses, but at the end of the day the Northumbrians were vanquished and York lay open to the mercy of the invaders.

What happened next is not entirely clear: it seems that Hardrada decided not to enter and plunder York, presumably because he now assumed that it would become his own city where he could spend the next winter. Instead, he moved his depleted and battle-weary army northwards to Stamford Bridge at a crossing of the river Derwent. There he intended to receive hostages and supplies from the Wolds and the Vale of Pickering. But on Monday, 25 September, the Norsemen were taken completely by surprise when King Harold appeared from the direction of York with a formidable army of foot soldiers, 3,000 royal housecarls, professional fighting men, reinforced with an equal number of militia recruited on the way from London. Tostig recommended to Hardrada that

11

they retreat down the Derwent to their ships and Olaf's men, but the Norwegian replied that he would stand, fight and die there if necessary. His pride would not allow him to run away from the English. In that case, said Tostig, he too would stay there and fight to the end.

Before the battle began King Harold offered his brother Tostig peace and the whole of Northumbria - a third of his kingdom. In reply, Tostig wanted to know what his brother had to offer his ally Harald Sigurdsson. 'No more than seven feet of English ground', answered Harold, 'since I understand that he is taller than other men.' With that defiant gesture the slaughter commenced and continued that hot afternoon. As at Fulford, five days earlier, no quarter was offered or asked for. Both sides fought to bloody exhaustion. When Harald, the battle-scarred veteran fell, next to his royal standard, the 'Landwaster', Tostig still refused to give in, until he too was cut down in the mêlée. By the time that Eystein Orri arrived with reinforcements from the ships, it was too late to save the day: the Norsemen were routed. Of the 300 longships that had brought Hardrada's army to Yorkshire, only 24 were enough to carry the survivors back home. Three days after the battle of Stamford Bridge, while the English were still binding their wounds and burying the dead, William, Duke of Normandy, landed unopposed on the coast of Sussex, 250 miles away.

The invasion of Yorkshire in 1066 by Hardrada and Tostig had momentous significance: it was the last Scandinavian attempt to conquer the country. Further incursions from the north were exercises in plunder not conquest. But for Hardrada, William, Duke of Normandy, might never have become William the Conqueror. If Harold Godwinsson had not been compelled to hurry north, commit his seasoned troops at Stamford Bridge, and then force-ride the survivors another 250 miles back to Sussex, the Normans might never have reached Hastings. Harold would have been on the shore at Pevensey to meet them. The history of the North might also have been different: its losses in leaders and fighting men at Fulford and Stamford Bridge were colossal; and though Northumbrians refused to accept the decision at Hastings, after Hardrada's campaign they lacked the strength to hold out against William and his Normans.

One of the local consequences of Hardrada's invasion was the temporary disappearance of Scarborough. Though now it became the property of King William, the manor of Falsgrave and its far-flung dependencies survived; but it took another three generations before the rebirth of a seashore community under the shelter of the rocky headland with the name of 'Skarthi's burg'.

Tostig's fatal error was to assume that he had the support of the Northumbrians and in particular the farmers and townsmen who lived in what had been his manor and soke of Falsgrave. He and Hardrada also assumed - wrongly as events proved - that because Yorkshire had once been a Scandinavian kingdom and was densely populated by people of Norwegian and Danish origin they would receive a warm welcome when they landed there. Alternatively, having harried Cleveland and made an example of Scarborough, Hardrada probably expected Yorkshiremen to be cowed into submission. Again, he was mistaken. Harold Godwinsson might not have attracted enthusiastic loyalty north of the Humber, yet he was clearly far more welcome than Tostig, who was remembered there with fear and loathing, and Hardrada, who was regarded with no more affection than a hungry wolf.

The native attitude to Hardrada's would-be conquerors is well illustrated by a story told by Snorri Sturluson in his saga. After the disaster at Stamford Bridge, Harald's marshal, Styrkar, was one of the few survivors who managed to escape. He found a loose horse and rode away from the battlefield. As the night drew in a cold wind blew over the Wolds and Styrkar, who was wearing only a shirt and a helmet, soon began to feel the chill after the heat of the day and the battle. However, he soon met a cart-driver who was dressed in a fur-lined leather coat.

Styrkar asked the peasant to sell him his coat but he refused saying, 'Not to you: you're a Norwegian, I can tell that from your speech.' 'And if I were a Norwegian, what would you do about it?', asked Styrkar. 'Why I would kill you', said the carter, 'but unfortunately I have no weapon with me.'

'Then since you cannot kill me,' said Styrkar, 'I must kill you.' And then Styrkar swung his sword at the man's neck, sliced off his head, took his warm coat, and rode off down to the ships.

The carter was probably descended from Scandinavian settlers and recognised a Norwegian by his language, but by 1066 he thought of himself as a native Englishman and Styrkar as a foreign enemy.

3. Albemarle and Anjou

About half way between Amiens and Rouen in French Normandy, tucked away in the valley of the river Bresle, lies the old town of Aumale. On a hill that separates Scarborough's Victoria Road from Westborough, a semi-circle of Victorian houses forms what is called Albemarle Crescent. On the face of it there seems to be no connection between the two, but in fact Aumale and Albemarle are alternative, inter-changeable names for the same place. What links an historic town in Normandy with Britain's oldest seaside resort is the name William le Gros, Lord of Holderness, Earl of York and Albemarle, who was the first to build a castle on the headland and possibly the refounder of the settlement of 'Scardeburg' below it. The first to hold the title of Earl of Albemarle, William le Gros, should not be confused with the eighteen-year-old Arnold Joost van Keppel, who in 1688 arrived in England from Holland as the catamite of William III and was subsequently rewarded with the revived earldom of Albemarle. His descendant, the tenth Earl, still holds the title.

William the Fat was the grand nephew of William the Conqueror. His grandfather, Odo of Champagne, had been married to the Conqueror's sister, Adela or Adelaide. According to one tradition, after 1066 the Conqueror had agreed to give his brother-in-law the County of Aumale and the lordship of Holderness in Yorkshire on condition that Odo acted as a standard bearer and provided twelve knights in any military campaign. However, Odo found Holderness so infertile and wet that he asked for land that would grow wheat, not just oats; and so William also granted him the lordship of Bytham in Lincolnshire. Odo's son, Stephen of Aumale, was therefore able to feed his own son, William, a growing boy, with bread made from wheat.

After Henry I died in 1135 without leaving a legitimate male heir (he had at least 19 illegitimate children), civil war broke out between followers of the two main contenders for the crown of England. On one side was Henry's daughter, Matilda, married to Geoffrey, Count of Anjou, and on the other, Henry's nephew, Stephen, Count of Blois and Champagne. Stephen was crowned king but Matilda and her supporters refused to accept him as sovereign.

One of the barons who rallied behind Stephen was William le Gros. As a young man he had won a reputation for vigour, strength and military prowess, and soon after his coronation Stephen had made him custodian of all the royal lands in Yorkshire. It was therefore natural that, in Stephen's absence in the south, William should command his army in the north. In August 1138 Matilda's most powerful ally, King David of Scotland, crossed the Tees with a huge marauding army and began to plunder and terrorise Yorkshire.

Led by William, the Yorkshire barons assembled at York with their fighting men. Amongst them was Earl Walter de Gant, Lord of Bridlington, Walter Espec of Helmsley, William de Percy of Whitby, Robert de Stuteville of Kirkbymoorside, and Roger de Mowbray of Thirsk, who alone could call on the services of 140 knights. After they had fasted for three days, the aged archbishop Thurstan of York gave them absolution and his benediction. He was too feeble to go into battle with them but he sent his archdeacon and at least one bishop. A great ship's mast surmounted by a silver cross was set up on a wheeled cart to which were also attached the banners of St Peter of York, St John of Beverley and St Wilfrid of Ripon. This was no less than an organised crusade of Yorkshiremen and saints against the Scots, 'more barbarous than any race of pagans'.

The two hosts came face to face on Cowton Moor, north of Northallerton, early in the morning of 22 August 1138. The Picts of Galloway charged the English men-at-arms in the front line, but broke against the 'iron wall' of their linked shields and under the hail of arrows from bowmen behind them. The Scots were routed; those who could fled back northwards, but the slaughter was enormous. The English lost only one leading knight and a small number of soldiers. There were no more Scottish invasions of Yorkshire during the remainder of Stephen's reign.

The battle of the Standard, as this victory was called, confirmed William's power in Yorkshire. Stephen rewarded him with the new title of Earl of York, but according to contemporary chroniclers, 'he ruled like a king' in the county. His letters were addressed to 'his steward and his sheriff and all his barons and ministers, French and English' in terms very similar to those of King Stephen. None of the other northern barons dare cross him. After William Fossard had seduced his sister and then fled abroad, in revenge le Gros destroyed his motte and bailey castle at Mount Ferrant, near Birdsall on the Wolds, and gave its timber to his newly-founded abbey at Meaux.

The earth and timber, motte and bailey castles were characteristic of this time of troubles; every baron had at least one. As yet the stone castle was beyond the means of even the most ambitious lord. The only towers of stone in the kingdom were in London and Colchester, both the work of William the Conqueror. Apart from Alan the Red's hall at Richmond all the strongholds in Yorkshire were of earth, timber and

15

thatch. Most of the mottes or mounds were man-made piles of soil, timber and rubble. William the Conqueror had raised two such artificial mounds crowned with wooden towers at York after quelling a rebellion there in 1069. Henry I had a deep ditch and an earth mound piled up inside it at Pickering when in 1106 he had chosen it as administrative centre for his new royal forest. However solidly constructed, such earth mounds were unable to bear the weight of heavy stone towers, or donjons as the Normans called them.

William le Gros had command of several motte and bailey castles. Chief among them was at Skipsea in Holderness where Drew de Bevrere's mound, nearly fifty feet high, rose abruptly from the surrounding flat countryside. Thanks to his wardship of the lands of other Yorkshire barons, such as de Roos, Brus and Fossard, he also controlled castles in other parts of the county such as Eskdale, Cleveland and the Wolds; but unlike all these, the castle at Scarborough was his own creation.

All that we know about Albemarle's castle at Scarborough is derived from a single source — William of Newburgh's chronicle which he called 'Historia Rerum Anglicarum', or a History of English Events. William was a monk who was born at Bridlington about 1135 and lived all his adult life in Newburgh Priory near Coxwold. His history was written down in the last years of his life, between 1197 and 1199, at the end of the reign of Richard Lionheart. Though William probably never ventured often from his priory and almost certainly never visited Scarborough, he had privileged access to the libraries of the neighbouring monasteries of Rievaulx and Byland as well as his own, and he must have listened to many travellers who had stayed as guests at Newburgh.

William's chronicle started in 1066 with the Norman conquest of England, but it provides the best detail for events in the north during the reigns of Stephen (1135-54) and his successor, Henry II (1154-89). The following is a modern translation of what he wrote in Latin about Scarborough:

> A rock of wonderful height and extent, and inaccessible because of the steep cliffs on almost every side of it, stands into the sea, which nearly surrounds it except at one point on the west where it is joined to the land by a narrow promontory. On the top of this headland is a broad grassy plain, sixty acres or more, and a little well of water springing from the rock. At the entrance, which is difficult to reach, stands a stately tower.

The town below the headland entrance spreads north and south of it and westwards where it is defended by a wall; on the east, however, it is protected by the castle rock and on both sides by the sea. William, surnamed le Gros, Earl of Albemarle and Holderness, observing this place to be well situated for a castle, increased its natural strength at great expense by enclosing the headland with a wall and building a tower at the entrance. But this tower was so decayed and fallen through age that King Henry the Second ordered a great and noble castle to be raised on the same site.

Clearly, William of Newburgh's description is marred by several errors and misunderstandings. The headland plain might have been sixteen acres in area, but it could never have been sixty acres; Scarborough is open to the sea on its eastern side, and sheltered from the north by castle hill; and at this time it could not have been more than a small fishing village: it would be many centuries yet before it spread north of the headland. In these respects the chronicler had been misinformed by travellers who told tall tales.

On the other hand, the 'little well of water springing from the rock' probably refers to what came to be called the Well of Our Lady, a natural source of surface water near the sea cliff which explains the location of the Roman watchtower and its successor there, a Christian chapel built about 1000 AD and destroyed by Hardrada in 1066. Also, though the headland rock is not nearly surrounded by sea, it does have precipitous cliffs and is accessible only from the west by a narrow ridge of land.

So what had William le Gros actually built on this rocky headland jutting into the sea? Though Albemarle might have been 'more truly a king than his master' in Yorkshire, he did not have a king's resources. The castle he had built at Scarborough was on land that formed the waste of the royal manor of Falsgrave, but in effect it was his castle, not Stephen's. The site was indeed well chosen for its natural strength. There was no need to throw up an artificial mound and on three sides the cliffs presented an insuperable climb to all but the most determined and athletic. Even if William had commanded the means to build a circumference wall long enough to 'enclose all that plain upon the rock' such colossal expense would have been unnecessary: the sea cliff and that overlooking the holms to the north were sufficient deterrent. All that William had to do was to construct a tower on the highest point of the headland which conveniently overlooked and barred the entrance to the plain from the west. No doubt he also dug a ring ditch around the tower and put up a drawbridge across the natural dyke which cuts across the narrow entry from the west.

Many commentators have assumed that Albemarle's tower and a perimeter wall around it were of stone. The assumption is no more and no better than that. For all his exaggeration William of Newburgh wrote nothing of a stone tower or a masonry wall. Of Albemarle's keep he wrote only that it was so decayed and weakened by the passage of time that Henry II replaced it with a grander one of his own. Since Henry's first recorded expenditure on the castle at Scarborough was in the financial year beginning Michaelmas 1157 and William's tower was unlikely to pre-date 1138, this means that it was only twenty years old when it was 'decayed and fallen through age'. In other words it was either a jerry-built stone keep or one made of wood. And if Albemarle's tower was of timber then his walls were probably no more than a stout palisade wooden fence standing on an earth bank inside a ring ditch closely surrounding it.

As for Scarborough town, there is no evidence of any kind that it was re-founded during Albemarle's time, though it does seem likely that there were some people living there before 1154. All five boroughs in Yorkshire noted by the Domesday clerks — York, Pontefract, Tickhill, Pocklington and Bridlington — were closely related to adjacent castles, though as early as 1086 only York was a recognisable town; the other four were mere villages with freemen burgesses who had the right to hold a weekly market. The neighbouring castle was their guardian and in return they supplied it with labour and provisions. At Skipsea there was a small cluster of houses on the south side of Albemarle's castle, and something like the same was the situation at Scarborough. At the latter, the earliest settlement was probably alongside a stream, subsequently called the Damyot, which ran out into South Bay. All that is known for certain is that William le Gros rebuilt the chapel of St Catherine on the headland to serve his castle up there.

The death of King Stephen and the peaceful succession of Matilda's son, Henry, Count of Anjou, to the English throne at the end of 1154 changed everything for William le Gros, as it did for other barons who had ruled like petty monarchs in their own little kingdoms. None of these English lords had the power to withstand Henry, now arguably the most formidable ruler in western Europe, since he was also Duke of Normandy, inherited from his mother, and lord of Aquitaine, by reason of his marriage to the duchess Eleanor.

Henry's immediate purpose in England was to recover lands lost by the Crown, and eliminate the independent power of the magnates by destroying their unlicensed castles and reasserting royal authority over their territories. Within a month of his coronation Henry marched north to York. Wisely and reluctantly William le Gros submitted to him, surrendering the royal properties which included the manor of Falsgrave and his stronghold at Scarborough. The earldom of York was allowed to lapse. In compensation, William received the valuable manor of Driffield, though it is possible that the king also promised to restore to him the county of Aumale and his family lands in Normandy which had been lost when Henry's father, Geoffrey of Anjou, overran the duchy in 1144. Henry treated William with due respect: after all, the earl was related to the king of France and by marriage to the royal house of Scotland. In effect, William, who was now nearly sixty years old, was being compelled to retire honourably. Henry was only twenty-one-years-old.

If William le Gros had a professional eye for the best castle sites, so had Henry the Second. Instead of demolishing and abandoning Albemarle's stronghold at Scarborough, the king now chose the place for one of his principal castles. During the next thirty years Henry's expenditure on his castle at Scarborough was exceeded only by that spent on those at Dover, Newcastle, Nottingham, Orford, Winchester and Windsor. Altogether, between 1157 and 1187, the Pipe Rolls, or annual accounts sent by the sheriff of Yorkshire to the Exchequer in London, record that £682 15s. 3d. was spent on Scarborough castle. Most of that money was put to building Henry's 'stately tower', averaging nearly a hundred pounds a year in six consecutive years from 1158 to 1164.

Henry's money was well invested. The great square stone keep of three storeys rising to a height of about one hundred feet has now survived nearly eight and a half centuries of wind, rain and frost. Only the heaviest cannon at the time, fired repeatedly at point-blank range, was able to bring down its west wall in 1645. Since then it has hardly changed. Henry's monument of royal power and wealth stands today as proudly as ever to form Scarborough's most familiar and oldest architectural feature. If Albemarle ever saw Henry's gigantic stone tower, built on the site of his poorer predecessor, he must have marvelled at its size and strength. When he finally died at Bytham castle in Lincolnshire at the age of 83 in 1179, Henry's splendid new castle at Scarborough was finished.

Also by that time Scarborough had been re-founded as a royal borough. Between 1155 and 1163, both years when Henry was at York, he granted to the burgesses of the town the same customs, liberties and privileges already enjoyed by the citizens of York. In return, each house in Scarborough with its gable towards the street would pay four pence yearly and those lengthways to the street six pence a year to the Crown. This came to be known as the gablage tax. From Michaelmas 1163 the sheriff of Yorkshire began to account for a new income to the Crown of £20 a year, described as 'the farm of Scarborough'. By 1169 the farm had risen to £30 a year, and by 1172 to £33, suggesting that the town was growing rapidly in population and prosperity. By the end of Henry's reign, there are references to Scarborough merchants trading overseas in wool, to Scarborough's weavers, to Roger the vintner, and to officers called reeves. After the holocaust of 1066, Scarborough's re-birth owed something to William le Gros but much more to Henry the Second, the first of the Angevin kings of England.

4. Lionheart and Lackland

On 12 December 1189, Richard the First sailed from Dover to Flanders on the initial stage of his long, eventful journey to Palestine — a journey that in history came to be known as the Third Crusade — to rescue Jerusalem from the possession of the Moslem Saracens. The previous day at Dover Richard sealed a royal charter which granted the revenues of 'the church of Scarborough…in pure and perpetual alms to the abbot of Citeaux, to find provision for the abbots at the time of the general chapter'. In this curious way, a link was forged between Scarborough and a French house of monks which was to last more than two centuries.

Richard's tomb in France

Richard's purposes were plain enough. Explicitly the gift was made for the health of his soul and for those of his dead father, Henry II, and his living mother, Queen Eleanor of Aquitaine. In immediate practical terms however, Richard was providing himself and his army with favoured hospitality as it passed across France on its long, land route to the port of Marseilles. By 1189 the mother house of Citeaux already had 491 'children' and most of these monasteries were in France. Given Richard's record and his subsequent behaviour, it seems that he was more likely to be motivated by material considerations than by piety. The price paid by Richard was a bargain for him: the income of St Mary's church at Scarborough at this time was between 100 and 120 silver marks, that is between £66 and £80, a year. Though the money was earmarked to pay the expenses of the triennial general chapter at Citeaux which lasted three days, a second charter of 1198 guaranteed that any surplus left over when these expenses were met was to be kept by the Cistercians. Whether the arrangement was a bargain for the people of Scarborough is less certain.

The sources of St Mary's revenue were described in the original charter of 1189. They included all the gifts and offerings made to the church and its chapels, the personal services paid by servants in kind and in cash, rents from its properties in the town, and, above all, tithes from the parish. The tithe particularly mentioned in Richard's charter is that of

'Droguedrave', that is the codfish caught in the North Sea off the Dogger Bank.

The fish tithe, literally one fish in every ten landed at Scarborough, was clearly the most valuable of all 'the tithings of land and sea', since apart from the codfish there was the enormous annual harvest of herring. Only when a new revised agreement was drawn up in 1251 between the burgesses and the abbot of Citeaux do the details of the fish tithe become apparent. Until 1251 all Scarborough's fishermen were obliged to bring their tithe of fish, fresh or salted, to St Mary's church door. Afterwards only the pence received for the sale of the fish tithe was to be brought to the altar. The fish were to be delivered on the harbour quay, except for Dogger Bank cod which was still carried to the altar 'within a month of catching'. After 1251 fishermen paid a tithe of every fortieth Dogger Bank catch and a twentieth of herring and other fish. Even the wages of the servants of fishermen were tithed every Lent.

The second charter of 1198 confirmed that Richard's grant covered more than mere revenues: it gave the Cistercian monks a virtual monopoly of the religious institutions and life of Scarborough, including St Catherine's castle chapel on the headland. By this time three other churches — of the Holy Sepulchre, St Thomas and St Nicholas — already existed in or just outside the town, but no new churches, chapels or altars could be established without the consent of the Cistercians.

Secondly, the abbot of Citeaux was given the right to choose the vicar of St Mary's for presentation to the archbishop of York. The first recorded instalment of a parish vicar, Richard de Chauseye, by this method is dated 1226. Thirdly, Richard's second charter also refers to 'the proctor of Citeaux', meaning the abbot's resident agent or representative in Scarborough, whose duty was to collect his revenues and oversee his property and interests. Thus, in effect, Lionheart's charters to Citeaux set up a permanent cell or priory of two or three Cistercian monks under their proctor. Scarborough was to be the only place in England with resident foreign monks from Citeaux.

The Cistercian presence in Scarborough had both beneficial and detrimental consequences for the town. Though other religious houses such as Bridlington, Malton and Watton priories, and hospitals such as St Leonard's at York and St Giles' at Beverley, had substantial properties in Scarborough, the Cistercian abbeys of Yorkshire were well represented there. Fountains had land in Sandgate; Byland had property on Sandside and in Bakstergate; and Rievaulx had at least one herring house and several other properties in Cartergate and Stainardgate. What is now King

Street and before that Apple Market or Helperby Lane was first called Rievaulx Lane.

On the negative side, the privileges exercised by the proctor and his brother monks at Scarborough diminished the revenues which might otherwise have remained in the town or the country, instead of going abroad to France. Moreover, the proctors at Scarborough evaded their full gablage on eight of their messuages by enclosing them and then claiming they were only one property; so instead of paying 3s. 10d. in gablage they offered only one payment of sixpence. When the case came before the King's court, it ruled that the proctor should pay four shillings a year in rent directly to the Crown, so that the town was still the poorer for loss of gablage.

The Cistercians were so jealous of their special status in Scarborough that they tried very hard to exclude all other religious houses from the town, particularly the friars. When the Grey Friars or Franciscans first arrived in Scarborough in 1240, the Cistercian monks objected immediately and strongly to their presence. The dispute raged for the next five years. Both orders appealed to the Pope. Eventually, rather than 'offend the monks', the friars retired to a site outside the town at Hatterboard, though without abandoning their right to be in Scarborough. However, thanks to a generous grant by Reginald the miller of an extensive plot of land in the heart of the old town astride the Damyot stream, the Franciscans returned in 1267, this time permanently.

Nevertheless, the Cistercians still continued to grumble. When the Grey Friars began to re-build and enlarge their church of the Holy Sepulchre in 1281, they were then ordered out of the town and threatened with excommunication if they attended services there. Finally, the Franciscan archbishop of Canterbury intervened to protect his brothers. The Scarborough Cistercians were told to abstain from opposing the public sermons of the friars there, both Franciscans and Dominicans, and threatened with severe penalties if they persisted with their persecution. Even so, as late as 1285, the general chapter at Citeaux complained to Edward I that because of competition from the friars their revenue from Scarborough was now hardly sufficient to pay for the entertainment of the abbots for one day out of the three they were there. Soon afterwards, when Edward taxed the church to pay for his wars, the rectory of Scarborough was assessed at the very high figure of £106 13s. 4d., and the vicarage taxed at £5 6s. 8d. a year.

Richard Lionheart was ever willing to tax the English to finance his wasteful foreign wars, but most unwilling to spend any money in and on his kingdom. In a reign of ten years he stayed less than six months in the country of his birth; of all the kings of England he was the least English. Scarborough castle received not a penny from him, whereas Richard's magnificent fortress on the Seine, Chateau-Gaillard, cost £11,500! In the greatest contrast, Richard's younger brother and successor, John, lost not only Chateau-Gaillard, but the entire county of Anjou and the duchy of Normandy to the king of France (hence his nickname 'Lackland'); but during his reign he spent more money on Scarborough castle than any other in his kingdom.

Between 1199 and 1212, John's expenditure on Scarborough castle altogether reached £2,291 3s. 4d. — a colossal total. After modest improvements in the early years of his reign, in 1209-10 the figure rose to £620, in 1210-11 to £542, and in 1211-12, to a staggering £780, three times more than on any other fortress. The last sum paid mostly for the leading of the keep roof, whereas previous investment was mainly on a stone curtain wall with solid half-round interval towers running all the way from the keep to the edge of the south cliff of the headland.

From his first visit in February 1201 to his last just fifteen years later, King John came to Scarborough four times. Though he never spent more than two nights at the castle (John only rarely slept more than three nights in any one place), on each visit he made sure that his residence was comfortable and spacious. Instead of having to sleep in the draughty, cramped keep, he had a hall and solar built against the wall of the outer bailey which after later re-building came to be called Mosdale Hall after a subsequent castellan.

King John's concern for the strength and security of the castle at Scarborough had more to do with the safety of his crown than the comfort of his body. John had never reconciled himself to the loss of Anjou and Normandy to King Philip of France and tried repeatedly to raise an English army to recover them only to find the English barons unwilling to cross the Channel. Most of them no longer had territorial interests on the Continent; and some of them who did had already pledged loyalty to Philip as their feudal overlord. John found himself caught in a dilemma: unless he recovered Anjou and Normandy by force he could not hope to win back the power, wealth and prestige he had forfeited by losing them; but every effort on his part to raise the necessary money and men for such an expedition provoked further baronial resistance in England.

Baronial opposition was particularly serious in Yorkshire, and like his father, Henry II, John regarded Scarborough castle as a place of the greatest importance in asserting royal authority in the county. Not only did he spend a fortune strengthening the castle's defences with stone walls and towers, but he saw to it that its garrison was well provisioned with numbers, food and armaments. In 1212 when a rebellion in the North was expected, £200 were invested in munitions and supplies for Scarborough and John's other neighbouring castle at Pickering. In 1214, as John sailed for France, in what proved to be a disastrous campaign to recover Anjou, he sent orders north to replace all perishable foods stored at his castles at Knaresborough and Scarborough.

As far as Scarborough castle was concerned, John was fortunate with his choice of governor. Whereas other castellans proved untrustworthy, Geoffrey de Neville at Scarborough remained steadfastly loyal and courageous. By 1215 he had 60 sergeants and ten crossbowmen under his command and later that year the garrison strength was increased to ten knights, 72 sergeants and 13 crossbowmen. Many of these professional soldiers were probably foreign mercenaries from Aquitaine and Poitou, but one local baron who brought his following into the king's castle was William de Fors. In reward for his support King John later gave him the manor of Driffield which his grandfather, William le Gros, had once held.

Even when the 'northerner' rebel magnates were able to compel John to accept Magna Carta in the summer of 1215, Scarborough remained one of the few royal centres to hold out for him. John ordered 100 marks to be sent to Geoffrey de Neville for the maintenance of Scarborough castle in June 1216, though it is doubtful that his instruction was obeyed. Nevertheless, Geoffrey stood fast and paid for the provisions of his garrison out of his own purse. It was not until the next reign that Geoffrey's son, John, was allowed 1,000 marks from the royal treasury to cover his father's expenses in King John's service at the castles of Pickering and Scarborough. Nothing is recorded of the siege of Scarborough by the rebels in 1215 except that they attempted to break into the town but were repulsed at its western wall.

Perhaps Geoffrey de Neville and his business associates, Robert Woodcock and Lawrence of Dunwich, made a handsome profit out of the civil war. With several of the king's fighting galleys at their disposal in Scarborough harbour, they appear to have employed them in acts of piracy. In 1216 and 1217 there were several complaints from foreign merchants that their wool, silver and wine had been illegally seized by the royal galleys based at Scarborough.

As for the burgesses of Scarborough, they were not spared from the heavy burdens of King John's exceptionally harsh taxation. In the first year of his reign they had to pay 40 marks to the Exchequer for confirmation of their charter of privileges, and then 60 more marks in tallage, the tax on boroughs that had once been part of the royal demesne. When John made his first visit to Scarborough, 4-5 February 1201, he granted the burgesses the 60 acres of demesne land and the common and meadow rights that were attached to them that comprised the royal manor of Falsgrave. Until this time the burgesses had no arable fields of their own; for their wheat and barley they depended on supplies from the neighbouring farmers of Falsgrave and Scalby. However, this new grant was not a gesture of royal generosity: it arose out of John's insatiable need for ready cash. The townspeople of Scarborough were required to pay a high price for acquiring their own arable and pasture land: John raised the annual farm to the Crown from £33 to £76. Still not content with this, in 1208 John took the farm out of the hands of Scarborough's burgesses and gave it to the town's richest resident, John Ughtred. Presumably, Ughtred had to pay the king an increment on the old farm. In the meantime, during his second stay at Scarborough castle in 1203, John had levied another tallage on the town.

Richard Lionheart had ignored Scarborough castle and given Scarborough's parish church to foreign monks. His brother John had spent a mint of money on extending and strengthening the castle to assert his royal authority in a region where it was notoriously weak and threatened. Financial necessity had driven him to squeeze more revenue out of his manor of Falsgrave by handing it over to men who could afford to pay him well for it.

Scarborough's burgesses had no more reason than the rest of the English population to thank Richard for being their absentee king. To add penalty to neglect, in 1195 the town had to find £100 as its own contribution to Richard's ransom. On the other hand, in the long term John had done the town a considerable service. The royal castle was now the most formidable fortress on the east coast of England; John's enormous investment in effect committed his successors to future care and consideration. Secondly, his gift of the Falsgrave demesne to Scarborough set another precedent. Whereas previously the site of Scarborough had been part of the royal manor of Falsgrave, in future the royal manor of Falsgrave would become part of the borough of Scarborough. The child had outgrown the parent.

5. The Third Henry and First Edward

Geoffrey de Neville might have been a steadfast servant of King John and his nine-year-old son, Henry III, who succeeded him in 1216, but he showed no respect for the charter rights or corporate privileges of Scarborough, either as governor of the castle for twenty years, or as sheriff of Yorkshire and later chamberlain of England. From sometime in the 1220s there has survived a lengthy complaint of the burgesses of Scarborough against him, his castle garrison, and his under-sheriff, Simon de Hal.

When wine, corn and salt came into the king's port at Scarborough the sheriff and his deputies seized them and then paid only half the market price. When they did buy goods legitimately they would often pay little for them and sometimes nothing at all. During the summer herring season the sheriff was known to come down to the harbour and insist on taking the whole catch for himself at only half the normal price. Should any townsman or fisherman dare to protest he was threatened with imprisonment 'or to have his house burnt'. Cattle passing through the country on their way to Scarborough market or butchers had been stolen by the sheriff's men; some of them had been killed for their meat, others ransomed back to their rightful owners. According to Scarborough's burgesses, the castle garrison and the sheriff had stolen 'bread, flesh, ale, corn, salts, cloths and other chattels' to the value of £300 6s. 4d. As a result some townspeople had been reduced to poverty and others had left the borough to find a living elsewhere.

In the face of Geoffrey de Neville and Simon de Hal the king's travelling justices had proved powerless. Stolen property had not been restored; culprits had not been punished. On the contrary, complainants had been arrested, imprisoned in the castle, deprived of their land and goods; hence this appeal from the burgesses directly to the king and his council.

Their appeal seems to have been heeded. After all it was not in the king's interest that Scarborough should be so impoverished that its burgesses could no longer pay the annual farm or that its harbour should be shunned by merchants, both native and foreign. That Henry was alive to the actual and potential value of Scarborough is confirmed by a royal grant of 1225. For the first time the borough was permitted to collect murage and quayage tolls, the former levied on carts and carriers bringing goods into the town by land, the latter on vessels carrying cargoes into the port. Carts were charged one penny, fishing boats twopence, larger vessels sixpence, and the largest merchant ships one shilling and sixpence. Murage money was intended to pay for the upkeep of the town's walls, quayage for the repair and maintenance of its harbour. As an indication of his interest, Henry gave the burgesses 40 oaks from his royal forest of Pickering. After 1225 royal grants of quayage and murage were renewed regularly for three, seven or ten years. Toll rates varied, but eventually they settled on sixpence for a merchant ship, fourpence for a five-man, fishing boat, and twopence for a coble. In retrospect, the grant of 1225 marked a key point in Scarborough's history as a trading port and a safe haven.

If Henry had regard for Scarborough as a port of growing importance neither did he neglect the castle there in which his father and grandfather had invested so much of their money. Even to maintain the fabric of the buildings was a costly business. The hall and the keep were repaired in 1223-4, and more than £100 spent at Scarborough and Pickering in the years 1225-7 on further repairs and improvements. In the winter of 1237 a storm damaged the lead roof of the keep and the hall which cost £42 to replace. Four years later another £63 were needed to rebuild a wall which had been brought down by a landslip. Next year repairs to the bridge over the dykes cost a further £40. During the years 1243-5 work took place to construct a new gateway with flanking towers on the outside of the dykes which altogether cost £81 7s. 3d.

In 1253, John de Lessington, then keeper of the castle, was allowed to spend up to £100 on necessary repairs, but it seems very unlikely that he did so. By 1260, when Hugh Bigod had become castellan, there were serious defects reported in all parts of the castle — in the keep, the hall, the walls, the barbican and the two drawbridges. Lead roofs were missing, wooden doors, floors and bridges were rotten, battlements and alures were damaged, and there was a total lack of crossbows, arrows and 'all manner of arms necessary for its defence'.

A succession of past governors, who were not salaried for the office, had pocketed the income due to the castle instead of using it for maintenance. Since they did not live in the castle they had no personal interest in making it weather proof or even defensible. Not until governors were required to reside in the castle and were given both a salary and allowance earmarked for specific repairs was there much hope of improvement.

On the other hand, the absence of a castle keeper and his avaricious garrison would have been welcomed by Scarborough's burgesses. Thanks to a series of royal charters, the middle years of the reign of Henry III were a golden age for the borough: between 1252 and 1256 its privileges were substantially increased.

In one charter Scarborough's status as a major port was confirmed. Tolls on merchant ships and fishing boats using the harbour were fixed on the understanding that the burgesses would employ them 'to make a certain new port with timber and stone towards the sea whereby all ships arriving thither may enter and sail out without danger as well at the beginning of flood as at high water'. In other words, all manner of vessels would be able to sail into and out of the harbour during twelve in every twenty-four hours.

From this time onwards Scarborough harbour began to take shape. A new quay, built at the foot of the sandhills along the line of modern Quay Street, provided a solid landing and mooring place. A new pier of timber frame and rubble core running southwards from it gave shelter against heavy seas coming in from the east. Since no other quay was permitted between Scarborough and Ravenser-Odd at the mouth of the Humber, all North Sea mariners came to regard Scarborough as a refuge of essential value.

A safer haven meant that merchants and fishermen were encouraged to use Scarborough rather than elsewhere. One of the most prized provisions of a royal charter of 1253 was the grant of an annual forty-five day fair. The fair was to be held from the Feast of the Assumption, 15 August, until Michaelmas, 29 September, to coincide with the passage southwards down the east coast of England of great shoals of herring. This annual migration of fish attracted increasing numbers of fishermen from all the shores of the North Sea. The unprecedented duration of the fair — one of the longest in Europe — indicated the special consideration now given to Scarborough. Norwegians, Danes, Germans, Flemings and Hollanders, as well as Scots and English, brought their herring into Scarborough harbour and sold it in the open market on the sands for salting and smoking. For forty-five days of the year Scarborough became the busiest fish market in western Europe.

And it was not only fish that could be bought and sold at Scarborough. Since one royal order prohibited the loading of ships anywhere else between Ravenscar and Flamborough and another closed the neighbouring rural markets of Brompton, Sherburn and Filey, Scarborough soon secured a monopoly along the coast and deep inland. Farmers as well as fishermen, craftsmen and pedlars — all had to come to Scarborough's Thursday and Saturday markets. Moreover, just as the town's bailiffs had the power to regulate its weekly markets, so also they were granted the right to hold a court of piepoudre (literally 'dusty feet') to settle any disputes arising at the annual fair.

There were two more royal charters, both dated May 1256. The first of them gave final confirmation of the extension of the borough boundaries to include the whole manor of Falsgrave. From now on Scarborough had its own arable fields, its own pastures and commons, its own windmill on Bracken Hill and its own water-mills in Ramsdale, and even its own fresh water lake, Byward Wath. Not least of the assets now permanently won by the town was access to an adequate supply of clean water. After the Franciscans returned from Hatterboard in 1267 they made an arrangement with the burgesses to bring water down into the town from Gilduscliff (Spring Hill) in Falsgrave by underground pipeline. The inadequacy of its deep draw wells and the pollution of the Damyot stream made such a pipeline essential for the health and expansion of Scarborough's population. Eventually the pipeline ran through the heart of the borough filling three conduits or public troughs at St Thomasgate, St Sepulchregate and the top of West Sandgate. For all these additional gains Scarborough was to pay an extra fee farm of £25, bringing it to a total of £91, due at the royal exchequer every Michaelmas.

Falsgrave was to provide Scarborough with more than its fields, pastures and water supply: the burgesses were also granted exclusive rights to hunt its wild life, a right known as free warren. Previously, Falsgrave manor had formed part of the royal forest of Pickering and had been subject to the king's forest law. Henceforth, his foresters and verderers would be excluded, so that the townspeople would have access not only to the wood, turf, brackens and whins of Weaponness (Oliver's Mount), Ramsdale and Falsgrave Moor, but also to their hares, rabbits, partridges and pheasants. In practice, however, there was no free warren for all. Apart from the borough's official warrener, only those who bought licences from the bailiffs were allowed to hunt, shoot and fish within the borough. Anyone taking ground game without the licence of the bailiffs was liable to a penalty fine of £10.

An earlier charter of Henry II had already granted Scarborough's merchants freedom from 'all tolls, lastage, wreck, pontage and passage' throughout England, Normandy, Aquitaine and Anjou, and through all ports and seacoasts of England. In short, wherever they travelled in the kingdom and the king's domains overseas they were not required to pay tolls of any kind. Scarborough's acquisition of Falsgrave now gave its burgesses freedom from chiminage, the toll charged for passage through the royal forest. From now on the burgesses of Scarborough and the men of Falsgrave could bring wind-fallen wood, turf and fern through the neighbouring forest land without charge or hindrance from the foresters.

Finally, Scarborough's judicial privileges and immunities were confirmed and enlarged by Henry III's charters. The borough's own coroners were permitted to try the pleas of the Crown so that the king's travelling justices would be in future excluded from its courts. The rights of Scarborough's own justices were to be extensive and final: they included 'infangthief', literally jurisdiction over a thief caught in the criminal act; 'gallows', the power to pass and execute the death sentence by hanging; 'pillory', to punish convicted offenders by exposing them to public shame and ridicule; and 'tumbril', which was the power to punish, usually female scolds, by binding them to a ducking-stool and ducking them in the harbour.

Scarborough's magistrates were soon to gain a notoriety for dealing with thieves and robbers in such a way that the proverb, 'Scarborough warning', meaning a blow delivered without warning, came to have widespread currency. As a later Tudor ballad explained, 'This terme, Scarborow warnyng grew (some say) / By hasty hangyng for rank robbery theare'. Clearly, Scarborough was a town where the gallows were in constant use.

Situated in the market place, the pillory at Scarborough was most often used to humiliate craftsmen and traders who broke what was called 'the assize of bread and ale'. Two official town breadweighers were given scales to check that the standard loaf was sold everywhere at the same weight and price, and that its contents met their requirements. Similarly, two borough 'alefyners' examined the quality, price and measures of the other essential of life. All ale brewed in the town or sold there had to conform to a minimum level of strength and retail in measures equal to the borough's standard 'pinte pott' and 'quart potte'. To control all the borough's internal commerce all transactions were required to take place within certain time limits and some were confined to particular market sites. Medieval Scarborough had a flesh shambles, a fish shambles, and markets specialising in live cattle, apples, corn and butter.

In 1274, when King Edward's justices investigated the liberties and rights of 'the men of Scarborough', they noted that the Cistercian proctor of the parish church of St Mary's claimed 'pleas of withernam'; but they could find no convincing warrant for such a claim. On the other hand, the king's justices discovered that there was no doubt that the burgesses of the town did possess 'pleas of withernam', that is the legal right to recover debts by arrest of debtors and distraint of their goods. By this date the borough probably already had its own special civil court of pleas which met almost daily to deal with disputes concerning cases mainly of trespass and debt. Registers of this court have survived from as early as 1400, and it is known for certain to have operated from 1298.

Another right claimed in 1274 by 'the men of Scarborough' was 'wreck of the sea'. Any vessel and its cargo wrecked on the shore or stranded on the sands could be taken legitimately as property of the borough, if there were no survivors to claim them. In practice, this 'liberty' was often abused. For instance, as the justices of 1274 recorded, 'the heirs of Sir Peter de Brus (of Cleveland) take wreck of the sea when men from the shipwreck have survived, just as when they have died'. However, whereas other local claimants to wreck of the sea, such as the abbot of Whitby and the earl of Holderness, could offer no warrant for it, Scarborough's claim was amply justified by royal charter.

Henry III did more for Scarborough than any monarch before or since, yet never visited it; his son, Edward I, held court in Scarborough castle in 1275 and came back there in 1280, but seems to have cared little for the castle and even less for the town. In 1278 it was reported that it would cost an estimated £2,200 to repair the castle roofs, the wooden bridge between the barbican and the main gate, and over a thousand yards of curtain wall. But Edward exhausted his treasury building magnificent modern castles in Wales instead of renovating old ones in England. His only use for the castle at Scarborough was to keep Welsh hostages and Scottish prisoners in it. John Sampson, the governor, was allowed fourpence a day for his 12 Welshmen in 1295, but only twopence a day for each of his four Scotsmen in 1304. Were Welshmen twice as costly to keep as Scotsmen, or hostages considered twice the value of prisoners?

Neglect of the castle fabric was not necessarily unwelcome to the people of Scarborough, but Edward's accession in 1272 signalled the start of a short period of misfortune for the town. What kings granted they could also withdraw, and it seems that after Edward's constable, William de Percy, lodged a complaint against the burgesses for their 'excesses and trespasses', the king refused to renew his father's charters. Instead, Scarborough was subjected to the direct rule of the king's sheriff and his castle constable, William de Percy.

Naturally, the burgesses protested at this loss of privilege and independence. In particular, they complained that rents from houses and mills 'built with the moneys of the burgesses' and for drying fishing nets formerly used to maintain the quay had been seized by the king's sheriff. As a result, the quay had not been repaired, houses down there had been destroyed 'by the raging of the sea', and seamen were now reluctant to seek shelter in the harbour.

Consequently, a royal commission of inquiry was appointed to investigate these complaints. Of the town rents, which were due to the exchequer as part of the annual farm, and which should be retained by the burgesses for their own purposes? The net result of this investigation seems to have been a verdict largely in favour of Scarborough. In 1276, the borough was granted a pardon, fined £40 for its misdemeanours, and its charters restored in full.

As other inquiries about the same time suggested, William de Percy and his family and retainers were guilty of more 'excesses and trespasses' than the people of Scarborough. Percy's garrison at the castle amused themselves by barricading the highway in and out of Scarborough and exacting illegal tolls on all who tried to pass. They stole grain from the abbot of Rievaulx's grange, a cart from the prior of Malton, and carts and goods from many others. Lady Elena de Percy of Seamer was a notable offender in the same way: she had obstructed the road in Burtondale and blocked the bridge between Scalby Hay and Raincliffe. Meanwhile Sir William was hunting in the king's forest without his licence, and using forced labour from the town to thrash his stolen corn. His 'janitor' at the castle lured town pigs into the dykes by scattering oats there and then extorted money from their owners before he would release the pigs; and his deputy constable had taken cloth worth 40 shillings from one of Scarborough's merchants and not paid for it. Since the castle was outside the jurisdiction of the borough there was no way that the townspeople could protect themselves from these criminals.

Compared with this lengthy list of offences, Scarborough's own illegalities were few and relatively minor. Some of their traders had sold sacks of wool to foreigners without paying duties on them; sometimes ships anchored outside the port had been forced to pay tolls; and the burgesses were accused of carrying off a great whale from Filey that had come ashore there.

Edward I made only one significant addition to Scarborough's privileges. Of the twenty 'cities and boroughs' summoned by him to send two of their 'wiser and apter citizens' to his forthcoming parliament at Shrewsbury in September 1283, one of them was Scarborough. The royal writ was addressed 'to the Bailiffs' indicating that already by this date these two annually elected officers were regarded as the borough's leading magistrates. The only other place in Yorkshire to receive the same summons was York. Though Scarborough's bailiffs did not always respond to the royal summons delivered by the sheriff of Yorkshire, from 1283 onwards there were few parliaments during the next 700 years when the borough was not represented in what came to be called the House of Commons.

6. The Second Edward and Piers Gaveston

Piers Gaveston was a Gascon knight favoured by Edward II above all others in his kingdom. There can be no doubt that the two young men were physical lovers: as the chronicler of Meaux abbey in the East Riding crudely expressed his contempt: the king 'particularly delighted in the vice of sodomy'. However, Gaveston was hated by the English barons not because he was a lowly-born foreigner and the king's lover, but because of the excessive wealth and power granted to him by Edward: their grievances were personal and political, not moral.

As soon as he succeeded to the throne in 1307 the young Edward had summoned his favourite back from exile in France, made him the earl of Cornwall (a title hitherto given only to members of the royal family), and conferred upon him for life the lordship of five honours which included Knaresborough and its castle. Lesser but still heartfelt injuries suffered by his fellow earls were Gaveston's habits of beating them in armed tournaments and calling them by insulting names. For instance, the earl of Warwick he described as 'the black dog of Arden'. Such indeed was the strength of baronial hostility to the Gascon that, to avoid civil war, Edward had to consent most reluctantly to his favourite's banishment to Ireland in 1308, and later, for the third time, his exile to France in 1311. Consequently, when the king once again defied the English earls by permitting his favourite's return at the end of 1311, civil war seemed certain; both sides now prepared for it. The outcome would decide the fate of Piers Gaveston.

In January 1312 the king and Gaveston were again together at York. There Edward announced that his companion was a loyal subject, his banishment had been illegal, and that all his titles and lands were restored. In reply, the earls declared Gaveston an outlaw, and the archbishop of Canterbury pronounced him excommunicate. Two earls, Pembroke and Warenne, were authorised by the others to seek out and arrest him.

York was not well fortified. Gaveston might have sought the security of one of his Yorkshire castles at Knaresborough or Skipton, but instead he chose Scarborough's, presumably because it gave him an escape exit overseas should it be necessary. In March Gaveston strengthened the castle garrison with his own 48 men-at-arms and foot soldiers, and soon he was joined at Scarborough by his brother, Arnand-Guillaume, who brought with him another eleven men from York. Between April and July 1312 a total of £48 was spent on repairs to the castle and provisions for its stores. To win the support of Scarborough's burgesses, Edward confirmed their charters of liberty and granted them the right to levy and collect harbour dues or quayage for the next eight years.

At York, on 4 April, the king had given Gaveston custody of his castle at Scarborough and a mandate to hold it indefinitely at all costs. Piers swore that he would not yield the castle to anyone, not even to the king himself if he came to claim it as a prisoner of the earls. If Edward died Piers was assured that he could keep the castle for himself and his heirs. On the same day, a royal writ, addressed to 'the mayor, bailiffs and good men of the town of Scardeburgh', notified them of this extraordinary arrangement.

The following day Edward and Gaveston left York and travelled north to the greater safety of Newcastle. There they remained for several weeks because the earl was ill. A doctor and a local monk were each paid £6 13s. 4d. for providing him with a cure. However, before the royal party was ready to depart, an army led by the king's cousin, Thomas, earl of Lancaster, Robert de Clifford and Henry de Percy, suddenly and unexpectedly reached the Tyne.

Percy had his own particular grievance against Gaveston. Four years earlier the king had given him permission to live with his wife and household in Scarborough castle, and later, in October 1311, he had been made 'superior custodian' there. However, the following January, Percy received an order from the king at York to deliver up the castle to William le Latimer and, when he failed to do so, he was summoned to the royal presence to answer for his open disobedience. Distrusting Edward now that he was accompanied by Gaveston, Percy defied a second instruction from York to surrender the castle to Robert de Felton. Only when the king gave him assurances of safe conduct for 15 days did Percy finally and grudgingly consent to vacate the castle and allow Gaveston to occupy it. He must have been more than a little displeased to have lost a home as well as the strongest fortress on England's east coast to Edward's detested favourite.

The surprising appearance of the northern barons outside Newcastle prompted the pell-mell departure of Edward and Piers down river to Tynemouth. In their extreme haste, the two fugitives left behind their treasures, arms, and horses, as well as the pregnant, sixteen-year-old Queen Isabella. From Tynemouth they took the first available ship to Scarborough.

At Scarborough king Edward made a decision which he was to

regret deeply for the rest of his life. Assuming that from there he could raise an army sufficient to overawe the rebellious lords, he went on to York, leaving Gaveston behind in the castle. It was a fatal miscalculation. Lancaster, Clifford and Percy, now joined by earls Pembroke and Warenne, descended rapidly on Scarborough. Gaveston was besieged in the castle and effectively separated from his royal guardian.

The siege of Scarborough castle lasted about ten days; Edward commanded his barons to lift it but they ignored him. Lancaster's three hundred soldiers, 'all clad in green jackets, arrayed and led by John Dalton, his bailiff of Pickering', sealed off all Gaveston's escape routes. Gaveston surrendered himself because his supplies were running low, there seemed no hope of rescue, and he was offered terms more than generous. On 19 May 1312, at the altar of the church of Scarborough's Friars Preachers, Pembroke, Warenne and Percy swore on the consecrated host that they would conduct the earl of Cornwall in complete safety to St Mary's abbey at York where they would discuss a settlement of his future with the king and the earl of Lancaster. If no agreement could be reached by 1 August, Gaveston would be allowed to return unharmed to Scarborough castle. In the meantime the castle garrison there would be provisioned and permitted to remain in occupation. Later it was rumoured that the earl of Pembroke had accepted a bribe of £1000 from the king in return for his guarantee of Gaveston's physical immunity.

At first all seemed to be going well for Gaveston. Though he was kept in confinement away from Edward, his captors met the king at York and there agreed that a parliament should be called to Lincoln on 8 July to determine his fate. On 3 June an order went out from the king to the keeper of his manor at Burstwick in Holderness to ship 300 quarters of wheat to Gaveston's garrison at Scarborough. Edward raised no objections when Pembroke took Gaveston into his personal custody and took him south where he was thought to be safer. Of all the rebellious lords Pembroke was the one that Edward distrusted least.

Unluckily for Gaveston, however, the earl of Pembroke could not resist a visit to his wife and left his prisoner insufficiently guarded. The following day, Guy Beauchamp, earl of Warwick, seized Gaveston by force and carried him off to his castle. As the author of the life of Edward II wrote gleefully, 'he whom Piers called Warwick the Dog has now bound Piers in chains'. Nine days later, 19 June, in the presence of three earls, Lancaster, Hereford and Arundel, Gaveston was executed by two Welsh swordsmen in Lancaster's employ: one ran him through the body and then the other struck off his head.

Edward had no other political choice than to pardon Gaveston's murderers, but privately he could neither forget nor forgive what had been done by them. Towards the end of July 1312 the sheriff of Yorkshire was given a royal order to seize Henry Percy and all his lands on the grounds that he had been a principal surety for the safety of Gaveston and had failed to surrender himself to the king after the murder. Yet before the end of the year Percy's lands were fully restored, though not his custody of Scarborough castle.

The king found it easier to punish Scarborough than to revenge himself on his powerful barons: 'for certain causes', wholly unspecified but not inexplicable, the town lost all its corporate privileges and was brought directly under the control of Edward's appointees. At least four Scarborough men — John Lok, Robert Fitzrobert, Reinard le Charetter and Robert le Coroner — were named in the general pardon, published in October 1313, of those known to have been involved in Gaveston's betrayal and death; but this was small compensation for the tribulations that were soon to descend on the whole community. For the next fourteen years, as long as Edward II remained on the throne, Scarborough was subjected to the most ruthless exploitation to which its people retaliated with exceptional violence.

A succession of constables of Scarborough castle, who were also given the title of keepers or wardens of the town, now acted as virtual dictators. Scarborough was bought and sold like any market commodity. In 1317 John de Mowbray in effect paid £100 a year to the king for a lifetime possession of Scarborough. According to the terms of their bargain, if Edward decided to restore the borough to its burgesses, Mowbray would have their fee-farm of £91 a year and the remaining £9 from other royal revenues. Sometime later, Robert Wawayn paid the king's new favourite, Hugh le Despenser the younger, £120 a year for custody of both town and castle.

Local resentment against Robert Wawayn is well reported. In 1316 an investigation was made into his complaint against eighteen townsmen that they had plotted his death. Wawayn alleged that they had hired William of Filey as an assassin, assaulted him, dragged him out into the street by his hair, and abducted a minor and heiress in his custody simply because 'he wished to bring them to justice for certain trespasses'. It seems that Robert had found it impossible to hold courts in the town, levy fines, or even collect customs. Some indication of what 'trespasses' were being committed in Scarborough at this time is to be found in this and other subsequent inquiries. Twenty-three Scarborough men were accused of intercepting incoming fishermen while they were still at sea, seizing their catches, and then selling them illegally at profit, thereby forestalling the market. These same men had also taken wreck of sea which by rights belonged to the king, refused to pay his custom duties on exports of wool and hides, and even stolen corn which was intended to supply the king's garrison at Berwick-on-Tweed. Early in 1319 the king had to send an armed force from Beverley to rescue Wawayn who was beleaguered by Scarborians in his own house. Only after most of these named wrongdoers had been convicted and heavily fined for their 'divers trespasses and usurpations against the king' were they granted royal pardons. Not even the king's freshwater fish were safe. Wawayn was one of the royal commissioners charged with investigating losses from the king's millponds, stanks and stews; and Henry Carter was actually imprisoned for daring to take a royal pike.

A glance at the list of Scarborough lawbreakers during this period of extraordinary lawlessness reveals that the culprits were not common criminals: among them were several leading burgesses and at least two priests. Roger Ughtred had sat for Scarborough in no fewer than four parliaments; John of Hatterboard, Robert of Helperthorpe, Adam of Seamer and Henry of Ruston were also former or future members of parliament. Wawayn had had to contend with four of the Carter clan — William, Reginald, Henry and Adam — who were all major property and office holders in the town. On the other hand, that Adam of Seamer joined Wawayn as collector of the wool custom in 1320 and Reginald Carter was appointed with Wawayn as customer two years later suggest that at least two of the former 'poachers' had become 'gamekeepers'.

Nevertheless, not surprisingly during these turbulent times, the economy of the town suffered losses. Though there is no truth in the repeated Scottish propaganda that Scarborough was burned to the ground by Robert de Brus in 1318 and plundered again by the Scots in 1322, there is evidence that its trade was damaged by Edward's disastrous wars and the misgovernment of his favoured appointees there. For instance, in 1316 there was a complaint that, though 'large sums' were being levied on merchants bringing goods into the port, the collectors of quayage had converted the receipts to their own use and spent 'little or nothing to the repair of the quay'. Judging by Wawayn's well-kept accounts that have survived for eighteen weeks in 1320 he had tried to restore order and efficiency into harbour management and maintenance; but later reports of serious damage there indicate that he had been unable or unwilling to effect more than temporary improvements. The quay provided not only essential refuge for shipping: without its sure protection the whole length of the Sandside frontage was at the mercy of tide and gale.

The deposition of Edward II and the succession of his son in 1327 brought Scarborough prompt relief. Within days the town's precious liberties were restored in full. Moreover, when the burgesses petitioned that they had paid a double fee-farm of £91 13s. and a fine of £14 17s. 6d. when the crown took over in 1312, the barons of the exchequer were instructed by the king's council to allow Scarborough this credit when the next fee-farm was due. When Robert de Baumbergh was made 'watchman' of the office of quayage at Scarborough for life in 1330 in reward for his service to Queen Isabella, it seemed that the era of exploitation by favourites had returned, but the grant was soon revoked. The men of Scarborough must have been delighted to read that 'it appears to the King and council that the quayage should be collected by men of the town and not by others'. From now on if Scarborians had complaints about the condition of their harbour they had only their own number to blame.

7. Carters, Accloms, Sages and Rillingtons: Scarborough's Unfair

There is no detailed description of how the borough of Scarborough was constitutionally governed before 1356 because seven years earlier 'Adam Reginaldson Carter of Scarburgh then one of the chamberlains ... to the impoverishment of the people and burgesses ... did maliciously break into small pieces tear and burn the said composition'. Adam Carter's motives for this outrageous action cannot be known for certain, but what is known of him and what was written down in the new composition or constitution of 1356 provide plenty of clues. The truth was probably that Adam Carter was one of a small number of very rich and unscrupulous merchants who were determined to exclude all but themselves from the government of the borough. His principal objection to the old composition was its declared purpose 'to do justice between rich and poor' for 'the security of the peace and the improvement ... chiefly of the middling and poor people of the town'.

According to the new composition granted by letters patent to the burgesses of Scarborough by Edward III in 1356, every year on Michaelmas day (29 September), or the day after, a meeting would be called to the Common Hall to elect the borough's officers for the forthcoming year. There, two coroners would be chosen by 'the most creditable and substantial of the whole commonalty', and then two bailiffs elected by 36 men 'sworn by the consent of poor and middling people'. However, whatever might have been written down, in practice men like Adam Carter had not the slightest intention of permitting even 'middling' residents to have any say in the government of the town. Scarborough was to be run by and for the benefit of a small number of local mafia.

Scarborough might not have enjoyed the same degree of liberties as York, but by the middle of the fourteenth century it was largely self-governing. A long line of royal charters dating back two hundred years to Henry II had endowed the town with many franchises and immunities. Along with York and Hull it was one of only three Yorkshire boroughs regularly invited to send two burgesses to Parliament. Scarborough's officers sat as justices of the peace in its own courts, regulated its own markets and fair, collected pavage and murage to repair its streets and walls, and quayage to maintain its harbour. From time to time its liberties were infringed by overbearing castle constables or challenged by grasping county sheriffs, but such intrusions had become rarer by the mid-fourteenth century.

Moreover, Scarborough was then still a place of considerable size and wealth. York, Newcastle, Beverley, Scarborough and Hull, in that order, were the only five northern towns assessed at more than £330 in the Lay Subsidy list of 1334. When six years later the richest burgesses were taxed at one ninth of the value of their moveable goods, 105 in Scarborough were judged to own possessions of more than a pound in value. According to the incomplete Poll-Tax returns of 1377 to 1381, with at least 1,480 paying adults, Scarborough was one of the 30 most populous provincial towns in England. In the north of the country it was exceeded in population only by York, Newcastle and Beverley, and was still bigger than Hull, Durham or Carlisle.

There is no evidence that the new composition of 1356 increased the security or extended the electoral rights of the 'poor and middling people' of Scarborough. On the contrary, for the next half century and beyond the town suffered from chronic lawlessness and exploitation, not only as a consequence of the attacks of French and Scottish privateers but also as a result of the criminal behaviour of its own borough elite.

The most infamous privateer and profiteer in Scarborough over a period of more than 40 years until his death in 1407 was Robert Acclom. The many 'enormities' for which he and others were responsible included the repeated misuse of the office of bailiff. In 1357 there were complaints that the cargoes of ships wrecked on the shore at Scarborough were being stolen by 'malefactors', instead of being handed over to their rightful owner, the king. One of the 'malefactors' frequently named was Robert Acclom. Ten years later, an inquisition considered a long string of offences said to have been committed by Robert Acclom, most of them when he was acting as Scarborough's bailiff. In 1360, as bailiff, he had extorted four pounds in money and a boat from Robert Grynglee; he allowed the export of a cargo of peas, beans and wheat to Flanders, contrary to an explicit ban on such goods leaving the country unless licensed by the king; and he had bought up all the wheat coming into the town so that the bakers had to pay his extortionate monopoly price for it. Three years later, when he was again bailiff, this time with Adam Carter as his partner, without Carter's knowledge, he had allowed a fisherman from Dunwich to escape with his illegal catch of herrings in return 'for a gift'. In 1366, again as bailiff, this time with Thomas de Scalby, Acclom had permitted a cargo of ale worth £16 16s. to be exported to Flanders, knowing full well that such trade was illegal and that Thomas had forbidden it. No doubt Robert Acclom's private licences were bought at a high price. Not only had he repeatedly robbed the crown of its right to seashore wrecks, Acclom had also deprived his fellow burgesses in the

Common Hall of their customary right to share bargains of purchase and sale. Nevertheless, though the sheriff of Yorkshire was ordered to arrest him, being 'indicted for divers oppressions, extortions and concealments', Acclom seems to have escaped punishment or even disgrace. In 1369 Robert Acclom was chosen by his fellow burgesses to represent them in the Westminster Parliament!

During the 1370s the situation in Scarborough deteriorated from bad to worse. Instead of being ruined by his nefarious abuse of power, Robert Acclom continued to prosper and even gained promotion. In 1372 yet another royal commission was set up to investigate the 'many treasons, felonies, trespasses, conspiracies, oppressions, extortions, damages, grievances and excesses ... in the county of York' alleged to have been committed by 'Robert Acclom, bailiff of Scarborough'; but as before nothing came from these charges. Acclom survived unscathed. In 1376 he was appointed commissioner to search ports for gold, silver and letters of exchange and prevent their export abroad to potential foreign enemies, and made deputy to William Neville, then the king's Admiral of the North. The thief was still a thief, but now he wore a policeman's uniform. Also, far from protecting the rights and privileges of his fellow townsmen, as an Admiralty official Acclom tried to prevent them holding their customary fish markets and annual fair on the sands between Castle Cliff and Ramsdale on the grounds that they belonged to the crown not the borough.

Not content with practising extortion, forestalling and customs evasion, by the late 1370s Robert was personally involved in at least two cases of criminal theft and assault. In October 1378, Henry Percy, earl of Northumberland, complained that Robert, his son John, William Scarborough and others had carried away the goods of his late kinsman, Sir Peter Percy, from his house at Hunmanby. Less than a year later, the same earl was asked to investigate a complaint of Matthew le Hosyer, a Scarborough merchant, that Robert and others had broken into his close and town house, assaulted him and his servants, and carried off his goods. But again nothing happened: it seemed that Acclom was a law unto himself.

The depredation suffered by Scarborough as a result of the prolonged wars with Scotland and France came to a climax in 1378. It appears that John Mercer, a leading Scottish merchant from Perth, who had acted as a spy for the French, was imprisoned in Scarborough castle before his ransom and release. However, his son Andrew, in an act of revenge against the town, led a naval attack on shipping in its harbour.

Many Scarborough seamen were killed, several ships were destroyed or towed away, and a number of prominent ship-owners and merchants were carried off to Boulogne. The following year it was reported to Parliament that the town had lost £1000 in prizes and ransoms paid to the French.

The Mercer raid alarmed the government in London and for a time paralysed the commerce and fishing industry of Scarborough. However, investigations made into the raid soon revealed an appalling situation. Though the king's council had required east-coast ports to build warships 'against attacks of the enemy', at Scarborough those who had property in the town had refused to contribute to its defence. Even worse was the revelation that one leading member of the oligarchy, Robert of Rillington, had bought ships and goods from the enemy which they had captured from the king's subjects, supplied Mercer with victuals and money, and then had led his men by night into the town to inspect its defences and those of the castle.

Rillington and Acclom were friends and business partners, though in this case the former seems to have acted alone on his own initiative. Rillington was fortunate to get a pardon for his treason for which he had to pay 100 marks (£66 13s. 4d.), though there is strong possibility that Henry Percy, earl of Northumberland, who was appointed by the king to examine the charges against Rillington, was already well disposed towards him.

The so-called Peasants' Revolt or English Rising of midsummer 1381 is usually thought of as an episode in the history of the south-east of the country, but there were three urban communities in Yorkshire — in York, Beverley and Scarborough — where violent demonstrations of public discontent took place. At York, there were physical attacks on the religious houses in the city; at Beverley, a leading burgess had his brains beaten out and his corpse thrown into the local beck; whereas at Scarborough there seems to have been no overt act against church property or personnel and there was no loss of life. Nevertheless, in common at all three places, there was organised resistance to the collectors of the third Poll Tax, and angry assaults launched by the aggrieved 'outs' against the ruling 'ins'; or, in the Latin language of the time, the 'viri mediocres' against the 'potentiores'.

What happened at Scarborough between 23 and 30 June 1381 is fairly well documented and understood. A number of so-called 'rebels' made a pact with each other after hearing about the risings elsewhere. They swore an oath 'to the whole commons of England' and then in great numbers they attacked the homes of several 'liegemen of the King', namely Robert and John Acclom, William Shropham, Alan Waldyfe, John Stokwith, William Carter, William Sage and William Percy. John Acclom was robbed of a hauberk worth 50 shillings; John Stokwith had 10 pounds in money taken from him. But plunder was not the purpose of the 'rebels'. Their captives were taken off to prison and kept there until they agreed to take oaths of loyalty to the commons. Though some townsmen were threatened with death, none suffered worse than severe bruising. Robert Acclom escaped to the sanctuary of the Franciscan friary; others sought the protection of St Mary's church; yet no attempt was made to seize them from there by force. However, it is clear that the insurgents intended to change the form and membership of Scarborough's governing body: the two bailiffs at that time, Henry Ruston, the elder, and Robert Acclom, were deprived of their offices.

John Stokwith was an obvious target because he was one of the local collectors of the Poll Tax. This new tax had first been levied in 1377 at a flat rate of fourpence per head on every person of 14 years and older. Two years later, a second Poll Tax was imposed. This time there were many more evasions but at least it was a graduated levy rising from fourpence on the poorest to four pounds on an earl. However, it was the third Poll Tax of 1380-1 which sparked off general resistance and rebellion because again it was a flat rate on all adults and this time it was a demand for a shilling per head. Stokwith was fortunate to escape alive. Some of the Scarborough rebels wanted him beheaded, others preferred to see him hanged slowly. He was kept in custody even though his son-in-law, Henry Ruston the younger, said he was willing to pay any ransom for him and settle any complaint against him whatever the cost.

In the main, however, the revolt at Scarborough, as elsewhere in Yorkshire, was directed at the richest rulers of the community — the 42 members of the so-called 'potentiores' who filled all the offices of municipal government year after year and monopolised the borough's parliamentary representation. Robert Acclom had been Member of Parliament in 1369 and bailiff half a dozen times during the previous twenty years; his son John had sat in the Parliament of 1373; William Shropham had been elected three times to sit in the House of Commons, in 1372, 1373 and 1379; John Stokwith had sat at Westminster in 1377; and Henry Ruston and Thomas de Burne, two more of the 'potentiores', were currently Members of Parliament at the time of the rising. Since the parliamentary franchise was exclusive to members of the Common Hall, only members of the Common Hall were ever chosen to represent Scarborough at Westminster.

Against this self-regarding, self-perpetuating elite was the opposition party of men of means who had been permanently excluded from public offices and could no longer tolerate their abuse. Of the seven men named in the court indictments as 'rebels', three of them are known to have been well-to-do burgesses. William Marche, described in more than one source as a draper, three years later was said to have a flock of 200 sheep, two shops and a town house with several servants. Another prominent 'rebel', Robert Galoun, as recently as 1380, had taken out a licence to endow a charity of considerable value; and only days after the rising in July 1381 the chantry was instituted at the altar of St James in the parish church of St Mary. When Galoun died in 1391 the property he left as endowment for the chantry consisted of various tenements in the town, several closes, and a house in St Mary Gate, altogether worth £6 a year. In his will he also left a gold ring with a sapphire to first his widow, then his daughter, and ultimately to the chantry chaplain at St James's so that all who sought healing might benefit from its powers.

So this was neither a peasants' revolt nor a typical town mob riot: it was a well-organised, well planned 'coup de ville' that would have earned the admiration of a later revolutionary such as Karl Marx or Lenin. A distinctive uniform of white hoods with red tails was worn by the insurgents; violence was employed against the 'potentiores', but only to frighten them into submission; lives were threatened and not taken; personal property was damaged and ransoms demanded, but there was no indiscriminate looting and arson as in London. No attempt, it seems, was made to occupy the castle. Marche, Galoun and the other leaders never lost control of the commons who were said to number five hundred. Alice de Wakefield, sister of Henry Wakefield, then bishop of Worcester, complained that a 'great number of evil doers' had taken away her rents and lands in Scarborough, but that was the worst of her complaints.

The Scarborough coup lasted just one week: it petered out after Sunday 30 June when Robert Acclom's house was besieged 'for quarter of a day'. No doubt news of the death of Wat Tyler and the collapse of the risings in Beverley and at York by 1 July disheartened Scarborough's insurgent leaders. There could be no revolution in Scarborough if there was none elsewhere. Nevertheless, the government in London took no chances. On 14 August 1381, 'for the better maintenance of his knightly rank', Sir Ralph Standish was granted custody of the royal castle of Scarborough for life. Until 15 June Standish had been no more than an esquire of Richard II, then on that day at Smithfield with one thrust of his sword he had killed Wat Tyler and effectively burst the bubble of rebellion. Soon afterwards he was rewarded with a knighthood by his grateful king. Now he was given further reward with a salary of 60 marks or £40 a year. Such was the reputation of Standish and the strength of Scarborough castle that Alexander Neville, the archbishop of York, applied for and received permission from King Richard to stay in his castle at Scarborough 'with his household and men', since he no longer felt safe at York.

On 26 August 1381, Henry Percy, earl of Northumberland, presided over an inquisition which met in Scarborough. There he heard the statements of 36 sworn jurors, 12 from the town, 12 from the East Riding wapentakes of Buckrose and Dickering, and 12 from neighbouring Pickering Lythe. Since their evidence is the only narrative account we have, and since it is so detailed, vivid, precise and consistent, it is tempting to accept it as the truth, or even the whole truth. However, such perfect consistency suggests pre-arrangement and rehearsal, and the names of some of the jurors indicate that their versions of events must have been partial and prejudiced.

Of the nine Scarborough jurors known by name, at least three of them, John Stokwith, Alan Waldyfe and William Pereson, are also listed as members of the 42 'potentiores', the victims of the insurrection. Not surprisingly, therefore, there is no hint in their evidence of the reasons behind the events of that extraordinary week, the grievances of the so-called 'malefactors', or their purposes in taking over the town. Galoun, Marche and the others are all equally and vaguely condemned as 'enemies and rebels to the lord king', intent only on settling grudges against the king's loyal and law-abiding subjects.

Still, some justice was done. Instead of blaming and punishing only the known rebel leaders and their followers, the whole town was made to pay. In October 1382, a general pardon was granted to the burgesses and commonalty of Scarborough, excepting the 'xl persones des mieultz vanez Burgeys', the 40 most substantial burgesses who sat on its ruling body. To these 40 excepted from royal pardon two more names were added — Robert Acclom and Robert Rillington. These 42 were now required to pay a fine of 500 marks (£333 6s. 8d.), whereas the remainder of the community was fined 400 marks (£266 13s. 4d.). In other words, even if the sworn jurors did not, the king's justices appreciated that what had happened at Scarborough was provoked by the lawless behaviour of men in authority there. Acclom and Rillington were singled out as special culprits.

Nevertheless, as so often before and afterwards, whatever royal justices might judge and decree, what actually took place at Scarborough was determined by those in power there and not in York or London. Galoun and Marche paid 150 of the 400 marks owed out of their own pockets, whereas it seems improbable that the notorious 42 ever handed over all the 500 marks demanded from them.

Moreover, at some time before December 1384, Robert and John Acclom, John Stokwith, William Sage, William Percy and Henry Ruston, the younger, made a pre-arranged violent attack on William Marche and his property. His home and two ships were broken into and ransacked, 200 of his sheep and other goods valued at £20 were stolen, his men and servants assaulted, and two men who had been accused by him of theft were released from the town gaol. In short, nothing much had changed: the old gangsters were still in charge and now taking revenge.

The same men and families who had dominated Scarborough's Common Hall and parliamentary representation before 1381 continued to do so long after 1381. There were no more poll taxes for the next 600 years, but Carter, Sage, Acclom, Percy, Seamer and Rillington, generation after generation, served as bailiffs, coroners and chamberlains, and sat in the House of Commons for the borough. When new names did appear on the parliamentary list, such as Thomas Carthorpe and John Mosdale, who sat in the parliaments of Henry IV and Henry V, they were not the names of former malcontents. Carthorpe, who was bailiff at least ten times between 1399 and 1425, had the doubtful distinction of being Robert Rillington's son-in-law. Like his infamous father-in-law, he too was involved in acts of piracy as well as legitimate trade, and died a very wealthy man. In contrast, John Mosdale was the king's serjeant-at-arms who was paid 12 pence a day for his service and was constable of Scarborough castle from 1393 for the next 30 years. Unlike most previous and subsequent constables, Mosdale actually had a home in the castle and did much to improve its defences and its accommodation. Also, he was the only medieval castle constable ever to sit in parliament as Scarborough's Member. Yet it seems that not even Mosdale was entirely above suspicion of malpractice: in 1410 the sheriff of Yorkshire was ordered to inquire into the allegation that the constable 'had converted to his own use' the 50 marks a year he was given to repair the castle.

Meanwhile Robert Acclom's son John and John's two sons, Robert II and John II, were keeping up the family tradition. John I was outlawed for murder in 1386 but soon secured a royal pardon; in 1388 and again in 1399 he used his position as bailiff to acquire a seat for himself in the House of Commons. In 1397 he paid 40 shillings for a pardon —

this time for 'selling bread, wine, ale and other victuals in gross and in retail whilst he was bailiff of the town and in trading in them at that time contrary to the ordinance'. When he died in 1402 he left a substantial property estate to his widow, his eldest son, Robert II, and his other sons, who included John II.

Robert II sat in the parliaments of 1401 and 1404. With his partner in crime, William Harum, in 1405 he seized two ships belonging to Hamburg merchants and carrying a cargo of beer, linen, wood and iron valued at £300. Though the Hanse owners petitioned the king's council for redress and two royal commissioners were appointed to investigate the offence and punish the offenders, Acclom failed to turn up at Westminster when summoned and the sheriff of Yorkshire claimed that he could not be found!

Finally, John II, who was bailiff of Scarborough at least four times and MP for the borough in 1421 and 1426, was one of several Scarborough defendants charged in 1412 with robbing at sea a Danzig merchant of goods worth about £200. Other names on the list of culprits included Sage, Percy and Carter. It seems that North Sea piracy had become a common commercial pursuit of Scarborough's foremost burgesses: clearly it was more profitable than legitimate trade or fishing. Even if caught and convicted the worst that might happen to them was a modest penalty fine.

Perhaps it was more than merely a coincidence that just when Scarborough was being misgoverned and terrorized by a criminal oligarchy, it became fashionable to endow perpetual chantries where priests were employed to say prayers for the souls of the dead in purgatory. In his will John Acclom I set aside 62 marks (£41 6s. 8d.) in rents for gifts to religious houses, priests and the poor. If he had a guilty conscience about a lifetime of misdeeds then it was evident only in the terms of his testament. Robert Rillington, whose record was perhaps even worse, was the first in Scarborough to endow a perpetual chantry inside St Mary's parish church. Only weeks after the rising, in September 1381, a deed of foundation established a chantry there at the altar of St Stephen. The original endowment was only two properties in the town valued at five shillings. A chaplain was to say prayers for Robert himself, Henry Percy, earl of Northumberland, William Rillington and Emma his wife. However, when Robert died ten years later, and was buried in his chantry chapel before the altar of St Stephen, in his will he left two ships to be sold and the money to be spent for the welfare of his soul. There is no record of how he acquired the ships.

8. The Third King Richard

'...for the special affection which we have towards our Town of Scardeburgh in the County of York and the Burgesses of the same and in consideration of their good and faithful behaviour and for their more secure immunity and quiet...' — with these opening words King Richard III confirmed his grant of a new charter to Scarborough on 8 April 1485. Richard's 'affection' must indeed have been 'special' since by this charter he conferred on the borough extraordinary privileges never previously enjoyed by it or more than a handful of other English towns. Unfortunately for Richard and for Scarborough, however, within little more than four months after this confirmation he was dead and his charter had died with him.

Richard's association with Scarborough had begun at least ten years earlier when as Duke of Gloucester he surrendered to his eldest brother, King Edward IV, his lordship of Chesterfield and manor of Busshey in Hertfordshire and in exchange received part of the manor of Cottingham near Hull, the advowson of Cottingham church, and the royal castle, lordship and fee-farm of Scarborough and Falsgrave. For 300 years since Henry II had conferred royal borough status on Scarborough, the town had owed its liberties and fee-farm rent for them directly to the Crown: now it was answerable to the king's younger brother.

In fact, Richard's hold on Scarborough also included its hinterland. The castle at Scarborough consisted not only of the headland on which it was built but also the adjacent manor of Northstead to the north of it — about 200 acres of woodland and pasture drained by Peasholm beck. To this, in 1476, Richard had added the derelict manor of Hatterboard out of his brother's duchy of Lancaster — another 280 acres to the north of Falsgrave. So that even before he was crowned king of England in July 1483, Richard had more interest in and control over Scarborough than any previous monarch.

Richard's interest in Scarborough was mainly naval. Since the age of nine he had held the title of Lord Admiral of England, and unlike other previous holders of this office was not unwilling to go to sea himself. First as duke later as king he regarded Scarborough as a place of key naval importance — as a base for privateering forays, as an assembly port for the royal war fleet in operations against the Scots, and not least as a provisioning refuge for warships employed to protect English fishing boats in the North Sea and off Iceland. Newcastle was too far north and vulnerable to Scottish raids across the border, yet Scarborough was far enough north to be safe from French or Breton marauders. Scarborough was also the most natural and convenient port for the heart of Richard's power which sprang from his lands and castles in Yorkshire at Skipton, Richmond, Middleham, Helmsley, Sheriff Hutton and Scarborough itself; and Scarborough was less than a day's ride from Richard's northern capital at York.

Scarborough harbour was generally regarded then as the only safe haven between the Tyne and the Humber. In the days when ships were extremely vulnerable to adverse tides and winds, when navigation was crude, and conditions on board were primitive and unhealthy, a secure refuge like Scarborough was essential even for the most seaworthy and best-handled vessels. The castle headland gave natural shelter from the north to Scarborough's shore but it was open and exposed dangerously to the south and east and therefore its harbour had to have a strong, well maintained pier. Ever since 1252, when Henry III had granted the burgesses the right to construct 'a new Port with Timber and Stone towards the Sea', Scarborough's reputation as a secure anchorage and its prosperity as a fishing and trading port had depended on its ability to maintain this bulwark 'against the rage of the sea'.

Once having decided to make Scarborough his principal northern naval base, Richard did all that his limited means and time allowed to preserve and strengthen the harbour's defences. For instance, he ordered 300 oaks from the forest of Pickering to be used for Scarborough's jetty and quay. When John Leland visited Scarborough in the 1540s he lamented that the 'peere wherby socour is made for shippes is now sore decayid' and that 'a bulwark ... made by Richard the 3' was then 'yn ruine by the se rage'. Leland's implication was that Scarborough's decay was the result of more than half a century of neglect since Richard's time there.

Leland also noted that Scarborough town was 'waullid a litle with ston, but most with diches and waules of yerth'. King Richard, he wrote, had begun ' to waul a pece of the town quadrato saxo [squared stone] ', but clearly this wall was incomplete at the end of his reign and there was no one with the money or the desire to have it finished. The location and extent of Richard's stone wall are well defined by a sketch or plat of Scarborough drawn in 1538. Since the plat was the work of a military engineer employed by Henry VIII its accuracy as far as the town's landward defences are concerned can be assumed. Though the western extension of Scarborough's original settlement had been called Newborough from as early as the twelfth century, it seems that unlike the

51

old borough it was protected only by an enclosure of earth rampart and ditches, not by a stone wall. Evidently, King Richard was concerned to give 'more secure immunity and quiet' to the people of Scarborough and therefore considered its Newborough ditches and earth rampart inadequate defences.

As a result, work was begun on fortifying the two main gateways into the town and stone walls constructed behind the ditches on either side of them. However, the wall running north from Newborough Bar never met that coming west from Oldborough Bar: a crescent of earth rampart and wide ditch, known for centuries afterwards as the New Dyke, separated them. John Cossins's New and Exact Plan of Scarborough, drawn in 1725, shows a surviving length of stone wall running to the west of Oldborough Bar, which he described as 'the new wall', whereas the ditch in front of it was labelled 'the old mote'. A short section of Richard's 'new wall' of squared stone has survived as the perimeter of the old Convent site linking the northern ends of St Thomas and Queen Streets.

During his brief and eventful reign it was unusual for Richard to spend much time in any one place: he was a restless, busy, nervous monarch. That he came to Scarborough at least twice in the summer of 1484 and that he stayed there about two weeks in all indicate not so much 'the special affection' he had for the town as the important role he had chosen for it. We know that he was at Scarborough castle on 22 May and that he returned there on the last day of June because writs, warrants and other documents were sealed by him there on these days. There followed a succession of royal orders given at Scarborough or at Scarborough castle on the 4, 5, 7, 8 and 11 July. By 12 July King Richard was back at York.

What Richard was doing at Scarborough during these summer days is revealed by the many writs issued from there under his personal seal. On 22 May he told all mayors and sheriffs to whom it might apply that he had given Richard Gough his commission to buy 'whete, bere, fisshe and flesshe' to provision 'the workes at Dunbarre' and to employ 'artificers and labourers with ship[s] and maryners' to carry 'the stuf' there. Following the English invasion of Scotland led by Richard when he was Duke of Gloucester in 1482, the Duke of Albany had been made lieutenant-general there to represent English power and interest. Though Albany was soon driven out of the country by the Scots, his garrison in the castle of Dunbar on the coast had continued to hold out against half-hearted siege operations. Maintaining 'the workes at Dunbarre' was therefore part of Richard's continuing campaign against the Scots. Two months after granting Gough his commission, Richard ordered his treasurer to pay William Todd of York the sum of £28 4s. 8d. 'due to him for beeves[beef], salt, shofold[?] and woode of him boughte by Richard Goghe for vitailling of oure shippes at Scardburghe'. So the supply ships to Dunbar had been loaded at and had sailed from Scarborough.

When Richard returned to Scarborough on 30 June his purpose was to assemble there a fleet of warships and fit it out for naval operations in the North Sea against Scottish ships. John Papedy was authorised to recruit sailors, soldiers and 'vitalle' for them. Whether Richard took personal command of his war fleet when it put to sea from Scarborough is not known; however, it is certain that on this occasion his ships won a significant victory over the Scots and one usually reliable source attributes the victory to Richard's 'own skill'.

By 4 July Richard was back in Scarborough. Local legend says that he lodged in what has long since been called 'Richard the Third's House' on Sandside. The present building in question contains no architectural features earlier than Elizabethan, but it stands on a quayside site occupied by a former structure. Richard might well have found the location here beside the harbour more convenient than at the castle. Also, writs and warrants issued by him on 22 May and 5 July were 'given at the castel of Scardeburgh', whereas those issued after 5 July were 'given at Scardeburgh'.

The house is thought to have belonged then to Thomas Sage, one of the town's leading burgesses and richest shipowner. Thomas was the latest in a long line of Sages who had lived and prospered in Scarborough since the early fourteenth century. His grandfather, great-grandfather, and great-great-grandfather had all sat in Parliament for the borough, and he himself had been a Member in 1472. That he was a very wealthy man well-disposed towards Richard is suggested by a royal warrant of December 1483 commanding the bailiff of Pickering Lythe to pay Thomas 100 marks — 50 at Michaelmas and 50 more a year later — in repayment of a loan.

On 7 July, all merchants, fishermen and mariners then in the vicinity of Iceland were informed by Richard that he had appointed William Combersale, captain of the royal ship *Elizabeth*, to be their escort and guard. They were to obey his instructions or otherwise forfeit their ships and goods. They were to sail together in convoy under Combersale who would bring them south to 'mete withe othre of oure Armye now being upon the see'. This was not the first time Richard had expressed concern for the safety of Scarborough's Icelandic seamen. Earlier that same year he had ordered them to sail northwards in escorted convoy 'well harnessed and apparalled for their own safety', having first assembled in the Humber estuary. Now that they were returning home he was anxious to protect them from hostile Scots or Norwegians.

While still at Scarborough Richard was not exclusively preoccupied with his northern war fleet and the Scottish campaign. On 8 July he commissioned Richard Forthey to buy '200 beefe, 200 muttons, 200 hoggs' for shipment to the English garrison at Calais. If the loyalty and security of Scarborough were vital to Richard's policy, his secure hold on Calais mattered to him in many ways. Not only was Calais a base for privateering operations against the French and Bretons in the Channel, there was a danger that it might be used as a springboard for invasion of England by the greatest threat to Richard's rule — the Lancastrian claimant in exile, Henry Tudor. Not least of Calais' importance was its role as Richard's only bastion and forward intelligence post on the Continent. Richard needed to know when Henry Tudor was coming, from where he was coming, and where he was expected to land. Scarborough might provide him with advanced warning if Henry came ashore on the North Sea coast, whereas from Calais he hoped to learn if it was to be an invasion across the Channel.

Richard's stone wall, his harbour bulwark, and his presence at the castle and in the town were testimony to his genuine concern for Scarborough's wealth and welfare; but altogether they were overshadowed by his supreme gift to the borough — its new charter of liberties. Richard had made financial concessions to Hull, Beverley and Newcastle; to Pontefract he had granted borough status; but Scarborough he converted into a shire incorporate, a status hitherto enjoyed by only London, Bristol and Norwich, and most recently, York. Considering Scarborough's relative size in terms of its population, wealth and commerce, Richard's charter was an astonishing preference.

According to the terms of Richard's charter, Scarborough was to become a county separate from Yorkshire with its own sheriff, who would have the same power and jurisdiction in the town as sheriffs elsewhere had in counties throughout the kingdom. Secondly, Scarborough was to become a seaport, separate and independent from Hull, to which it had been formerly subordinate. One practical consequence of this newly-acquired independence was that in future Scarborough would have the wool staple or monopoly of the wool-exporting trade over a wide area of north-east Yorkshire and along the whole length of the coast from Teesmouth in the north to Filey in the south. Thirdly, Scarborough was to be exempted from the jurisdiction of the Lord Admiral's court, and its mayor, as admiral, would exercise authority along the entire coastline and shore from 'Scaryhale' in the south to 'Nothland' in the north.

Scarborough had never had a mayor before: previously its government had been in the hands of two bailiffs, two coroners, four chamberlains and 36 burgesses, in all 44 members of the Common Hall. Now the borough was to have a mayor, a coroner and 12 aldermen. Richard himself chose the first mayor, Peter Percy, the elder, and the first sheriff, Robert Maylyerd, while the 36 burgesses were permitted to elect from amongst their own number the 12 aldermen and the coroner. After the first year of this regime in effect the aldermen would have become Scarborough's new ruling body with power to choose future mayors, sheriffs and coroners. In short, it seemed that Richard wanted an even smaller oligarchy to govern Scarborough, since only the 12 aldermen would be able to elect their successors. Presumably, he assumed that 12 men would be easier to control than 44.

In return for all these additional, extraordinary privileges, Scarborough might have expected to have had to pay a higher fee-farm annual rent to the Crown. For some time past the farm had been fixed at £91 a year, £66 for Scarborough itself and another £25 for Falsgrave. However, just to underline 'the special affection' he had for the town, Richard remitted £10 of the £66 previously paid into the Exchequer every Michaelmas, so that the total owed was reduced from £91 to £81. King Edward III had granted £22 11s. out of Falsgrave's £25 to the Warden and Scholars of King's Hall, Cambridge, and Richard II had added to it another £20 out of Scarborough's £66, but Richard III insisted that King's Hall, which later became Trinity College, should continue to receive its full allowance annually of £42 11s.

Even before the final confirmation of Richard's new charter to Scarborough it had been put into effect. Peter Percy, the town's first mayor, was in office and the 36 burgesses of the Common Hall had already elected 12 of their company to act as aldermen. Moreover, now that the borough had a new government its leaders decided to draw up new rules of practice 'to the honour of the lord the king and the security and utility of this town of Scardeburgh'. In future any burgess who refused to take up one of the municipal offices was to pay a fine, ranging in value from £40 for refusal to serve as mayor to £10 for refusal to be one of the two chamberlains. To draw attention to their importance and dignity, it was decreed that the mayor, sheriff, aldermen, chamberlains and burgesses should all wear distinctive robes of scarlet or blood-red. Again, failure to dress properly would incur heavy penalty fines. These officers were also required to set good examples by walking in procession up to St Mary's on Sundays and holy days and there sit in their appointed places in the choir. Penalties for deliberate, inexcusable non-attendance were measured in pounds of wax to be paid to the parish church.

Just in case attendance at masses did not guarantee honest conduct, the two chamberlains, who dealt with 'the issues and profits generally pertaining to the commonalty', were required to present their weekly accounts every Saturday in the Common Hall before the mayor and at least two aldermen. Among the heavy responsibilities of the chamberlains was their duty to pay the mayor his salary of £20, in three equal instalments of 10 marks, in May, September and December. However, their principal care was 'to repair and amend the quay'. Even if this meant going into debt, the chamberlains had to make sure that the wages of workmen on the quay were paid promptly and in full.

Finally, in the interests of public hygiene and freedom of public movement, it was ordained that no inhabitant of Scarborough should use the street or lanes outside his dwelling to dry salt fish or to store timber or stones. Free-range pigs were also a nuisance: owners were to keep their pigs in their houses and not allow them out on to the street, except on Saturdays for the market. Every pig found in the street on any of the other six days of the week would cost its owner fourpence.

The death of Richard III on the battlefield of Bosworth and the succession of Henry Tudor were double blows to Scarborough. Richard had given the town privilege and priority well in excess of its perceived importance, and when he was killed the charter died with him. There was no reference to Richard's charter in the final charter granted by Henry VII in 1492: it was as though neither he nor it had ever existed. Peter Percy and Robert Maylyerd had no successors. The office of sheriff of Scarborough disappeared for ever and that of mayor was revived only 200 years later when another king, Charles II, tried to alter the town's form of government.

Richard's Newborough wall was left unfinished; Richard's quay and bulwark were allowed to decay. Scarborough's long decline continued and accelerated; the Tudors had only occasional interest in its castle. After Richard III the next reigning monarch to visit Scarborough was Queen Elizabeth II, just 500 years later — by which time it was too late. As for Scarborough castle, no English king or queen has ever set foot in it since Richard and his Queen Ann lived there in the summer of 1484. In the eyes of many, Richard the Third might have been one of the most evil men who ever disgraced the English throne, but to Scarborians he was the best royal friend they ever had, and his premature death was an unmitigated disaster.

9. Sir Ralph Eure the Younger

In October 1536, the protest movement against Henry VIII's threatened closure of religious houses, known as the Pilgrimage of Grace, spread like a wind-driven priarie fire across the whole of Yorkshire: starting in Lincolnshire, it crossed the Humber, took hold in the East Riding, and soon engulfed Hull, York, Wakefield and Pontefract. By the end of that month a huge peasant army of at least 10,000 ill-armed men, marching southwards, had reached Doncaster.

Throughout the entire county only two strongholds remained loyal to the king — the castles at Skipton in the west and Scarborough in the east. Skipton castle belonged to and was the chief residence of Henry Clifford, first earl of Cumberland, one of the few northern magnates who opposed the Pilgrimage. Scarborough castle belonged to Henry VIII, and it was held for him by his deputy constable there, Sir Ralph Eure the younger.

As early as 17 October, when the popular rising in Yorkshire was little over a week old, it was reported to the king that 'great numbers' had occupied the town of Scarborough and were besieging its castle. The 'great numbers' concerned must have been villagers from the neighbourhood, since Robert Aske, the leader of the Pilgrimage, denied any responsibility for or even knowledge of the siege until it had already begun. According to one of the lesser-known North Riding Pilgrim captains, George Bawne, Scarborough castle had become the only refuge in the area for the enemies and victims of the rebels, so that he was determined to win it 'or hassard his life'. This is confirmed by another report that some of archbishop Lee's servants, who had fled from the commons at York, were first captured by the besiegers at Scarborough but then rescued by Sir Ralph's men who brought them into the safety of the castle. We also know the names of several of Scarborough's leading burgesses—William Lockwood, William Langdale, Guy Fysh and Launcelot Lacey—who had fled into the castle in fear of their lives.

About 27 October supplies of 'victual and gunpowder' were sent by sea up the coast from Lincolnshire by the duke of Suffolk, acting directly under King Henry's instructions. Since Eure was related to several Pilgrim ringleaders, and other Yorkshiremen had first sworn allegiance to the king only to surrender tamely to the commons or even join them, there was a risk that Sir Ralph would do the same. However, Henry believed that he could be trusted with the munitions because, as he put it to the duke in a letter, 'Ivers [Eure] had promised to do a notable act.'

Sir Ralph received his supplies safely through the port of Scarborough probably because when they arrived there a truce had been made between the Pilgrim leaders and the king's envoy, the duke of Norfolk, at Doncaster. The siege of the castle had been lifted. But the king never intended the truce to be more than a temporary, tactical manoeuvre: he was playing for time in the hope that the onset of winter weather would force the Pilgrim host to disperse and return to the warmth and comfort of their homes. Consequently, in clear breach of the terms of the truce, further supplies of 'ordnance, victual and gunpowder' were dispatched from Grimsby by sea 'in a small crayer'. The ship also carried £100 in money and letters of encouragement from Thomas Cromwell, the Lord Privy Seal, and the king himself addressed to Sir Ralph. However, this vital cargo never reached Eure: it was intercepted and captured by one of the East Riding Pilgrim captains. Whether the money was shared out amongst the Pilgrims or sent to Aske at Doncaster is not clear, but the content of the letters and the true intentions of Cromwell and Henry were clear enough: the negotiated truce was a cynical and deceitful stratagem. Henry's objective was suppression and revenge, not concession.

Strengthened by their captured munitions, the Pilgrims resumed the siege of Scarborough castle. For twenty days Sir Ralph and his hard-pressed garrison held out. By now they had only bread to eat and the castle well water to drink. In March 1538, two of Henry's inspectors of the defences of Scarborough castle reported to him that the north wall, overlooking the holms, was 'clene decayed and fallen down' for 75 yards in length. Three months earlier, Sir Ralph had told Cromwell that this same north wall, 'betwixt the gatehouse and the castle', had been 'shot down' during the recent siege. In other words, the Pilgrims had used cannon against the castle, and what was probably a decayed wall had collapsed under the impact of artillery fire.

At the beginning of December the Pilgrim leaders, with astonishing innocence, accepted the king's offer made through Norfolk of a full, free pardon and a new parliament to meet at York the following spring. The commons were told to return to their homes. The siege of Scarborough castle was lifted, and Sir Ralph was given a pledge of safe conduct southwards when he was summoned to London.

Eure must have expected handsome reward from the king for his 'notable act': against the odds he had held out at Scarborough and defied the Pilgrims. In the event, he was made constable of the royal castle for life and granted the tenancy of the adjacent royal manor of Northstead at an annual rent of £24. Though in the past previous constables of Scarborough castle were also allowed part of the town's fee-farm rent to the Crown, there was no specific reference to any salary, only that Eure was to have a permanent, paid garrison of one hundred armed men under his command.

When a second invasion of Scarborough, this time by Wolds men of Sir Francis Bigod, took place in the evening of 16 January 1537, Sir Ralph had not yet returned to the castle. Both town and castle were open and undefended. Nevertheless, so timid and scrupulous were the invaders that instead of occupying the castle they merely mounted a guard outside it!

A week later, Sir Ralph was writing to the king to tell him that he was master of Scarborough and that the rebel leaders had surrendered themselves without a fight. He had given the people 'comfortable words' so that the neighbourhood was now quiet and loyal. However, he thought it prudent to strengthen the castle and hold it with the promised garrison of a hundred soldiers. On the same day, Eure also wrote to Thomas Cromwell, asking for the lands and offices of Sir Francis Bigod, whose insurrection had collapsed and who was now an abandoned fugitive.

There was no love lost between the Bigods and the Eures, and between Sir Francis and Sir Ralph there had developed a personal animosity and rivalry of great, indeed murderous, intensity. The two men hated each other. Sir Francis had been a gentleman of considerable power and influence in the locality. His property in Yorkshire consisted of two main groups—one centred on Mulgrave castle, which included the manors of Seaton and Hinderwell, and a larger one in the East Riding which took in the manors of Settrington, Birdsall, Hunmanby and other lands in the Malton area. Not least of his offices was the stewardship of the Liberty of Whitby Strand, granted to him for life by his patron, the earl of Northumberland. By the standards of his time, Sir Francis was a highly literate and scholarly young man. As a ward of Wolsey, he had profited from the best education then available in the cardinal's household and at the university of Oxford. Above all, Bigod was a disciple of the New Learning—a radical reformer of the church and the religious houses.

In the sharpest contrast, Sir Ralph Eure was uneducated and illiterate. His dictated letters betray not the slightest interest in the revolutionary changes that were currently transforming church and state in England. If Sir Francis was in debt, Sir Ralph was just poor. His home was neither draughty castle like Mulgrave, nor modern mansion house like Bigod's Settrington. His grandfather, the old Sir Ralph, who lived until 1539, had his residence at Ayton castle, and his father, Sir William, the first Lord Eure, occupied the new family house at Malton. Sir Ralph the younger had therefore to make do with a tenancy of the farm house and demesne of Foulbridge, which he leased from the Knights of the Hospital of St John at an annual rent of £17 6s. 8d. Foulbridge had once been the only crossing of the river Derwent between Ayton and Malton and on the main north-south route across the carrs of the eastern end of the Vale of Pickering, but by Sir Ralph's time the bridge had gone, replaced by one at Yedingham, a mile downstream.

The feud between Bigod and Eure had come to violence even before the two took opposing sides on the Pilgrimage. Sir Francis was so shocked by the deplorable conduct of the monks and servants of Whitby abbey, in particular the notorious abbot, John Hexham, and his bailiff, Gregory Conyers of Bagdale, that he tried to remove both from their places. At Whitby fair, on St Hilda's day, 25 August 1535, Conyers and some servants of the abbey were attacked by Bigod's retainers and narrowly escaped with their lives. The following March, Bigod's servants attacked and murdered one of Sir Ralph's in Malton. In January 1537, it was Gregory Conyers, said by the duke of Norfolk to be 'in great trust with young Sir Ralph Evers, his master', who seized Bigod's property at Mulgrave castle and very nearly caught its owner as he fled northwards.

Bigod was eventually cornered, conveyed to London in chains, convicted of treason, and, along with other Pilgrim leaders, executed at Tyburn in June 1537. He was not quite 30-years-old. But Sir Ralph failed to profit from his downfall as much as he expected. Three times he wrote to Cromwell, reminding him of his recent service and asking for Bigod's attainted lands. One of the letters was headed 'from my poor house' at Foulbridge, but the Lord Privy Seal ignored the hint. Eure had to be content for the time being with Bigod's stewardship of Whitby Strand: the prizes which he coveted most—Mulgrave and Settrington—were retained by the king.

Sir Ralph's conspicuous failure to secure what he considered his just deserts might explain why he helped himself to rewards. Even by the low standards of that unruly time, he acted with exceptional rapacity and dishonesty. After the siege of Scarborough castle he had stripped the lead from the roofs of its towers and turrets, used some of it to make himself a 'brewing vessel' for his house at Foulbridge, and sold the rest to buy 'French wines'. He had done the same injury to the parsonage mansion house at Scarborough, thereby 'suffering it to decay'. As for his tenancy of the royal manor of Northstead, he had sub-let it at a profit to himself of six pounds a year and still allowed the manor house there to fall into ruin. According to the sworn testimony of one of his servants and captains, William Lockwood, who was with him in the castle and had brought money to him there from the duke of Norfolk, Sir Ralph had received £356 to maintain his garrison but had paid out less than £100 for this purpose. If this was true it contrasts with Eure's repeated requests to Cromwell to make good his soldiers' wages which he claimed were in arrears.

There were even more damning accusations levelled at Eure by Lockwood and other witnesses. One serious allegation was that he had received stolen goods belonging to the former prior of Guisborough when he was arrested at Easter 1537 on charges of aiding the Pilgrims. The goods in question were the prior's treasury of coins and jewellery which he had kept in locked caskets. One of these caskets had been brought to Sir Ralph when he was out hunting on the North York Moors. Eure had eagerly forced open the metal box with his dagger and found inside a purse full of gold and silver coins—'realls, ducats and angels, and some crowns of 5 shillings'. After his count of the gold coins had reached '200 angels', he put them back into the purse and rode off with it. The ex-prior's household furniture and livestock were declared forfeit; the prior, James Cockerell, was executed; but his caskets were never seen again.

Yet none of these outrageous acts seem to have upset Cromwell as much as a disrespectful reference to himself found in one of Sir Ralph's letters written at Scarborough castle. When challenged, Eure pointed out that he could not write more than his own name so he could not have been the author. Suspicion then fell on Lockwood. He was accused of having forged the letter in Eure's name. Interrogated by both Norfolk and Cromwell, Lockwood steadfastly denied responsibility. The matter remained unresolved: both Eure and Lockwood escaped punishment, though the latter was probably the culprit.

The cloud that now hung over Eure perhaps explains why he never was rewarded with the forfeited Bigod lands he so coveted: he had to make do with their stewardship and fees of a mere £5 a year. It must also have been galling to him that when Whitby abbey was dissolved in 1539 another of his local rivals, Sir Richard Cholmley, was granted the lease of the monastery demesne for the next 21 years. Cholmley had not joined with the Pilgrims, but neither had he actively resisted them.

Sir Ralph was hardly likely to feel satisfied with the unpaid and onerous offices he was given after the Pilgrimage. In 1538 he became justice of the peace in the North Riding, and in January 1542 he was elected to serve with Sir Nicholas Fairfax as one of Scarborough's representatives in the House of Commons. He might have been chosen by Scarborough for the earlier parliaments of 1536 and 1539-40, but the names of the members of the House of Commons in these have been lost.

Eure was clearly no parliamentarian, and the king soon found more suitable employment for him—employment which he doubtless relished, not least because it offered new opportunities for plunder. First he was appointed keeper of the notorious Northumberland border areas of Redesdale and Tynedale and then, from 1544, lord warden of the Middle Marches. The outbreak of war with the Scots in August 1542 meant that he was to spend what remained of his life fighting them in the borderlands.

For a military leader, described by the earl of Shrewsbury, a fellow campaigner in the Lowlands, as 'a fell cruel man and over cruel, which many a man and fatherless bairn might rue', Sir Ralph's demise was fitting. On 27 February 1545 he and his army were outmanoeuvred and annihilated on Ancrum Moor between Selkirk and Jedburgh. In retaliation for the barbarities he had committed on the ancestors of the earl of Angus at Melrose abbey, Eure's corpse was mutilated before burial in the same place. Though since his grandfather's death he was no longer called 'the younger', Sir Ralph was still only 35-years-old.

Ironically, the Bigod lands in the East Riding, Settrington and Birdsall, which Eure had wanted most of all, eventually came into the hands of the Scottish Lennox family. The royal castle at Scarborough, which he had both protected and pillaged, along with the manor of Northstead, which he had exploited, passed from his family to Sir Richard Cholmley, 'the great black knight of the North'. The Cholmleys, not the Eures or the Conyers, were to be the principal beneficiaries of the dissolution of Whitby abbey. Even Mulgrave escaped Eure's clutches. After Bigod's execution his widow Katherine wrote from there to the bishop of Worcester thanking him for his intercession on her behalf. Though the Act of Attainder was passed against her husband, it was repealed in 1547 and the Mulgrave estate was restored to Sir Francis's grandson. Another of the many ironies of this time was that George Dakins, who as a Bigod servant had murdered one of Sir Ralph's men in Malton in March 1536, succeeded Eure as the tenant of Foulbridge.

It is not easy to classify people, especially if there are only three categories to choose from, but in the case of Sir Ralph Eure it is evident that he was neither honest hero nor harmless eccentric. He used the Pilgrimage of Grace, a relatively idealistic demonstration, as a fortuitous opportunity to destroy his arch-enemy Sir Francis Bigod and win favours from the king and his chief minister. But for the Pilgrimage he might have remained in his 'poor house' at Foulbridge and risen no higher than deputy constable of Scarborough castle. Fortunately for him, king Henry's acute need for unscrupulous northerners to replace those who could no longer be trusted outweighed his natural distaste for rapacious adventurers. The religious issues raised by Henry's Reformation were entirely lost on Sir Ralph: only his material self-interest mattered. His greed was so great that it nearly ruined him, but in the end he got his just deserts.

10. The Gates of Seamer

Little is known about the early life of Sir Henry Gates. He was born about 1515, the son of Sir Geoffrey Gates and the younger brother of the better-known and ill-fated, Sir John Gates. By birth and upbringing Henry was a southerner. In his will he described himself as of Kilburn in Middlesex; he first sat in the House of Commons as burgess for Shoreham in Kent in 1544; and he was first appointed justice of the peace in Suffolk in 1547, the year of his knighthood and the birth of his eldest son, Edward. Sir Henry continued to prosper until the death of Edward VI in 1553 when, unfortunately for him and even more so for his brother John, they tried to put Lady Jane Grey on the throne and exclude the Catholic, Mary Tudor. John was executed for his treason and Henry was imprisoned indefinitely in the Tower of London.

John's death and his own lengthy incarceration may well have converted Henry into a lifelong champion of the Protestant Reformation, so that Mary's early death in 1558 and the succession of her Protestant sister, Elizabeth, must have brought great joy and relief to him. Sir Henry was immediately released from the Tower and the charges against him dropped.

The new queen badly needed friends and active allies in the North, particularly in Yorkshire, where there remained a dangerous majority of followers of the old Roman Catholic faith. A survey of the religious convictions of the principal gentlemen in Yorkshire about this time revealed that in the East Riding only six out of 12, in the North Riding, only nine out of 22, and in the West Riding, only eleven out of 31 were known to be reliable Protestants. In these unpromising circumstances the government had to import southern Protestants into predominantly Catholic areas to act as informers, propagandists and law-enforcers. Sir Henry Gates was chosen to be one such Protestant import.

The list of offices—judicial, administrative and military—held by Gates from 1558 onwards was a tribute to his exceptional energy and loyalty. At once he was made a member of the Council in the North, the most powerful instrument of royal authority in the region, and served on it for the rest of his life. He was appointed justice of the peace in the North Riding in 1559, in the East Riding in 1561, and in the West Riding in 1569. Later, he served as magistrate in four other northern counties—Durham, Cumberland, Westmorland and Northumberland. As deputy constable and steward of Pickering Lythe, he exercised considerable authority over the area which included Pickering and Scarborough.

Apart from his seat in the Council at York, which qualified him for an annual 'stipend and diet' of £20, few of his many onerous offices were paid, and most of them incurred heavy expenses. Gates needed land and income which would give him means, status and location. Ever since the Percys had fallen foul of Henry VIII their manor of Seamer, three miles inland from Scarborough, had been forfeited to the Crown. In 1559 the queen granted Sir Henry the lordship of the manor and the lands attached to it. The following year from her he also received the rectory of the parish church of St Martin's at Seamer and the chapels of nearby Cayton and East Ayton, which had once belonged to the dissolved abbey of Whitby. In subsequent years Gates added several other properties to his Yorkshire estate, but his home he made permanently at Seamer.

Sir Henry amply justified and repaid the trust placed in him. At the lowest level, as justice of the peace, he was assiduous in seeking out and punishing persistent Catholics who refused to conform to the established Protestant church. One typical case concerned Thomas Williamson, Scarborough's bailiff for the year 1583-4.

Soon after Williamson's election, William Taylor, curate of Scarborough's St Mary's, wrote to Sir Henry at Seamer pointing out the perils of having such a man in such an office. According to Taylor's testimony, Williamson seldom attended church and his wife never came at all; when he ought to have been in his bailiff's place to listen to sermons or take communion 'he used to shifte himselfe into the countrey the morning before'; and recently he had 'perswaded a widowe that if shee should marry a mynyster she shuld loose hir creditte'.

Sir Henry sent Taylor's letter up to London, adding his own condemnation: 'Williamson hath of late procured his dwellinge upon or nere unto the sea coast, to no good purpose at all.' His recommendation was that because Williamson was 'a man of a verie shrewde wytte, great wilfullness and evillie affected in Religion', he ought to be removed from his dwelling at Scarborough as well as his office of bailiff there. Williamson was duly taken into custody on a charge of obstinant recusancy and under suspicion of plotting treason, and imprisoned in York castle, though the worst that could be proved against him was that he had imported Catholic rosaries and crucifixes, not Spanish spies or Catholic priests.

At a much higher level, the service of Sir Henry to the queen and the Protestant church in England was inestimable: in particular, during the rising of the Northern earls in 1569 he played a key role. As early as July 1568 he and his friend John Vaughan warned the queen's principal secretary, Sir William Cecil, of the danger of an imminent insurrection in the northern counties in support of the Catholic Mary, Queen of Scots, who had recently fled into England. 'The Scottish Queen,' they wrote, 'wins the affection of many, especially the simple ... Religion waxes cold, and is going backward.' Cecil was advised to take precautionary military measures, and in particular secure and strengthen Scarborough castle.

In October, as soon as rumours of a rebellion led by the earls of Northumberland and Westmorland leaked out, the Lord President of the Council in the North, the earl of Sussex, then at Cawood, sent for Sir Henry, who was staying with Vaughan at Sutton upon Derwent, eight miles away. Gates and Vaughan came at once: arriving at Cawood between five and six in the morning, they found his lordship still in his night-gown and bare-legged. Sussex was clearly in a panic, believing that he was about to be taken hostage by the rebels. The following day Gates rode off to Seamer to raise the loyal men of Pickering Lythe and arrange the safe custody of Scarborough castle. If the earls had planned a rising they now thought better of it: when summoned to York there they expressed their total innocence. In the meantime Gates's presence calmed the countryside, or, as he put it, 'the bruits have ceased'.

When the rebels did finally break cover in November 1569, and the sheriff of Yorkshire, Richard Norton, joined them, Cecil's first choice for his replacement was Sir Henry Gates. However, though Sir Henry's spirit was more than willing, his body could not respond to the invitation. When Sussex went to see him he found Gates 'lying very sick' and 'much troubled that through sickness he cannot serve in that office nor venture his life in the field'. By the time that Sir Henry's health had begun to improve, the rebels had turned back from Tadcaster, their furthest point southwards, and retreated to Durham. In the vain hope that Spanish troops might come ashore there to assist them, one rebel group had taken possession of Hartlepool. Though there was never any real danger of a Spanish landing, this threat was taken seriously by Sussex, who sent a force of 600 men with field ordnance under Sir Henry to retake and hold the port. After he had occupied Hartlepool, Gates spent Christmas there with 300 of his own men drawn from Pickering Lythe.

In the aftermath of the rising Sir Henry was entrusted with several important and dangerous duties. For instance, he was sent by Queen Elizabeth to Edinburgh with her letters for the Scottish regent Moray; but his mission there came to an abrupt end when Moray was assassinated. Sir Henry himself was a target for the rebels who made more than one attempt to murder him; only a strong bodyguard prevented their success.

Sir Henry's public activities were not confined to combating rebellious northern Catholics: during the thirty years from the queen's first in 1559 until his death in 1589, Gates sat in nearly every one of Elizabeth's parliaments. He was chosen as Scarborough's senior Member in 1559, 1563 and 1572, and as one of Yorkshire's county representatives in 1571 and 1586. Only for the parliament of 1584-5 was he absent from Westminster. His name appears frequently in the brief journals of the House of Commons, usually when religious bills were being drawn up and debated. As everywhere else, Sir Henry was a steadfast champion of the settlement of the Protestant Church of' England under Queen Elizabeth its Supreme Governor which had been established by Acts of Parliament.

Though Gates himself had no training in the law, either at University or at one of the London Inns of Court, the breadth of experience he had gained as a magistrate, collector of taxes and customs, royal courier, captain of militia, and Member of many Parliaments explain why he was so often chosen for vital state responsibilities. Sir Thomas Gargrave, sheriff of Yorkshire and deputy to the Lord President of the Council in the North, recommended that Sir Henry should live permanently in York so that he would always be present for Council meetings; but the queen rejected this advice on the grounds that she might need him for a variety of travelling commissions.

Given Sir Henry's favour with the queen's government and his predominant local influence, it is hardly surprising that in 1577 he re-opened Seamer's fair and market. As lord of the manor of Seamer, he invoked the charter granted to a predecessor, Henry Percy, first earl of Northumberland, by Richard II in 1382. Whether Seamer's Monday market and annual July fair were ever held for long by the Percys seems unlikely. As early as 1256 Scarborough's burgesses had secured a local commercial monopoly for their Thursday and Saturday markets by closing those at neighbouring Sherburn, Brompton and Filey; and Seamer's probably soon suffered the same fate. For nearly two hundred years, therefore, the royal charter had been dormant.

By 1577, if Gates was strongly placed, Scarborough was scarcely strong enough to stand up to him: the town's chronic, economic depression and demographic decline were all too evident. A visitor to Scarborough in the 1540s noted that whereas 200 years previously it had 'many good ships and rich merchants, now there be but few boats and no merchants of estimation'. Once the town had a population of 2,500, but now there were fewer than 1,000 inhabitants. To keep its precious pier in repair, the burgesses had sold the lead off the roof of St Thomas's church and auctioned the contents of the church of the Holy Sepulchre. The queen was sufficiently moved by Scarborough's poverty that she gave it £500, 100 tons of timber from her forest, and six tons of iron to build a new harbour pier.

If Sir Henry had prevailed, then Scarborough might have become little more than a fishing village, and Seamer might have grown as large as Malton or Pickering, but the borough refused to concede defeat. For the next 35 years there was almost continuous open warfare between the Gates family and Scarborough's ruling burgesses.

The war was fought out mainly by lawyers in the courts. As the case dragged on in one court after another year by year, Scarborough was said to have paid out £2,000 in legal fees, and it could hardly have been much less costly to the Gates family.

However, it is clear that the borough's complaints against Sir Henry went far beyond his market at Seamer. In one bill presented before the Court of Exchequer in 1583 Scarborough's advocates alleged that he had deliberately trespassed by force on Falsgrave Moor, where the burgesses had exclusive pasture rights. Worse still, he had 'verie wrongfully and viciuselye turned and altered a great p[ar]te of the course of the water coming to the mylles', so that their value to the town had fallen by £20 a year. These water corn mills must have been the three in Ramsdale powered by the beck which ran out of Scarborough Mere, the borough's southern boundary with Seamer.

In his defence, Sir Henry denied all the charges and argued cogently that by re-opening Seamer's market and fair he had not acted for profit or out of malice towards Scarborough. There was no direct competition: Seamer's market was open on Mondays, Scarborough's were on Thursdays and Saturdays. Indeed, the poor people of the neighbourhood had welcomed the lower prices and the greater supplies of food and utensils the new market provided. Seamer was much better situated and more accessible than Scarborough for the exchange of goods between the people of Blackamoor (North York Moors) to the north, the vale of Pickering to the west, and Yorkswold (Yorkshire Wolds) to the south. In winter the roads into Scarborough were often so bad that carts and horses could not reach the town without danger.

As for Scarborough's impoverishment, Gates insisted that this had happened long before he had revived Seamer market, and was the result of the greed and foolishness of the borough's bailiffs and their 'consorts'. Once the burgesses had prospered because they were content to engage themselves in fishing, salting, boat-building, rope-making and other crafts associated with the sea; but for some time past they had neglected these proper occupations for malting and engrossing of corn thereby making the town 'impoveryshed almost without hope of recovery'. Corrupt officials and bailiffs had embezzled money intended to maintain the harbour and then had the impertinence to petition the queen for assistance. Not surprisingly, he went on, English and foreign traders no longer came to Scarborough unless they were driven into its haven by bad weather or hostile privateers. In other words, Seamer market was being used as a convenient excuse, when the burgesses of Scarborough had only themselves to blame for the decline of the town's economy.

By the 1580s Sir Henry seemed to be winning the argument, perhaps not in the courts but certainly on the ground. William Fysh, one of Scarborough's richest merchants, alarmed his fellow burgesses by setting up a shop at Seamer. The Common Hall on Sandside responded by forbidding all townspeople to attend, buy or sell in the Monday market on pain of imprisonment, a fine of ten shillings, and the loss of all burgess privileges in the borough. Whether Scarborough's self-elected oligarchy of 44 councillors really had the authority to pass and enforce such a draconian order seems highly doubtful, and there is no evidence that it ever had any effectiveness. Nevertheless, it shows how seriously they measured the menace of Seamer's market to their livelihoods.

Though now approaching his seventies, Sir Henry's influence in the locality was undiminished either by his age or by his drawn-out conflict with Scarborough. His eldest son and heir, Edward, had become justice of the peace in both North and East Ridings in 1579, and Sir Henry himself was again chosen to represent the county of Yorkshire in the Parliament of 1586. Ever since the rising of the Northern earls he had provisioned and maintained Scarborough castle at his own expense, even though the constable there was still officially Sir Richard Cholmley. However, after Sir Richard's death in 1583, Sir Henry made a successful plea to Sir Francis Walsingham, the queen's secretary, that henceforth his son Edward should be constable at Scarborough for life and tenant of the adjacent royal manor of Northstead.

As the war with Spain intensified and the execution of Mary, Queen of Scots brought the threat of an English Catholic rising and a foreign invasion closer, Elizabeth and her councillors placed great value on Sir Henry's loyal presence in a coastal area where the people were thought to be not entirely trustworthy. When Philip of Spain was preparing his Armada, Gates wrote to the Privy Council in London reminding it of how

Scarborough castle had been seized by seaborne enemies just 30 years earlier because it was then inadequately guarded. He asked for a grant of £200 to make repairs to the castle's crumbling defences and pay for a supply of ordnance, 'small shot, a last of powder, long bows, arrows, pikes, bills and a gunner appointed to attend' the artillery. Finally, he warned the Council that 'the unsettled affections of divers of the inhabitants [of Scarborough]' made that port a potential landing-place for hostile forces.

In the event, as Edward Gates lit Seamer's hill-top beacon to warn the neighbourhood, the Spanish Armada passed harmlessly by Scarborough on its way northwards to self-destruction. The national crisis of 1588 followed closely by the death of Sir Henry in April of 1589 seem to have brought about an armistice in the prolonged war between Seamer and Scarborough. Edward Gates and William Fysh were elected by Scarborough's Common Hall to represent the borough in the Parliament of 1589, and later that same year the latter was chosen by the same body to serve as the town's senior bailiff. Fysh died in 1591, but two years later Edward Gates was again returned to sit in Parliament for Scarborough.

But it was no more than a temporary cease-fire. By 1594 Edward Gates had re-opened Seamer market and the commercial war with Scarborough reached a new ferocity. The penalty fine imposed on any resident of Scarborough who went to Seamer on a Monday was raised to an astonishing £3 6s. 8d. All 44 members of the Common Hall were required to swear that Seamer market was 'a great hynderance to the town of Scardburgh' and that they had not spoken to the contrary.

By this time the dispute had been considered without verdict by the Court of the Exchequer, the Council in the North, the Court of Queen's Bench and the queen's Privy Council. However, and at last, in 1595, the earl of Huntingdon, Lord President of the Council in the North, ruled that Seamer market should be suspended for the next five years to see what result this had on the local economy in general and Scarborough's trade in particular. Three years later, when 'a dangerous infection whereby great mortalitie did ensue' visited Scarborough and closed its markets, as a temporary concession, the Privy Council lifted the embargo on Seamer market.

Nevertheless, after Scarborough had been declared plague-free in 1599, Edward Gates tried to make temporary concession into permanent right by refusing to close his market at Seamer. Again the question was referred to the queen's Privy Council in London. Scarborough's traders and craftsmen all declared that they had prospered during the recent suspension of the Monday market, but now they were being damaged by competition as well as fear of infection. In a desperate attempt to delay an adverse decision Edward conveyed his estate and his title to his eldest son, Henry, while his sister, Mary, wrote a long, well-argued letter in defence of Seamer market to Robert Cecil, now the queen's principal secretary.

But time had run out for the Gates family. Edward had neither the money nor the power of his late father, who was once accurately described by his Scarborough enemies as 'a man of great countenance with great frends, alyes and kinsmen in the countie of Yorke'. At the end of 1599 Seamer market was finally closed, and in 1602 forbidden ever to re-open.

Commercially, and with Sir Henry behind it, Seamer might have been able to break Scarborough's local market monopoly, yet after his death events moved against his son and grandson and their interest. The arrival in the district in 1596 of Sir Thomas Hoby marked the beginning of a new phase in local politics. In the parliamentary election of 1597 at Scarborough, Gates was ousted by Hoby, and Roger Dalton, a Gates nominee, lost his seat to Walter Pye, a candidate sponsored by the earl of Nottingham, the Lord High Admiral, who had recently become Scarborough's steward. Edward Gates had no patrons in high places to match Hoby and Nottingham; and Seamer could not hope to emulate Scarborough's importance as a port of refuge, or even as a source of income to the Crown. The Gates paid nothing to the Treasury for their market and fair, whereas Scarborough paid £91 every year for its royal charter privileges.

Scarborough's reaction to the final shut down of Seamer's weekly market was one of grateful relief. The Common Hall agreed to give £100 to Edward Gates and his son Henry in compensation for their loss—£20 at Michaelmas 1602, £20 at the next Annunciation, 25 March 1603, and £10 on each of the next six Christmas days. But the promise was probably never fulfilled: the Corporation records contain only one receipt for £10 signed by Henry Gates in April 1605 'in part payment of a more sum'.

Moreover, by that date, the Gates had sold out. As early as 1602 Sir John Thornborough from Hampshire had bought a 99-year lease on Seamer, and the following year he was granted the office of constable of Scarborough castle for life in succession to Edward Gates. Thornborough's interest in Seamer was merely speculative: in 1604 he sold it for £200 to another outsider, Thomas Mompesson of Wiltshire. Mompesson secured a patent to reopen Seamer market only to have it declared illegal by the Court of King's Bench on Scarborough's appeal.

Little remains today of the Gates family of Seamer. When Edward died in 1621 he was buried with his parents in St Martin's church, but by that year the family had moved out of the village manor house into a more modest dwelling at East Ayton. The great wealth accumulated by Sir Henry had been eaten away by inflation and litigation; and the predominant position he had established for himself and his son in the neighbourhood had been taken over by a new southern 'carpet-bagger', Sir Thomas Posthumous Hoby of Hackness. Only one of Sir Henry's many achievements has endured: every July the lord of the manor still proclaims the opening of Seamer's annual fair.

11. The Hobys of Hackness

Assuming that you first have the vicar's permission, take a torch and a step-ladder to the eastern end of the chancel of St Peter's parish church of Hackness and there you will discover on the north wall a black marble monument, bordered with a wealth of heraldic arms and inscribed with the following words:

> Here lieth interred, in the assured hope of resurrection, Arthur Dakins Esq.; who after he had attained the age of 76 yeares, died the 13th day of July, 1592. He left behinde him, by Thomazin his wife ... one only daughter and heyre named Magret, whom he twice bestowed in marriage in his lifetime; first unto Walter Devereux, Esq., second brother unto the right honourable Robert now erle of Essex, but he died in his first youth wthout issue by a hurte he receved in service before Roane in the year 1591, and then he married her unto Thomas Sidney Esq., the third sonne of the Honourable Sir Henry Sidney, Knt., and Companion of the Most Order of the Garter; but he, after he had outlived his wive's said father, died also wthout issue, the 26th day of July 1595, whos body was by his disressed widdow honourably buried at Kingston uppon Hull. And in the 13th moneth of her single and most solitary life, the said Margaret disposed of herself in marriage unto Sir Thomas Posthumous Hoby, Knight, the second sonne of Sir Thomas Hoby, Knight, who died in Paris in the yeare 1566, where he then remayned resident Ambassador from our most dread soveraigne the Q:Matie that nowe is.

> In dutifull memorye of the aforesayd Arthure Dakins, Sir Thomas Postumous Hoby & Dame Margaret his wife erected this monument, whoe alsoe repayred the chawncell the 9th day of Augt. 1597.

Historically, Lady Margaret Hoby has overshadowed her third husband, not because she was more worthy, able or distinguished, but simply because of an accident. Part of a diary which she kept from August 1599 to July 1605, consisting of 118 closely written folios, happens to have survived; and although it is probably only a small fragment of her personal record it is thought to be the oldest of its kind written by an Englishwoman. Like nearly all diaries never intended for public scrutiny or entertainment, Lady Margaret's is essentially pedestrian and repetitive, yet it is immensely revealing of a mentality and a way of life so totally foreign to anything experienced in England 400 years later.

Margaret's good fortune was that she was the only child and heiress of a man who had neither name nor breeding but had made a lot of money. Arthur Dakins had been a highly successful Elizabethan buccaneer and soldier. Contrary to wishful legend, nearly all adventurers and sea captains of that time, such as Drake, Hawkins, Raleigh, Frobisher and Grenville, died as failures: they were heroic catastrophes. Arthur Dakins was different. He retired a healthy, rich man and bought himself land and status with his wealth. His recently acquired coat of arms was decorated with anchors and carried the appropriate motto, 'Strike Dakins!'.

Margaret was born in 1571 and while still only a young girl she was sent from her home at Linton, near Wintringham on the Wolds, to York. Since there were no schools for girls the normal practice was for them to be educated in the household of a lady willing to take them into her care. Margaret was brought up in the house and the extended family of the Countess of Huntingdon, whose husband, Henry Hastings, third Earl of Huntingdon, was Lord President of the Council in the North from 1572 to his death in 1595. The Huntingdons were stern Puritans and zealous enemies of the old Roman Catholic religion, which still had many adherents in north and east Yorkshire. Margaret's whole life and outlook were to be fashioned by her Puritan upbringing at York.

By the time she was eighteen several suitors sought Margaret's hand in marriage. However, as in other matters, she was willing to accept the choice of her guardian, the Earl of Huntingdon, who favoured his 'cousin Wat', Walter Devereux. No doubt Margaret's parents were much flattered that they were to have the younger son of the Earl of Essex as their son-in-law. When it came to the question of an endowment for the young couple, Arthur Dakins put down £3,000, the Earl of Essex another £3,000, and the Earl of Huntingdon the remaining £500 for the manor and rectory of Hackness. At its dissolution in 1539 Whitby abbey had possessed Hackness as part of its extensive estate, but Queen Elizabeth had given it to Robert Dudley, the Earl of Leicester, her current favourite. Nine months later Leicester sold Hackness for £4,365 8s. 4d. to Sir John Constable of Burton Constable, who had now made more than two thousand pounds profit on his original purchase.

The lordship of Hackness covered an area of more than 11,000 acres; besides the 'town' of Hackness itself and the rectory of its church, it included the villages and farms of Langdale, Everley, Broxa, Silpho, Suffield and Harwood Dale, some properties over towards the coast at Cloughton and Burniston and southwards in Ayton and Hutton Buscel — altogether about 200 messuages and four water-mills on the river Derwent.

The new couple were ill-matched. Walter Devereux found Margaret dull; Huntingdon rebuked him for not spending more time with his 'Meg'. However, in 1591, after only two years during which they had seen little of each other, the high-spirited Devereux was killed by a stray cannonball at the siege of Rouen. The 20-year-old widow left Hackness Hall and returned to the household of the Huntingdons at King's Manor, York.

But Margaret was too young and too valuable an heiress to be allowed to remain single for long. Only weeks after Devereux's death the bishop of London granted a licence for her second marriage. Again the choice was made by the Huntingdons rather than by the Dakins family, and again they chose a relative, their young nephew, Thomas Sidney. Like his predecessor, Thomas was the younger son of a distinguished, southern, aristocratic family: his father was Sir Henry Sidney of Penshurst in Kent and his elder brother, the poet and hero, Sir Philip Sidney. Margaret's second husband was much more to her liking, so that when he died suddenly in 1595 she was said to be most distressed.

Margaret was so upset by her second widowhood at the age of 24 that she would not hear of another husband. Also, since her father was now dead, she had more say in her own future. Moreover, perhaps she felt that the loss of two husbands in six years was a sign of God's displeasure — that He did not intend her to marry and have children. Consequently, when Thomas Hoby first appeared at Hackness in October 1595 Margaret told him that she was not ready for a third husband, even though he carried letters of recommendation from Lord Huntingdon and his cousin, Robert Cecil, soon to be the Queen's Principal Secretary.

In November Thomas returned to Hackness; this time he was said to carry 'good store of fair jewels and pearls'. However, Margaret was not the kind of lady to be persuaded by precious stones whatever their number and value. Far more persuasive was a letter she received from her guardian and mentor, the Earl of Huntingdon, who was now close to death: 'Mistress Margaret for God's cause have care of our credits, and so handle the matter on his [Hoby's] coming again may be neither offensive to you nor displeasing to himself.' This last appeal from such a source must have been irresistible: in August 1596, after 13 months of 'solitary life', Margaret gave in and took a third husband.

Like his two unfortunate predecessors, Thomas Posthumous Hoby was a younger son of a leading southern family of Bisham abbey in Berkshire. His father was an outstanding scholar and linguist, who had translated Martin Bucer from German and Castiglioni from Italian, and a career diplomat. When he died of the plague in Paris at the age of 36, a few months before the birth of his second son, the elder Sir Thomas Hoby was Queen Elizabeth's ambassador to the French court there. Elizabeth was so grieved by his death that she wrote a personal letter of sympathy to the pregnant widow, and when Thomas Posthumous was born she agreed to be his godmother.

Elizabeth Cooke, young Thomas's mother, was as talented as her husband and even better connected by birth and marriage. Her elder sister, Mildred, was the wife of William Cecil, the first Lord Burghley and Queen Elizabeth's Lord Treasurer from 1572 until 1598. Mildred's two sons were Robert and Thomas. Robert Cecil became the Queen's Principal Secretary in 1596, a month before Margaret married his cousin, and Thomas Cecil was to be President of the Council in the North from 1599 to 1603. Another of the Cooke sisters, Ann, married Sir Nicholas Bacon and became the mother of Sir Francis Bacon.

In 1574, Elizabeth Hoby had taken John, Lord Russell, son and heir of the Earl of Bedford, as her second husband. Their household in London became the 'very centre of Puritan high society' and remained so even after Russell's death in 1584. Elizabeth lived on until 1609 when she was 81-years-old. The tombs that she had set up for both her husbands in All Saints' church at Bisham and in Westminster abbey and the lengthy Latin inscriptions she composed for them testify to her great wealth and learning. Her own tomb at Bisham, which she also designed, is one of the finest and most elaborate of its kind in England.

Thomas and Margaret were well matched. Thomas was as severe a Puritan and as much an enemy of Catholics as his wife. Indeed, Lord Huntingdon's support for him rested on his belief that the Protestant cause would be served best by Hoby's presence at Hackness, at the centre of an area dominated by Catholic gentry, in particular the Eures and the Cholmleys. This opinion was also shared by Hoby's Cecil cousins in London, who were increasingly worried by the possibility of a Catholic conspiracy in the North.

Consequently, with the backing of his Cecil relatives and Queen Elizabeth, his godmother, Sir Thomas's rise was meteoric. Though a complete stranger in the locality, within a short time he was made justice of the peace in the North and East Ridings, commissioner for musters of the trained bands and the collection of parliamentary subsidies, and a member of the Council in the North at York. Hoby's only failure was to secure one of Yorkshire's two county seats in the House of Commons; reluctantly, he had to settle for one of Scarborough's instead.

Not surprisingly, therefore, Hoby soon became the most hated man in his neighbourhood. His marriage to a rich, local widow, his southern origins, his small stature, his relentless persecution of Catholics, and his 'incessant litigiousness' made him the target of many vulgar insults and slanders. One court witness declared that he was 'the busyest, sawcie little Jacke in all the Contrie, and wolld have an ore in eny bodies bote'; another said that he was 'the little knight that useth to draw up his breeches with a shooting-horn'; and a third wrote that he was 'a troblesome vexatious neighbour who haveing married a widow ye inheritor of all Hackness lordship, haveing a full purse and no children (& it was thought not able to get one) delighted to spend his mony & tyme in sutes'. Before long Sir Thomas had quarrelled with nearly all his gentry neighbours — the Eures of Malton, the Dawnays of Ayton, the Hutchinsons of Wykeham, the Legards of Ganton and, most bitterly of all, in what became a life-long vendetta, the Cholmleys of Whitby.

Events moved inexorably to a violent confrontation. In August 1600, without invitation or even much warning, a hunting party arrived at Hackness Hall. The visitors included four local gentlemen — two Eures, Stephen Hutchinson and Richard Cholmley — with their servants. Given the bad blood that already existed between Sir Thomas and his neighbours, their arrival at Hackness was planned and provocative, not accidental. They knew that the only sport approved by Hoby was fishing, yet they talked of nothing but horses, hounds and falcons. They knew that Hoby detested swearing, yet, according to his later testimony, they exchanged 'lascivious talk where every sentence was begun and ended with a great oath'. They knew full well that the Hobys had forbidden gambling in their house and yet they spent the evening playing dice and cards. They drank wine and beer to excess, interrupted household evening prayers by stamping their feet and singing profane songs. Lady Margaret was so outraged that she took refuge in her private chamber. The next morning some of the guests were still drunk and were denied more wine and beer from the cellar. When Lady Margaret refused to come out of her room or admit any of them into it, one of her servants was assaulted when he stood in their way. As the party rode off they threw stones at the house windows, knocked down fences and trampled over a newly-laid courtyard. Sir Thomas alleged that in the presence of his wife he had been called 'scurvy urchen' and 'spindle-shanked ape', and that the riotous company had threatened to fire his house and pull down the parish church.

When Hoby got no satisfaction from the Council in the North he appealed to the Star Chamber in London. Though no official record of the court's judgement has survived, there is no doubt that the Hobys won. As Lady Margaret wrote triumphantly in her diary in May 1602, Lord Eure had come to Hackness to pay £100 'for riott comitted and unsivill behavour'. Even to this day Lord Downe of Wykeham pays Lord Derwent of Hackness £60 a year as part of a fine imposed on Stephen Hutchinson and his descendants for 'the Wykeham shame'.

Whatever Lady Margaret's feelings about them might have been, Sir Thomas pursued the Cholmleys with unconcealed relish and stamina. As lords of Whitby Strand, the Cholmleys possessed the greatest extent of land and the largest number of tenants in the vicinity; if he could disgrace them politically and ruin them financially he might be able to supplant them. Not content with Hackness, Hoby meant to be master of the entire locality. In the end he failed. Sir Henry Cholmley escaped disaster by openly conforming to the established church in 1599, thereby avoiding the political and financial perils of 'obstinant popish recusancy'. When Hoby then tried to use his favour with his cousin, Robert Cecil, who had become the Earl of Salisbury and King James's Lord Treasurer, by establishing judicial and administrative rights over the whole of Whitby Strand, the Court of Exchequer eventually ruled against him and for the Cholmleys. Finally, with the third generation, in the person of Sir Hugh Cholmley, the ageing Hoby met his match. In 1635 they clashed when both sat on the magistrates' bench at Malton, but now Cholmley had the backing of Lord Wentworth and Hoby did not. Wisely, Hoby withdrew his latest suit in Star Chamber against Sir Hugh and made peace with his more powerful neighbour.

Hoby's busy preoccupation in politics and litigation often drew him away from Hackness for long periods of time. When he travelled to London in his own horse-drawn coach—the first to be seen in north-east Yorkshire—sometimes Margaret went with him, but usually she stayed behind at Hackness. There was plenty for her to do there. Every moment of life was precious to her; wasting time in idleness she regarded as sinful. As lady of the manor, she visited and dressed the wounds of her sick tenants and servants, delivered their babies, gave religious instruction to their children, collected their rents, and paid their wages.

Lady Margaret's domestic duties were just as important and time-consuming as her manorial responsibilities. As head of a household of between 20 and 30 members, consisting of relatives, male and female servants and children in her care, she led morning and evening prayers, sorted the linen, picked fruit, made jam and ginger bread, tended the herbal garden, planted trees and made wax lights. The only recreations she allowed herself were fishing in the river Derwent for which she held a licence, the occasional game of bowls for exercise, and taking the air in her four-wheeled springless coach to visit her mother at Linton, the Gates at Seamer, or friends in Scarborough. Though she was never a natural mother, she was nurse, midwife, teacher, housewife, steward, bailiff and spiritual counsellor for a community of nearly a thousand people.

As we know from the privacy of her dairy, Lady Margaret's mind was dominated and directed by religious conviction. She enjoyed lengthy sermons, prayed as often as a nun, employed her own personal priest, and detested popery. Apart from the Bible, which she read every day, her favourite book was Foxe's 'book of Marters', a blood-curdling account of the sufferings of Protestants under the Catholic persecution of Mary Tudor. Margaret tortured herself with imaginary sins. When she experienced illness or pain she took them to be signs of divine displeasure; when the sickness passed then she believed that God had forgiven her for whatever wrong she might have done. In Margaret's world the devil was everywhere: Satan was always casting his malice on her and working ceaselessly to divert her thoughts from God's word and her activities from God's service. After three husbands Margaret's failure to conceive a child must have given her much mental anguish in an age when infertility was regarded at best as unfortunate and at worse cursed.

Given that you are still in possession of torch and step-ladder, on the opposite south wall of St Peter's chancel you will be able to read another inscription on an even grander marble monument, this one to Lady Margaret herself:

> After she had lived seven and thirty yeares and one month with her husband in mutuall entire affection to both their extraordinary comfortes: and had finished the woork that God had sent her into this world to performe; and after she had attained unto the beginning of the sixty-third yeare of her age, on the fourth day of the seventh moneth of that yeare, it was the will of Almighty God to call her forth of this vale of miserie. And her body was buryed in this Chancell, on the sixth day of the said moneth (beinge

September Ano.1633) so neer unto the bodies of her sayde father and of her sayde mother (which was interred by her sayde father's body, on the thirteenth day of November, Ano.1613) as all three will become one heape of duste.

> Non ero vobiscum, donec Deus ipse vocabit:
> [I shall not be with you until God Himself calls]
> Tunc cineres vestros consociabo meis.
> [Then I shall mix my ashes with yours]
>   Thomas Posthumous Hoby

Lady Margaret's death was a blow from which Sir Thomas never fully recovered. For the next year he was absent from the North Riding Bench, where he had been the leading magistrate for the past 30 years, and devoted himself entirely to fulfilling the terms of his late wife's will and his promises to her when she lay dying.

The Hobys had often noted how hard it was for the people of Harwood Dale, on the northern rim of the parish of Hackness, to attend St Peter's church three miles away on the other side of Silpho Moor. During her last illness Margaret had therefore asked Thomas to build a chapel of ease in the Dale 'for the good of the souls and bodys of the inhabitants' there. As a result, he spent the greater part of 1634 supervising the construction of St Margaret's chapel, and soon afterwards endowed it with the tithes of Harwood Dale, Harwood and Hingles for the maintenance of a perpetual curate for it. For more than 200 years the chapel and its surrounding and enclosed graveyard were used by the people of Harwood Dales until in 1862 a new and larger St Margaret's church was built by the Johnstones of Hackness in a more convenient position. This meant that unfortunately Hoby's chapel was abandoned and allowed to fall into ruin, and by the end of the twentieth century it had become an empty shell.

If Hoby finally lost his conflict with the Cholmleys, for a long time he remained at odds with Scarborough's oligarchy, and in particular the Thompson family who led it. Hoby's overbearing arrogance and Scarborough's acute sensitivity about its ancient privileges brought the two into frequent collision. When elected by the Corporation to sit in the Parliaments of 1597-8 and 1604-10, far from expressing any gratitude Sir Thomas had the impertinence to object to its choice of his partner. Only when he was himself senior bailiff of the borough in 1610-11 was he convinced that the town was being well governed. On some matters, such as his selection of preaching ministers for its weekly church lectures and schoolmasters for its grammar school, Hoby was permitted to have his way; but other issues caused friction and ill-feeling.

As justice of the peace and deputy lieutenant in the North Riding, Hoby never conceded that only the bailiffs of Scarborough had the right to inspect musters of the town's trained band or home guard. In 1629, after he had sent three different orders in five days from Hackness regarding such a muster in Scarborough, the Common Hall made an official complaint against him to Sir Thomas Wentworth, then Lord President of the Council in the North at York. Three years later, Hoby overstepped the limits of legality by summoning Scarborough's militia to a general muster at Hutton Buscel six miles inland, and demanding that the town send 36 armed men instead of the customary 30. In response to more indignant protests from Scarborough, Wentworth overruled Sir Thomas, who was told that since the town was 'a place of danger on the sea' its trained band should be mustered only within the borough and the traditional maximum of 30 should be observed.

Hoby's quarrel with the Thompsons of Scarborough arose out of their attempt to exclude him and other non-residents from the Common Hall, and to reduce the membership there from 44 to 14. A new royal charter, granted in 1626 by Charles I, would have effectively converted an existing oligarchy into a closed cabinet run by one family, but it seems likely that Hoby's intervention killed it. After Sir Thomas brought yet another action in Star Chamber, this time against the Thompsons, in May 1632 Scarborough's old charters and form of government were confirmed. However, there was no way that Hoby could oust the Thompsons from their predominant positions in Scarborough's ruling body, even though he made as much trouble for them as he could.

Hoby's last round with Scarborough occurred in 1636. He had presented the Corporation with a magnificent silver mace as a kind of peace offering for which the two newly-elected bailiffs, William Foord and Roger Wyvill, thanked him by letter. However, the reply from Hackness was characteristically abrasive. Sir Thomas addressed his letter to 'Mr Bailiff Foord' only, because, as he explained, 'by your charters Mr Wyvell ys not legally elected'. Hoby's real objection to Wyvill had nothing to do with the borough charters: the truth was that the Wyvills of Osgodby were Catholics, and Roger had sent his son and heir William to be educated abroad at a Jesuit college; but Sir Thomas had claimed that Roger was disqualified from election because he was a non-resident.

Since Hoby himself had been a non-resident when chosen bailiff in 1610 his argument was threadbare, and he must have known it.

In the words of the Hackness parish register, Sir Thomas finally succumbed 'about two of the clock on Wednesday night', 30 December 1640, after 'falling into a fit of cold palsy'. In some ways his life had been a failure: he had lost his battle with the Thompsons of Scarborough and his other old enemies, the Cholmleys of Whitby. When he died the Thompsons were still running the town: for the past four successive years, Christopher, Timothy, Richard and Francis Thompson had each served as senior bailiffs. As justice of the peace, colonel of the local trained bands and member of parliament for Scarborough, Sir Hugh Cholmley had supplanted Hoby as the leading figure in Whitby Strand and Pickering Lythe. Moreover, the Thompsons and the Cholmleys all had children and grandchildren whereas he had none to succeed him at Hackness.

Hoby had made many life-long enemies because by nature he was bad-tempered, dictatorial, intolerant and self-important. On the other hand, there is no evidence that he was corrupt, lazy or incompetent. On the contrary, for 40 years he took upon himself every kind of public responsibility, and he was immensely hard-working and efficient. His local enemies regarded this ceaseless activity as ambitious busybodying, but in truth he was a tireless and conscientious public servant. Like his Puritan wife he too regarded idleness as sinful. Above all, his knowledge of the law in general and local custom and practice in particular was unrivalled. Even after he had long retired from the magistrates' bench his legal counsel was still sought and valued. Rather than accept the partisan recollections of Sir Hugh Cholmley or the slanders of hostile witnesses, it would be fairer to record the verdict of a fellow justice in another Northern county: in his Journal Sir William Brereton of Cheshire wrote that Sir Thomas was 'the most understanding, able and industrious justice of the peace in this kingdome'. Even Wentworth, who had no reason to flatter Hoby, conceded that he 'had good abilities and great experience...'

Even Scarborough, that so often resented his hectoring interference, owes Hoby more than it was probably willing to admit. Today, all that remains of the Thompsons is a set of three battered tumblers amongst the Town Hall's silver which was given to the Corporation by godfather William when he died in 1637. These simple gifts compare very unfavourably with Hoby's great silver mace, which is still carried proudly before the town's mayors. Also, Scarborough's own grammar or high school, originally a medieval foundation, survived until reorganisation in

1973, but it might have disappeared long before if Sir Thomas had not rescued it with a generous new endowment.

Even in the privacy of her diary Lady Margaret usually addressed Sir Thomas as 'Mr Hoby', and only rarely as 'my husband', yet whatever their feelings towards each other at the beginning of an arranged, political marriage, as the years passed they grew very close and dependent. Not all their 37 years together could have been spent 'in mutuall entire affection to both their extraordinary comfortes', but Hoby's grief after her death was real enough. In his will he asked to be buried 'neither with superfluous cost, nor in over publique sort' and next to 'the dust of my most dear and only wife, the Lady Margaret Hoby'. To the day of his death he had worn a chain bracelet of gold to which was fastened a picture of his 'most dear and only wife deceased', emphasizing that she might have had three husbands but he had only one wife.

12. Mr and Mrs Farrer

That Scarborough's famous spa waters were accidentally discovered by a certain lady called Mrs Farrer is well known. The event was first described by Dr Robert Wittie in his promotional advertisement *Scarbrough Spaw*, published at York in 1667. According to the doctor, the discovery was made about 1627.

The date is uncertain. In his first edition of *Scarbrough Spaw*, which came out in 1660, Dr Wittie did not name Mrs Farrer: he wrote only that the springs at the foot of South Cliff had been found 'about thirty-four years ago'. Thomas Gent, who had a printing house on Bland's Cliff a century later, referred to 'Mrs Farrow' taking her momentous walk along South Bay sands about 1630.

Not that the particular year really matters: only the fact of Mrs Farrer's discovery has importance in Scarborough's history. Indeed, if not Mrs Farrer then almost certainly someone else would soon have made claims for Scarborough's waters at a time when spas were all the fashion and Bath, Epsom, Buxton and Tunbridge were already established recreational and health centres. It could hardly have been a mere coincidence that Dr Edmund Deane, 'the father of Harrogate', published his *Spadacrene Anglica, or, The English Spaw Fountaine* in 1626. Perhaps Mrs Farrer had a copy of it.

Dr Wittie was only a summer-time visitor to Scarborough and it is probable that he never met Mrs Farrer and heard about her only after her death. However, he does say that she was a respectable gentlewoman who lived in the town; that she was observant enough to notice how the springs stained the stones at the foot of the cliff reddish-brown; curious enough to taste their acidity; and sufficiently 'scientific' to know how their chemical content might be tested. By any standards, seventeenth or twenty-first century, Mrs Farrer was clearly no ordinary female.

Thomas Hinderwell's third, posthumous history of Scarborough, published in 1832, noted that Mrs Farrer (in the first and second editions of 1798 and 1811 the spelling had been 'Farrow') was the wife of Mr John Farrer, who in 1628 had founded the charity hospital for poor widows named after him. In 1882 Brogden Baker was the first to record in print that the 'John Farrar', who had been Scarborough's bailiff, was also 'the husband of the lady who first discovered and made public the efficacy of the Scarborough spa waters'. Surprisingly, however, since Baker's further revelation nothing more about the Farrers has come to light. Both Rowntree (1931) and Edwards (1966) disappoint the investigator: they add nothing to what Wittie had written about Mrs Farrer and ignore her husband altogether.

Having thus quickly exhausted the uninformative and unsatisfactory secondary authorities, what evidence of the Farrers can be found in the primary sources? Independent research is soon rewarded. Paver's list of Yorkshire's wedding licences reveals that in 1600 John 'Farrar' of Scarborough was given leave to marry Thomasin Hutchinson of Wykeham Abbey. That the wedding took place is confirmed by Dugdale's visitation returns, which also show that Thomasin was one of the ten children of Edward Hutchinson. Her father lived from 1543 until 1591. Edward had inherited the manor of Wykeham at the age of 17 and been granted arms in 1581. Thomasin's eldest brother, Stephen, like their father, was on one occasion Member of Parliament for Scarborough. One of Thomasin's elder sisters, Isabel, was the wife of Christopher Thompson, one of the richest merchants and a senior member of the most powerful family in Scarborough. In short, Thomasin Farrer was indeed a privileged lady with many influential relatives.

In 1600 John Farrer might not yet have been a gentleman but he was well on the way to becoming one. As early as 1589 he was already described as 'merchant"; in 1598 he bought a substantial tenement in West Sandgate; and the following year he was elected one of the town's two bailiffs: the other one was Christopher Thompson.

John Farrer was such a prominent burgess that his name appears frequently in the Corporation records. In 1600 he was one of eight Scarborough men granted the local monopoly of salt-making for the next seven years. They paid an initial 'fine' of £60 and thereafter an annual rent of £20. One of the other monopolists was Francis Thompson, nephew of Christopher.

Two years later, on the feast of St Thomas the apostle, 21 December 1602, 35 shipowners and 31 master mariners of Scarborough formed themselves into a society largely for the benefit of distressed seamen, their widows and orphans. Third name on the list of founding shipowners was 'John Farrar'; others on the same list included four Thompsons — William, godfather of the family, Francis and Richard, his two sons, and Timothy, son of his brother Christopher.

After his first election as junior of the two bailiffs of the town in 1599, John occupied the same office in 1602-3 and 1607-8, but from then on was senior of the pair in 1613-14, 1619-20 and finally 1625-6. As one of Scarborough's foremost burgesses, now honoured with the title of 'Mr', he took his turn in the borough's highest positions about every six years. At a time when Scarborough had fewer than 2,000 residents this record of municipal service was outstanding though not unique.

Scarborough men were once proud and jealous of their precious corporate privileges: one of them was their right to take a census of their own weapons, known as a review of arms. 'John Fayrer' is one of the 23 on a 1605 list of 'private men with their armes', that is men who owned and carried swords and possibly pistols as a mark of their status, as distinct from 'common souldiers' in the local militia or 'trained band'. On this occasion, John was also credited with a 'calliver' or short musket, whereas on later review lists he has only corslet or body armour.

Nowadays you have to be poor not to pay income tax, but in the early seventeenth century only the rich paid direct taxes, and even then only irregularly and infrequently when parliament granted subsidies to the crown. Scarborough was normally assessed at £40 and this was paid entirely by only twelve 'subsidy men' in the town. One of the twelve in 1621 and again in 1625 was 'John Farer'. On both occasions he paid £3, which represented probably only a small fraction of his income though more than a labourer then might earn in wages in a whole year.

In 1626 the new king, Charles I, granted Scarborough a new constitution of government. Instead of the traditional ruling body of two bailiffs, two coroners, four chamberlains and 36 capital burgesses sitting in three Twelves, in future Scarborough would be in the hands of a mayor, a coroner and twelve aldermen. Thomasin Farrer's brother, Stephen Hutchinson, was to be the first mayor, John, her husband, the first coroner, and five Thompsons—William, Christopher, Timothy, Francis and Richard—were named amongst the aldermen. For reasons which remain unknown, the royal writ was never executed: there was no Thompson take-over of the town, and no break in Scarborough's time-honoured form of self-government. Nevertheless, this extraordinary document is further illustration of the local prominence and power of the Farrers and their Thompson relatives.

Though his name is absent from St Mary's very incomplete burial register, which has survived only in the form of bishops' transcripts, and also from the York probate register of wills, John Farrer must have died about 1628. Probably he was many years older than Thomasin. In the words of the Charity Commissioners' Report of 1834, Farrer's hospital was then 'two small tenements or cottages under one roof, situate in Cook's Row, near the Low Conduit ... which are stated in one of the benefactors' tables in the church to have been given by Mr John Farrer, who died between 1627 and 1630, for the habitation of as many poor widows as the same could conveniently contain'.

In fact, a surviving fragment of a draft or copy conveyance shows that John Farrer, handed over his two tenements under one roof, which he had 'lately builded and erected', into the hands of the bailiffs and senior burgesses in June 1628. It is also clear from this conveyance that Farrer had built the cottages as a hospital or charitable home for two poor widows to live there 'without any rent during their lives'. Remarkably, Farrer's hospital cottages survived until the 1950s when they were demolished along with other elderly and not so elderly buildings. What had once been Low Conduit Street then became the south side of Princess Square and the site of the hospital was occupied by Dilt's fish restaurant.

Perhaps Mrs Farrer was already a widow when she took her historic walk on South Bay sands, but whatever the date of her husband's death the Corporation records indicate that she continued to live in Scarborough for many years more. As a widowed heiress she became a property-owner in her own right. Perhaps she lived alone. If the Farrers had children either they had died young or left the town before the death of Mr John Farrer. During the next three decades Mrs Farrer is the only one of that surname in Scarborough's records.

St Mary's parish church suffered more change and damage during the seventeenth century than at any other time before or after. In 1600 it was still Catholic and medieval in appearance—huge and majestic. During Mrs Farrer's residence in Scarborough it was transformed by Protestant reformers and then mutilated by two civil wars. In the past private church seats had been provided for notables and patrons only: ordinary parishioners stood, sat on the floor, or brought their own stools. The congregation occupied the nave; the chancel was reserved for priests and their servers. But in 1635 all this was altered at St Mary's.

For all practical purposes the eastern end of the church was abandoned, its altar was brought westwards to the crossing under the central tower, and the preaching pulpit was rebuilt in the centre of the nave. The rail that had once separated clergy from laity was abolished. The vicar in his pulpit was now surrounded by his parishioners, all seated in their family pews. Of St Mary's 155 new pews one was assigned to 'Mrs Farroe' which cost her £1 13s. 4d. The most expensive places were at the eastern end of the nave on either side of the middle 'great allee'. These were occupied by the Fysh, Thompson, Batty, Harrison, Foord and Headley families and reserved for the officers of the Corporation—the bailiffs, sub-bailiffs, coroners, aldermen and parish rector. Mrs Farrer's pew was third from the better eastern end, beyond the north 'back allee' and opposite the place provided for the four junior aldermen. From there she would have had a clear view of the vicar, William Simpson, as he stood in his newly-constructed pulpit.

In 1638 St Mary's needed some new windows. All the townspeople were assumed to be Anglican and all but the very poorest were required to make their contribution. The assessment lists for only two of the four Quarters, Newborough and Oldborough, have survived. They show that the highest sum of one pound each was expected to come from Mr Francis Thompson and Mr Thomas Foord. Both men were very rich. Second on the list of Oldborough residents, sandwiched between Robert Woodall, who was to pay 3s. 4d., and Roger Boyes, who was rated at 6s. 8d., a 'Mr(sic) Farer' was assessed at just four shillings. The hand that wrote 'Mr Farer' also contrived 'Mr Cath. Fysh', widow of Gregory Fysh, so perhaps all subscribers were regarded as males whatever their gender. If the assessment of Mrs Farrer was fair then she must have been regarded as well-to-do. On the same lists, William Penston, the grammar schoolmaster, with an annual salary of £10, paid only two shillings, William Oliver, the merchant, only three, and John Key, the prosperous tailor, also four shillings.

Only one document found in Scarborough Corporation records reveals Mrs Farrer's christian name. By a fortunate accident, the only surviving sheet of the town's Ship Money assessments for 1637 is that for the Quarter where she still lived—Oldborough. The second name on this list, again placed between her neighbours Robert Woodall and Roger Boyes, seems to read 'Mrs Tomyzin Farden widdow'. Her personal contribution towards a new warship in the Royal Navy was put at four shillings.

Though very variously spelt, Mrs Farrer's surname figures frequently during the war years of the 1640s. Like all Scarborians she was now being compelled to pay exceptionally heavy and continual taxation to both Roundheads and Royalists. In December 1642, 'Mrs Farer' paid another four shillings, this time as part of an assessment on the whole town of £50 'for making two pairs of gates'. Seven months later, after Sir Hugh Cholmley had taken Scarborough over to the king's side, 'Mrs Farrere' was required to find 4s. 6d. as her part of an assessment of £60. This time Robert Woodall paid the same and Roger Boyes eight shillings. Six years later still, on the last day of October 1649, Parliament's North Riding Committee presented its tax demand to Scarborough for the next two months. On this occasion, 'Mistress Farrer' was still at home in Oldborough but her low assessment at eight pence suggests that like many other town residents her income had been seriously eroded by recent years of siege, forced, unpaid billeting, and plague. Now she was considered no wealthier than Mr Penston the schoolmaster, still subsisting on his annual salary of ten pounds. The last time her name occurs on an assessment list for Oldborough was on Christmas day 1654. 'Mrs Farrer' was then expected to find ten pence, whereas Roger Boyes, now assessed at 4s. 4d., must have been one of the few town inhabitants to prosper during the civil wars.

Even at a time when he occupied the office of senior bailiff, John Farrer had not always been careful to observe the town's trading regulations. In 1624 he was in trouble for using an underweight measure in his shop, and later for failing to bring in his measures for their annual test. The following year he was presented before the sheriff's tourn for not submitting his weights and measures for examination, even though he had been elected to serve as the borough's senior magistrate only a few days earlier. Mr Farrer's widow was also not entirely blameless, though her offences were of a different kind. At the sheriff's tourn in April 1644, 'Mrs Farrer' was charged with blocking up or diverting the water out of a common sewer. In October 1647, she was accused of repeating the same breach of the town's sanitary bye-laws. As the court presentment reads: 'Mrs Faro for puttinge the water out of the course at hir backe doore'. In the same document we learn that she had a 'gardinge ioyninge to the kings streete'.

Another reference to the name Farrer in the contemporary records raises more questions than it answers; it occurs in the minutes of the Common Hall meeting of 13 February 1649. By that time Scarborough's ruinous civil wars were ended, but their costs were still being counted and borne. The old charnel chapel schoolhouse between St Mary's parish church and the castle barbican which Cholmley had used as a forward post in 1645 and Matthew Boynton, his successor as governor, had demolished in 1648, was not to be rebuilt. Instead, the town's rulers decided to put the boys and Mr Penston into St Mary's for the time being. As the clerk of the Hall wrote: '... and that Farrers Isle shalbe made fitt for a schoole house, and the money made of the charnell stones to be imployed towards that worke'.

Though the name is now obsolete, 'Farrer's Aisle' was, and still is, the south transept of St Mary's. During two sieges of the castle the south side of the church had suffered minimal structural damage, whereas the north aisle, north transept and eastern chancel had all been ruined. The north transept was never restored. The central tower above the crossing was so shaken by artillery vibration that it collapsed in a storm in 1659. So in 1649 the south transept was divided into two floors for two classes and a new doorway cut at ground level in the outside south-west wall so that the boys could enter without passing through the church. For the next two hundred years Farrer's Aisle was to be the makeshift home of Scarborough Grammar School.

But why was St Mary's south transept called 'Farrers Isle' in 1649? In the new pew list of 1635 it had been called 'the south ile next the quire'. Aisles, or side chapels as we would call them (they called aisles 'allees'), in the parish church had been formerly dedicated to Saints Nicholas, Mary, Stephen, James, Clement and others, and before the Reformation used by chantry priests to say prayers for the souls of their dead benefactors. So what had John Farrer done to merit this special memorial? In 1649 his widow was still living in the town. Had her husband been buried in the south transept twenty years earlier? This seems an improbable explanation: the south transept was not normally used for this purpose after the Reformation. Former bailiffs and leading burgesses had privileged graves in the north aisle or at the eastern end of the chancel beyond the high altar.

The most favoured explanation is that Farrer's Aisle derived its new name from the benefactor whose table in the south transept recorded John Farrer's foundation of an almshouse for Scarborough widows. Just over a century after John's death, Thomas Gent reported that he had seen the following inscription 'on a table in a place on the south side (of St Mary's) where formerly had been a chantry':

> Mr Thomas Farror of this Town, Merchant, by his Will gave two Hospitals near the Low-Conduit, in a Place call'd Cook-Row, adjoining the Quakers Meeting-House, for the Habitation of as many poor Widows, as the same can conveniently entertain for ever.

Somehow 'Thomas' had been mistakenly substituted for 'John', but clearly this is the same dedication referred to by the Charity Commissioners a century later.

Mrs Farrer was one of nature's hardy survivors. She had lived in Scarborough throughout the civil wars and seen the town twice besieged, bombarded and put through the tribulations of military occupation, food rationing and a final visitation of the bubonic plague. Her last documentary appearances locally are as a dispenser of charity in the parish's poor law papers. In May 1647 she was paying a penny a week and her neighbour Robert Woodall a penny ha'penny for the maintenance of a ten-year-old orphan boy called John Deeton, who was in St Thomas's poor house and not yet 'fitt to be put apprentice'. In 1654 she was still contributing a penny a week to the town's paupers. By then she must have been well over seventy years of age.

The civil wars had been particularly hard on Mrs Farrer's family and relatives. Her eldest brother Stephen Hutchinson had died in 1648. Of all her kin he had been the only one to take Parliament's side. His son and heir, and Thomasin's nephew, Edward Hutchinson, had fought as a colonel in the Royalist army, and was disinherited by his father for doing so. All her rich and powerful Thompson relations were active or passive Royalists and as a result, by the 1650s, all of them had suffered for their opposition to Parliament. In these circumstances it is remarkable that Mrs Farrer survived for so long, though not that she stayed put in Scarborough: there was nowhere else for her to go.

Mrs Farrer did not live to see the Thompson star rise again after the Restoration in 1660: after 1654 her name disappeared from the lists of Scarborough residents. The will of 'Thomasin Farrer widdow of Scarbrough' was dated 16 March 1654 and received probate in London two years later. The 'John, son and heir of John Farrar, Esq.', who was admitted to Gray's Inn in March 1620 might well have been her son, but there is no reference to him in her will. Her next of kin and administrator was named there as a niece called Agnes Syme.

Even as a widow Thomasin Farrer had been overshadowed by the memory of her husband. The almshouses in Low Conduit Street and the south transept of St Mary's were named after him, not her. Yet whatever the importance of John in his lifetime and the subsequent value of his bequest, it was Thomasin's curiosity that has justly given her a greater and more lasting fame. As Thomas Gent wrote more than two and a half centuries ago, her 'memory ought to be for ever precious'.

13. Sir Hugh and Lady Cholmley

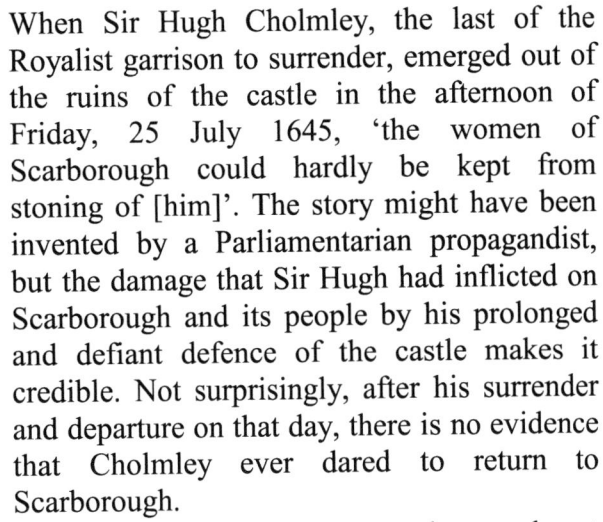

When Sir Hugh Cholmley, the last of the Royalist garrison to surrender, emerged out of the ruins of the castle in the afternoon of Friday, 25 July 1645, 'the women of Scarborough could hardly be kept from stoning of [him]'. The story might have been invented by a Parliamentarian propagandist, but the damage that Sir Hugh had inflicted on Scarborough and its people by his prolonged and defiant defence of the castle makes it credible. Not surprisingly, after his surrender and departure on that day, there is no evidence that Cholmley ever dared to return to Scarborough.

Hugh Cholmley was born almost exactly 45 years earlier in Roxby castle, on the west side of the village of Thornton, though by 1600 the centre of the Cholmley estate had moved out of Ryedale to Whitby. The Cholmondleys had shortened their name to Cholmeley or Cholmley soon after they came into Yorkshire from Cheshire, where the main branch of the family remained. Hugh's great-grandfather, Sir Richard, commonly called 'the great black knight of the North', had first established the Cholmley family's estate in the lands formerly belonging to the dissolved abbey of Whitby. When he died in 1583 this estate stretched from beyond Whitby town in the north as far south as Ravenscar and from the North Sea coast inland to the moors of Fylingdales—altogether about 26,000 acres, including the communities of Whitby, Sleights, Grosmont, Stainsacre, Hawsker, Fyling and Robin Hood's Bay. For his loyal service to the Crown, amongst many offices held by Sir Richard, was the constableship of Scarborough castle and a lease on the adjacent royal manor of Northstead.

However, after the death of the great black knight of the North, the fortunes of the Cholmleys declined rapidly. Under Hugh's grandfather, Sir Henry, who was head of the family from 1586 until 1616, debts mounted and the estate shrank as more of it was sold to raise ready money. In an era of raging inflation and fixed rental income, Sir Henry lived far beyond his means, wasting his time in hunting and hawking and his money on hounds and horses. By 1607 Hugh's grandfather had lost all his lands in the Vale of Pickering and left Roxby castle to fall into decay.

Hugh's father, another Sir Richard, was hardly an improvement on his grandfather. He too lived well beyond his income; bred more children than he could afford to support; and nursed public ambitions which made excessive demands on his purse. For instance, he represented Scarborough in the Parliament of 1621 and served as Yorkshire's High Sheriff in the year 1624-5, when both offices incurred great financial expense and no profit in return. By 1626 the Cholmley estate was effectively bankrupt: Richard had debts of £11,000 and an annual income of only £900. Foreclosure was imminent when Hugh then took over responsibility from his exhausted father.

Now in his 26th year Hugh Cholmley's past record was less than promising. According to his later memoirs, only God's timely intervention had saved him on numerous occasions from death or mutilation. Even before his baptism he might have perished but that his grandmother, who had a child of six months of her own, gave him and his aunt 'sucke for one day from her owne breasts'. At the age of three, he would have fallen out of an upstairs window at Roxby had not, 'by gods providence', a servant caught hold of his coat. At seven he fell off a galloping horse, but only his hat was crushed under its hooves. On his eighth birthday, he was rescued by his father's brave butler from the jaws of 'a great fearce sow', which was savaging him in the yard of Abbey House. At Beverley Grammar School he was taken dangerously ill with a fever. His mother came down from Whitby to nurse him, caught the fever and died of it. Hugh survived again. By the age of eleven he had already lived through attacks of smallpox and measles.

Such a young man might have counted his blessings and made profitable use of his privileged opportunities instead of wasting them like his grandfather and father before him; but Hugh followed in their misdirected footsteps. At Jesus College, Cambridge, between the ages of 13 and 17, and at Gray's Inn, London, from 18 to 21, he misspent his days and his father's allowance in drinking, gambling and 'all sports and recreations'. Not even marriage at the age of 22 and then the fatherhood of two sons had converted him to a life of frugal care and serious responsibility. His wife's dowry of £3,000 was soon frittered away; he had personal debts of six or seven hundred pounds.

What changed Hugh was the inheritance of his father's estate. In the spring of 1626 he was brought face to face with the cruel reality of imminent ruin. Again, Hugh just survived, though here, as he had to admit later, the estate was saved by more than 'gods providence & direction'. Crucial to the rescue was the financial help received from many friends and relatives, particularly his uncle John Legard of Ganton and his cousin and close friend Sir John Hotham of Scorborough. For instance, Sir John paid Hugh £4,400 for Fyling Old Hall and grounds, which was probably more than they were worth at the time.

What Cholmley failed to explain in his subsequent memoirs was that another major contribution to his solvency was the spectacular rise in local property values brought about by the new alum industry. In the second, third and fourth decades of the seventeenth century alum mining and manufacture at Sandsend and Mulgrave had made Whitby into a major commercial port. As lords of that port the Cholmleys were able to benefit handsomely without risking their own capital. All ships entering the harbour, all goods loaded and unloaded there, and all vessels taking shelter there had to pay dues to them. Moreover, what had once been worthless mudflats along the banks of the River Esk now became sought-after sites for warehouses, coal-yards and shipbuilding berths. Consequently, Hugh was able to convert much of Cholmley land in Whitby town into ready cash by selling thousand-year leases with very high entry charges.

With this newly-acquired wealth Hugh was able to convert Abbey House at Whitby into a fine mansion, and launch himself into a successful political career. His father had secured one of Scarborough's House of Common seats for him in the last Parliament of King James and the first two of King Charles, but the priority of saving the estate absorbed all his time and energy until he took a place on the North Riding Bench in 1632. Soon he was made deputy-lieutenant of the North Riding and commissioned colonel of the trained bands (home guard) of Whitby, Scarborough, Pickering and Ryedale. With the eclipse of his arch-rival, Sir Thomas Posthumous Hoby of Hackness, Sir Hugh, as he had now become, was the unrivalled leader of north-east Yorkshire. As he expressed it immodestly in his memoirs: 'My father being dead the Country looked upon mee as the cheif of my famuly and haveing masterd my debts I did not only appear at all publicke meetings in very handsome gentilmanly equapage but lived in as handsome and plentyfull a fashon at home as [any] gentleman of my ranke in all the Country; I had betweene 30 and 40 in my ordnarely famuly …'

Sir Hugh's political promotion had owed much to the patronage of the king's chief minister, Thomas Wentworth, Earl of Strafford. It was Strafford who secured a Privy Council licence for Whitby to make a national collection to pay for its new west pier—a project dear to the heart and profitable in the long term to the purse of Sir Hugh. But for reasons which are not entirely clear, Sir Hugh lost Strafford's goodwill in 1640 when he denounced the legality of the Ship Money tax in the Short Parliament of April in that year. From then on the two became implacable enemies. Sir Hugh was deprived of all his royal commissions and censured by the Privy Council. When a new Parliament was called towards the end of 1640, and Sir Hugh was again returned as one of Scarborough's MPs, he and other Yorkshire Members led a vindictive assault on Strafford. No mercy was shown: Cholmley, Hotham and the others were determined to have the earl killed. By Act of Parliament he was condemned to death and executed in May 1641.

Cholmley's association with the anti-Straffordians meant that when the Civil War between King Charles and Parliament began in the summer of 1642 Scarborough's senior Member of Parliament was committed to that side.

In the first months of the war the king's forces controlled most of Yorkshire. However, their failure to capture Hull either by persuasion or by force was a serious setback to the Royalist cause. To match Parliament's superior resources in manpower, money and armaments, Charles had to have help from the Continent. Such foreign assistance from France, the Netherlands or Denmark could reach him only by sea, but Parliament held all the south and east coast ports from Portsmouth to Hull and nearly all the warships of what had been the Royal Navy.

In these circumstances, Scarborough's strategical value was soon evident to both sides. If the king could not have Hull, and Newcastle was too distant and too easily blockaded at Tynemouth, Scarborough was his most convenient and safest port of entry for mercenaries and munitions. With this in mind, Sir Hugh was sent north in September 1642 carrying his former commission of colonel of the trained bands of Whitby, Scarborough, Pickering and Ryedale. His orders were to secure the town, harbour and castle of Scarborough, thereby denying them to the use of the Royalists.

Cholmley did all that was asked of him, and more besides. Within a few weeks he had gathered together a regiment of more than 600 armed militia, raised a squadron of cavalry, greatly strengthened the defences of the castle, and won the confidence of the people of Scarborough. When he refused to bring his men from Stamford Bridge across the Ouse to join the Fairfaxes at Tadcaster and instead withdrew them to Scarborough, he was reprimanded by Parliament for faint-hearted disobedience. Nevertheless, Sir Hugh's action was neither pusillanimous nor rebellious: his commission was to hold Scarborough, not to abandon it to the doubtful mercies of the king's cavalry. Within a few more weeks the Fairfaxes in the West Riding and Parliament in London were singing Cholmley's praises for his gallant, prompt and highly successful reaction to a Royalist advance on Whitby which had reached Guisborough.

Sir Hugh's first experience of bloody warfare sickened and saddened him. He was not in the least triumphant about a victory in which he took over 100 prisoners of the enemy and he had only two cases of wounded men on his side. On the contrary, as he watched his former friend and now opponent, Sir Guilford Slingsby, bleed to death slowly after both his legs had to be amputated, he wrote sorrowfully to his masters in London: 'I confess it grieves my heart to see how these calamities increase, and how I am forced to draw my sword not onely against my countrymen but many near friends and allies, some of which I know both to be well affected in religion and lovers of their liberties.' He now pleaded for a speedy settlement with the king even if this meant giving way to him on all contentious issues except that of religion. Two months later, Sir Hugh changed sides and went over to Charles.

Most commentators on Cholmley's sudden and surprising defection in March 1643 have concluded or assumed that it was the result of his secret meeting with the Queen, Henrietta Maria, at York; but this is to confuse coincidence with cause and effect. In fact, Sir Hugh had already come to a clandestine arrangement with the king's generals in Yorkshire before he saw the queen; their meeting was a diplomatic courtesy, not a dramatic and decisive moment, though more than one recent author has invented additional meetings between them in Scarborough and Whitby, which the queen never visited, to give spurious credence to this romantic silliness. Sir Hugh was no more dazzled by Henrietta Maria's delicate beauty than she was charmed by him. She never forgave him for his part in the death of Strafford, and they did not meet again.

Cholmley's motives were complex and remain controversial. In material terms, he had everything to lose by remaining loyal to Parliament. By March 1643 the Royalists dominated Yorkshire. The Fairfaxes were outnumbered and on the retreat in the West Riding; the Hothams were shut up in Hull; and Parliament's navy had failed to prevent either General Goring or the queen from bringing in enormous reinforcements by sea from Holland through Newcastle and Bridlington.

In February, Sir Hugh had sent a company of soldiers from Scarborough to intercept Goring's progress southwards, but it was annihilated at Yarm. In overwhelming numbers Royalist troops were advancing on Scarborough. Cholmley's birthplace, Roxby castle, was theirs; Fyling Old Hall, once his home, had been plundered by a Royalist raiding party. By comparison with the Royalists, his forces were puny, and he had no hope of supply or rescue by land or by sea. It was only a matter of time before the whole of the Cholmley estate and the towns of Whitby and Scarborough were overrun or forced to surrender. The only way he could save them from such a fate was to go over to the king.

In the event, Sir Hugh brought off his coup with brilliant success. He prepared the ground carefully for his declaration and timed it perfectly: the officers in the garrison who might have resisted were first taken completely by surprise and then wrong-footed when he told them they could leave Scarborough and go to Parliamentarian Hull. Captain Legard considered assassinating his colonel and then rejected the thought because it would be certain to send Sir Hugh's soul straight to hell. When confronted by his cousin outside Newborough Bar, Captain Browne Bushell handed him the keys to town and castle without even an argument. Scarborough passed from Roundhead to Royalist without a shot being fired or a drop of blood shed. Wisely Cholmley refused the offer of 1500 Royalist troops to intimidate the town: nearly all of its burgesses came over to him out of respect and deference rather than fear. Only four families preferred exile in Hull to living under a Royalist regime in Scarborough.

King Charles must have been as grateful to Cholmley as the people of Scarborough: the man that he had once threatened to hang, the man who had driven his best servant and most loyal friend, Strafford, to the block, he now made his governor of Scarborough town and castle, colonel of horse in the Royal army, and responsible for all maritime affairs between the Tees and Bridlington. However, whereas to the Royalist press Sir Hugh had suddenly become 'the gallant knight', in the words of the London newspapers he was now 'Judas', 'cowardly' and 'apostate'. After Cholmley's defection the House of Commons declared him unfit ever to sit there again and resolved that when captured he would be tried for high treason.

Unable to lay hands on Sir Hugh himself, the House 'being netled that they had lost a person soe usefull to them ... plunderd [his] wife of her coach horses and used [her] coarsely'. Elizabeth had stayed behind in London when Hugh went north to Scarborough the previous September, but now she and her two daughters, Ann, aged eight, and Elizabeth, only four, secured passes to sail to Whitby. They left behind the younger son and brother Hugh who was a boarder at St Paul's school, whereas William, the eldest boy of the four Cholmley children, now eighteen years old, had escaped the war altogether by crossing the Channel and travelling to Italy.

Elizabeth must have been confused and hurt by her husband's unexpected transfer of loyalties. In Sir Hugh's own words, she had been 'very earnest and fearce for their [Parliament's] party', and it took him some time and not a little patience to persuade her that he had taken the right course. Nevertheless, once persuaded, Elizabeth became as convinced a Royalist as her husband. After two or three days spent in Whitby, together they travelled to Scarborough and took up residence there with their two girls.

At first it seemed that Cholmley and Scarborough had gone over to the winning side just in time. The Fairfaxes were defeated at Seacroft at the end of March 1643 and then routed on Adwalton Moor three months later. The Hothams soon tried to follow Cholmley and betray Hull to the king but bungled their defection and were shipped off to London in chains. Apart from Hull all Yorkshire became Royalist territory.

However, Royalist successes proved indecisive and temporary: within little more than a year near victory had turned into total defeat. In September 1643 Sir Hugh took part in the frustrating and humiliating siege of Hull. The following summer from Scarborough he could only watch helplessly as a Scottish army in alliance with Parliament invaded Yorkshire from the north forcing the Royalists back into a besieged city of York. When Prince Rupert tried to break the siege in July 1644 his army and that of the northern Royalists under the Marquess of Newcastle were massacred on Marston Moor. A few days later York fell to Parliament. Whatever might happen elsewhere, the king had lost the war in the North and Cholmley's position at Scarborough had become untenable.

When the Marquess of Newcastle and his staff officers arrived in Scarborough directly from their crushing defeat at Marston Moor they told Sir Hugh that the civil war was lost and that he should come with them into exile. Cholmley provided the distinguished Royalist party with two ships to make the crossing to Hamburg but answered the Marquess that he would not desert his post at Scarborough until ordered to do so by the king himself. Word finally arrived from Charles in faraway Cornwall in August. The king thanked Cholmley for his 'faithful endeavours' and asked him not to be discouraged 'by the ill success of our forces' in the North, but to hold Scarborough if besieged, and not to yield it to the enemy until 'the last extremity'. The king's personal appeal to Sir Hugh's honour, courage and allegiance was well judged: from now on desertion was unthinkable.

Now that there was no longer a Royalist army in the North to be supplied through Scarborough, Parliament showed little immediate interest in that port. Of far greater priority was the capture of Sunderland and Newcastle, not least because of the vast stocks of coal on the banks of the Wear and Tyne which Londoners had been denied for the past two winters. However, if 'Scarborough horse', Cholmley's cavalry, were only minor irritants, Scarborough's 'pyrates' soon became a major menace to the vital sea-coal traffic to the capital. During the early winter of 1644-45 hardly a week passed without a report in the London newspapers of some new loss of colliers to Cholmley's audacious 'sea-rovers'.

Accordingly, to deprive Cholmley's marauding pinnaces of a safe, supply haven, Parliament ordered the seizure of Scarborough by force. At the end of January 1645, with an army of nearly 2,000 infantry, General Sir John Meldrum moved in on Scarborough town from his headquarters at Falsgrave. Sir Hugh had never entertained the ambition of defending the town and harbour: he knew that he lacked the men and firepower to hold them. In November he had summoned an extraordinary meeting of all the townspeople to St Mary's church and there assured them that he would retire to the castle rather than subject them to all the perils of bombardment and assault. And he was as good as his word. On Shrove Tuesday, 18 February 1645, when Meldrum launched a full-scale attack on Scarborough by land and sea, the Royalists simply retreated to the castle. As in March 1643, Sir Hugh gave the burgesses a free choice: they could follow him into the castle or stay behind in the town. There was no compulsion and very little bloodshed.

Parliament was delighted with the news from Scarborough. *Mercurius Britanicus* declared triumphantly that 'God was visible' there; Meldrum was promised £1,000 for his victory. But the Scottish veteran knew that neither town nor harbour was secure until the castle was his, and the defences of the castle were truly formidable. When Cholmley scorned Meldrum's invitation to surrender, Parliament was obliged to call up its heaviest artillery.

By the beginning of May, Meldrum's cannon-royal, the biggest piece in Europe, firing a 63-pound ball, had been mounted in the chancel of St Mary's church. For three days it was fired point-blank at the castle keep until finally the tower split in two and the western wall came crashing down with Cholmley's men still on it. The Roundheads assumed that the fall of the keep signalled the surrender of the castle, but they were much mistaken: it might have 'dislodged the Governor, his ladie and most of the gentlemen and officers of qualitie', yet it also provided the defenders with a huge barricade of masonry across the only entrance to the headland, and a huge arsenal of ready-made missiles. During the next few days there was savage hand-to-hand fighting as Cholmley and Meldrum both tried to gain control of the barbican and the bridges leading from it to the heart of the castle. Meldrum threatened no quarter; Elizabeth Cholmley begged her husband not to give way for the sake of the women, but to fight on for his honour and the king. Meldrum vowed that he would take the castle or leave his bones under its walls. Finally, in the thick of the battle, the Scottish General, now more than 60 years old, received a musket ball 'in att the bellie and out of the backe'; and within six days he was dead.

Under Meldrum's successor, Sir Matthew Boynton, the siege lasted another ten weeks. Cholmley's garrison was slowly reduced by thirst, scurvy and malnutrition until on 22 July Sir Hugh signed terms of honourable surrender. Of the 500 who had gone into the castle, after 22 weeks only about half that number came out alive, most of them carried out in blankets because they were too weak to walk.

Lady Elizabeth had stayed by her husband throughout these violent events. The two girls were sent off by sea to Holland before the siege began, but she would not forsake Sir Hugh whatever the danger. As her admiring husband later wrote, she 'shewd a courridge even above her sex'. After the keep was shattered, she had to sleep in a bivouac and as a result suffered permanently from 'a defluction of rume upon one of her eies', and never fully recovered from effects of the scurvy.

But now Hugh and Elizabeth had to part. Sir Hugh had intended to join the king who was then at Raglan in Wales; however, when he reached Selby he had neither the health nor strength for such a long journey and therefore turned back to Bridlington. From there, with only £10 left in his purse, he sailed to Holland. His purpose was to find his daughters and eventually reunite his family. Article 5 of the surrender terms allowed Lady Elizabeth to return to the Cholmley home at Whitby, but she learned that Abbey House was occupied by one of Parliament's officers who had no intention of quitting such comfortable quarters. Consequently, she had no choice but to seek the hospitality of one of her husband's friends, Christopher Percehay, who lived at Ryton, near

Malton. It was there that she heard that plague at Whitby had driven the Roundheads out of Abbey House and, though it was now mid-winter and the way deep in snow, she was determined to reclaim her home. With only a maid and a cook for companions she rode the thirty miles over vale and moor only to find Abbey House ransacked and empty. Nevertheless, though these were the saddest months of her life, in her husband's words, 'her sperret would not submit to make complaint & application to the Parlaments Committy at Yorke, as most others did ...'

Meanwhile Sir Hugh had found his girls in Holland, sent them back to their mother in Yorkshire, and moved on himself to France. According to his memoirs, in Holland he had, 'by gods providence', acquired £600, probably by selling or pawning jewellery in Amsterdam, and this was enough to pay all his expenses for some time to come. Finally, he was able to settle at Rouen where eventually he was joined by his two sons, William, who had come from Italy, and Hugh, who had now left St Paul's school. In the spring of 1647, Elizabeth and her two daughters came over from England to complete the family. It was the first time they had all been together for five years.

As a 'malignant' Royalist, Sir Hugh's estate had been sequestered by Parliament. However, fortunately for him and his family, in 1640, anticipating a time of troubles ahead, he had placed the whole of his estate, except for the manor of Fyling, in the hands of his younger brother Henry and other trustees. Unlike Hugh, Sir Henry Cholmley had kept faith with Parliament throughout the Civil Wars, so Hugh was allowed to re-possess his property on condition he paid a composition fine of only £850 on Fyling, which had been valued at only £170 a year. All this explains why the Cholmleys were able to return to Whitby in the summer of 1649, and also why Sir Hugh had the capital to start his own alum mine at nearby Saltwick soon afterwards.

Given his political record, Sir Hugh was closely watched for signs of Royalist conspiracy; but whatever he might have felt about the recent execution of the king and the establishment of a republic, he steered well clear of further trouble. His eight-week imprisonment in Leeds castle, Kent, in 1651, during the panic caused by Charles II's invasion, was a consequence of the Commonwealth's hyper-caution. The following summer the whole Cholmley family moved back to Abbey House, where they remained for nearly two years. It seems that Whitby was regarded by the government as a place of internal exile.

Lady Elizabeth was busy refurnishing the house, though not to the previous standard on account of the family's relative poverty and 'the unsetlednesse of the tymes'. Sir Hugh particularly prized his wife's fine needlework: in his memoirs he reminded his sons to take 'exstraordnary caire' of 'a suite of greene cloth hangeing with flowers' which she and her maids had sewn. However, 'gods blessing' did not spare her for much longer: soon after returning to London for her elder daughter's wedding, 'she fell in to a feaver' and died in April 1655.

Hugh was heart-broken: she was not yet 55 years old. Within a few days of hearing the news of her death, he left Whitby for ever, explaining that he could not endure the sight of those rooms and places where he had so much enjoyed her company. Instead he went south to live in the house of his brother-in-law, Sir Roger Twisden, at Roydon Hall, East Peckham, in Kent. There he spent the remaining two years of his life writing his memoirs. At the outset he had intended to write only in praise of his dear wife, but he soon realised that here was an opportunity to tell the story, as far as he could remember it, of his own ancestry and his own eventful life. There was time only to finish a first rough draft before he died in November 1657. His final tribute to Lady Elizabeth was to ask to be buried next to her in the local parish church of St Michael, instead of with his Cholmley forebears in Whitby.

Most funeral dedications are at least exaggerated if not downright dishonest, but Sir Hugh's inscription on Lady Elizabeth's black marble tombstone was an accurate description of his true feelings:

> Deposited the body of Lady Elizabeth Cholmley, daughter to Sir William Twisden of East Peckham, in the county of Kent, knight and baronet, wife to Sir Hugh Cholmley of Whitby, in the county of York, knight and baronet, by whom she had six children. She was very beautiful, of great ingenuity, and a discerning judgement; in great dangers had courage above her sex; of a most noble and sweet nature, compassionate to all in distress; a virtuous chaste, loving wife, indulgent parent, and true friend; and, which was above all, a most pious and religious person; and in belief and assurance of salvation and eternal life, by the death and merits of Christ Jesus, died the 17th of April, anno Domini 1655, in the 54th year of her age, after she had been married 32 years.

14. Admiral Lawson

Of all the many Scarborough men who have put to sea from there, none rose so far and became so mighty in his country as Admiral Sir John Lawson. Nevertheless, though he was thought to deserve a lengthy entry in the *Dictionary of National Biography* summarizing his achievements, in his own town he has been long ignored and largely forgotten.

Queen Victoria never set foot in Scarborough and warned her eldest son of its vices, yet she is the only subject considered worthy of a statue in the town. Scarborough has roads and streets, avenues and parks named after her, her sons and daughter-in-law; former prime ministers and explorers are well represented in street names; and even Lawson's Roundhead comrades, Cromwell, Fairfax and Ireton, none of whom ever came to Scarborough, have been honoured in the same way; but Lawson himself—who served the town loyally and became one of its most generous benefactors—has neither plaque nor place-name to commemorate his extraordinary life and merits.

Such ungrateful neglect perhaps owes something to the obscurity of his birth and early life. More than one so-called authority has alleged that he was born in Hull; the earl of Clarendon, a contemporary who knew him well, conceded no more than 'he was of Yorkshire, near Scarborough'; and, in the absence of a parish register of baptisms and Lawson's failure to leave an autobiography, there is no conclusive proof of the time and place of his birth. However, wherever John first saw the light of day, without any doubt he regarded Scarborough as his home and lived the greater part of his life there. On one occasion, he described two periods of enforced exile from Scarborough to Hull as 'banishment'; and in his last will he described Scarborough as 'the place of my nativity'.

Neither is it certain who his parents were and on this subject there are some striking conflicts of opinion. A recent account accepts that Lawson was born in Scarborough, but then asserts that he was 'probably of the Lawson family of Longhirst [in Northumberland] whose arms he used'. This is only a little less unconvincing than the *Dictionary of National Biography* which concluded that he 'doubtless belonged to a branch of that family'. In sharpest contrast to these flattering views are the more often stated opinions that Lawson's origins were of the humblest: 'son of a person in low circumstances', wrote the historian of Britain's admirals; 'son of a poor man', said one of the many editors of the diary of Samuel Pepys; and, perhaps the most disparaging of all, 'formerly a kind of fisherman (or little better)', whose father was no more than 'a common sailor', according to Lord Clarendon, who should have been better informed.

Though the surviving evidence is thin, there is just enough to indicate that John Lawson was neither gentleman nor plebeian by birth. His father was probably William Lawson, master mariner and shipowner—not one of the richest of Scarborough's mercantile oligarchy, yet certainly not 'a common sailor'. This William Lawson had a quarter share in one of St Mary's new pews when they were first allocated in 1635, and since there were only 155 such pews for 264 men of the parish with a population of about two thousand, this placed him amongst a privileged minority. A year later William is on record as master of the *Hopewell* of Scarborough and one of the four elected wardens of the Society of Shipowners, Masters and Mariners. Founded in 1602, this society was then Scarborough's most powerful and prestigious guild, and the office of warden was a position of local importance and trust.

John Lawson makes his first appearance in the records of the Society of Shipowners, Masters and Mariners in 1639 as master of the *Adventurer*. Later that same year, 'John Lawson, nautam', aged 24 of Scarborough received licence to marry Isabel Jefferson, spinster, aged 23. Isabel was the daughter of William Jefferson of Lythe, himself a shipowner and master mariner. The wedding took place on 5 January 1640 in Lythe parish church. In 1639 John had made only one recorded and long voyage in the *Adventurer*, yet in 1641 he was credited with as many as 26, and in 1642 a further five. Most of these voyages involved carrying coals from Sunderland or Newcastle to Scarborough, whereas the longer journeys were probably to continental ports such as Rotterdam or Antwerp. Significantly, in the account book of the Society, the names of William and John Lawson are always written on consecutive lines, and after the *Hopewell* William's ships are named the *John* in 1641 and 1642, and then the *Isabel* in 1643 and 1645. John Lawson had called his eldest daughter Isabel after her mother.

In short, John Lawson was probably born in Scarborough about 1615, the son of a successful master mariner. By the age of 24 he was already a master of a ship and had married the daughter of another shipowner. Three years later, at the outbreak of the Civil War, he was experienced in East coast trade and North Sea navigation. At the age of 27 he might have aspired to become a wealthy shipowner and merchant with a mansion house in Scarborough; he might have had ambitions to become a member of the town's ruling body, the Common Hall, and one day perhaps to occupy one of its highest offices such as bailiff, coroner or chamberlain. He could never have imagined what an altogether different and greater future fate had in store for him. As it did for tens of thousands of other young men at the time, the Civil Wars changed everything for John Lawson.

Whereas nearly all of his contemporaries in Scarborough and elsewhere in the country were reluctant or even refused to take sides openly and actively, from the outset of the war John Lawson volunteered himself and his ship to Parliament. Though there is no evidence that he belonged to any of the nonconformist religious groups that sprang up in Scarborough during and after the Civil Wars, Lawson is usually described as a baptist—in other words an extreme Puritan who regarded the established Church of England as far too close to the doctrines and practices of the detested Church of Rome. Such radical religious prejudices if strongly held would alone be sufficient to explain Lawson's wholehearted commitment to Parliament's cause; unlike the majority of Englishmen he was neither 'impressed' by force nor neutral by preference.

In 1642, at a time when most of Yorkshire was in Royalist hands, Scarborough was Parliament's most northerly outpost. In the first months of war, when the town, harbour and castle were under the control of Parliament's Colonel Sir Hugh Cholmley, Lawson and a few other like-minded sea captains, such as William Nesfield, were engaged in intercepting Royalist arms and supply traffic to Newcastle, the King's only major East coast port. Early in 1643 the House of Commons thanked him for seizing a corn ship on its way to Newcastle 'for the reliefe of the enemies there'. He was told to sell the prize and its cargo and use the proceeds to maintain Cholmley's garrison at Scarborough.

However, by the time the House approved this order, Lawson's loyalty had been put to the severest test: in March 1643 Sir Hugh abruptly changed sides and took Scarborough with him over to the King. According to Cholmley's own later account, there 'were not above 4 families' in the town which, rather than live under a Royalist regime, chose exile in Parliamentarian Hull. One of these families was Lawson's. For the next two years Lawson, his wife and their eldest daughter Isabel made their home in Hull. This 'banishment' was only the first of many 'tossings and removals' Lawson and his family suffered because of his service to Parliament.

Whether Lawson also took the *Adventurer* to Hull is not known, but it is clear that he was soon at sea again in command of 'a small ship of [his] own and partners'. This armed merchantman of 140 tons with a crew of 42 and carrying 12 cannon was aptly-named the *Covenant*, which was first listed in Parliament's North Sea summer guard of 1643. Though much of the time Lawson carried routine cargoes to supply Parliament's garrisons and its Scottish allies, there were other occasions when the *Covenant* did outstanding deeds. For example, towards the end of 1644 when Cholmley was being blockaded by sea at Scarborough, the *Covenant* intercepted, engaged and captured a Royalist supply ship. Such a success would have been more than enough for any ordinary merchantman, but Lawson transferred some of the enemy's guns to the *Covenant* and, 'for better advantage in chasing a man-of-war, cut off his own boat which was thereby lost'. Even heavily armed merchant ships rarely risked battle with enemy warships, even less gave chase to them, but Lawson was always looking for a fight regardless of the odds against him.

For Captain John Lawson the Civil War was a holy crusade: it was neither an adventurous game nor a disastrous distraction. To him Royalists were enemies of God as well as enemies of the state. The more often he escaped death and injury even in the most perilous circumstances the more convinced he became that God had spared him to fulfil His purposes. When Sir John Hotham, Parliament's governor of Hull, and his son, tried to follow Cholmley's defection, it was Lawson who uncovered their plot and helped to defeat it. In his own typically modest words, 'it pleased God to make mee an Instrument in discovering and (in some measure) preventing the intended treacherie of Sr Jo: Hotham ...'. The Hothams were arrested, sent off to London in chains, eventually found guilty of treason, and both executed in January 1645. Much to Parliament's advantage and the King's undoing, Hull remained securely in the former's hands throughout the war.

Under Lawson the *Covenant* served Parliament continuously during the First Civil War, but soon after Cholmley surrendered in July 1645 he brought his family back to Scarborough. As recognition of his recent service at sea and as a mark of the esteem he now had locally, 'Captain John Lawson' was elected at the end of September 1645 to a place in the First Twelve, in effect the town's governing elite. Other newcomers to this body, Captain William Nesfield, Mr John Harrison junior, and Mr Peter Hodgson, all shared Lawson's radical religious and political opinions, but they had previously served in the Second Twelve before Cholmley's defection, whereas Lawson came in as a complete outsider. Also, unlike these others, Lawson never accepted any senior administrative post during his membership of the First Twelve from 1645 until 1652; this was because he had more important duties to perform outside the borough.

Like many impoverished post-war towns Scarborough was hard-pressed to repair the damage done to property and yet still provide free accommodation to a garrison of unpaid and increasingly disaffected Parliamentary soldiers. Though the borough had two capable Members to represent its interests in the House of Commons—Sir Matthew Boynton and Luke Robinson—John Lawson was now so highly valued as an advocate that in 1646 and 1647 he spent more time in London on Scarborough's business than he did in Scarborough. However, Parliament was much more concerned about the security of Scarborough castle than about the well-being of potentially disloyal burgesses and in April 1646 Lawson was awarded a captain's commission and put in charge of the castle garrison of 100 soldiers. His principal responsibility was to man and guard 'the forts which command the harbour at Scarborough', and to serve this vital purpose he was promised a generous allowance of both money and cannon ammunition.

As a result of his profitable and distinguished service at sea for Parliament and his appointment as captain of the castle guard, Lawson was now regarded locally as a man of substance and influence. He is first described as 'gentleman' in an indenture copied into the Corporation minute book of September 1646. The same source also reveals that by this time from the Corporation he held a seven-year lease of the Garlands, an extensive pasture of 16 acres at the northern foot of Weaponness. Two years later, he took out a second lease of another Corporation property, Butt Closes. Both these tenancies were highly valued and usually held only by leading burgesses. According to Hinderwell, between these two leases which were later renewed on even more favourable terms, Lawson bought a mansion house, later known as 4 West Sandgate, opposite the lower end of Merchant Row.

However, Captain Lawson was allowed little time to enjoy his newly-acquired properties: for the second time in five years he was compelled to bring his wife and children out of Scarborough to exile in Hull. Towards the end of July 1648, Colonel Matthew Boynton, son of Sir

Matthew, and Parliament's governor of Scarborough, raised a red flag above the wall of the castle and declared himself a Royalist convert. As in 1643, there was no resistance from the soldiers of the garrison who tamely followed Boynton. As in 1643, Lawson would not live under a Royalist regime.

What particular part Lawson played in the second siege of Scarborough castle, which lasted from September to December 1648, is not recorded. All we know is that Captain John Lawson was one of Parliament's signatories to the articles of Boynton's surrender; that his company of soldiers took over the castle when it fell; and that subsequently he was appointed permanent captain of the castle guard on the recommendation of Parliament's new governor of Scarborough, Colonel Hugh Bethell.

Early in 1650 Lawson went back to sea. He had served a highly successful apprenticeship in armed merchant ships and was now launched into a professional career in the Commonwealth's navy. In his first command, as captain of the *Lion*, he again showed exceptional audacity and enterprise. Under the guns of Glückstadt fort and the noses of its Danish garrison, Lawson went boldly into the harbour, boarded a collier belonging to John Harrison of Scarborough but lately stolen by another Scarborian, the Royalist privateer, Captain Browne Thomas, and towed it out again. The *Lion* was out of range before the Danes could fire a shot. Harrison had his ship and cargo returned intact to Scarborough.

Lawson was rewarded with the command of the newly-built *Centurion*, a battleship of 40 guns. During the summer of 1650 he escorted transports taking supplies to Cromwell's army in Scotland. Early the following year, now captain of the *Fairfax*, he followed Admiral Sir William Penn southwards to join him at the Azores. For the next fourteen months, Lawson served in Penn's Mediterranean fleet.

The first naval war against the Dutch (1652-54) brought Lawson to the top of his profession: when it started, he was only one of dozens of warships' captains; when it ended, he was Vice-Admiral of the Fleet, the fourth most senior post in the Navy. Of the six major sea battles fought between the English and the Dutch in the Channel and North Sea, Lawson had a crucial and heroic role in at least four of them. On more than one occasion he rescued his superiors, the three Generals-at-Sea, Blake, Deane and Monck, from the potentially disastrous consequences of their inexperience. They were professional soldiers and only amateur seamen, and as such found themselves repeatedly outmanoeuvred and out-witted by the veteran Dutch commanders such as Marten Tromp and de Ruijter.

With the possible exception of William Penn, no English flag officer of that time had knowledge of navigation to compare with Lawson's.

Lawson's lowly origins, his background as a merchant seaman, his rough manners and broad vowels disqualified him from the highest ranks, even in the navy of the republic; but these same qualities gave him a unique affinity with the lower deck. Unusually for a flag officer Lawson was a champion of the welfare of ordinary seamen. After the victorious Dutch War he proposed a number of radical reforms which, if implemented, would have greatly improved morale and raised the quality of warship crews. He believed that forcible impressment could not be justified except in an extreme emergency of national defence; he thought that seamen should not be compelled to spend months or even years abroad in the West Indies or the Mediterranean; and that their dependants ought to be paid maintenance money during their long absences, and compensation if they were killed on active service.

Lawson made it his duty to know every man of his ship's crew personally. After seaman John Morris was killed on board the *Fairfax* in the battle off Portland, his captain not only signed a certificate to this effect for the benefit of his family, but added in his clumsy handwriting, 'The father of the above named is an Inpotent(sic) Aged man in great want.'

If Lawson was a professional seaman, in politics he had no craft at all. His profound distrust of Lord Protector Cromwell led him unwisely into the dangerous waters of intrigue and conspiracy, where he was easily outmanoeuvred. When Cromwell ordered him to accompany Blake on an expedition to Cadiz and promoted another untried soldier, Edward Mountagu, to be General-at-Sea above him, Lawson retaliated by resigning his commission. Presumably, he hoped that this dramatic gesture would cause a sympathetic mutiny of captains and seamen, but he was mistaken. When foolishly Lawson continued to conspire with other dissidents, Cromwell banished him to Scarborough. In 1657, at the age of 42, it seemed that the former admiral's career had come to a premature conclusion.

Two years later, however, after the death of Cromwell and the downfall of his son Richard, Lawson was summoned back as Vice-Admiral in command of the Channel Fleet—a post which gave him the means to determine the fate of all his fellow countrymen. When an army junta led by Generals Lambert and Fleetwood seized power in London, Lawson intervened decisively. In December 1659, the Vice-Admiral brought his fleet of 22 warships from the Downs up the Thames as far as

Gravesend. In the middle of winter, by blockading the river, Lawson had the capital at his mercy: Londoners would freeze and starve to death. On Christmas day Fleetwood capitulated, and parliamentary government was restored. Lawson was called to the Bar of the House of Commons there to receive the hearty thanks of the Speaker. As the historian of the Commonwealth's navy wrote, this was 'Lawson's finest hour': he had saved the nation from military dictatorship.

Five months later, he helped to save it from anarchy. The old republican baptist aided the restoration of the monarchy and the Church of England because reluctantly he accepted that there was no stable alternative to them: by 1660 the state was sliding speedily into chaos and bankruptcy. Lawson's realistic reconciliation to the return of Charles II was a crucial condition of his peaceful restoration. Without Lawson, the republic had no popular leader; without his fleet, it had no defence and no authority. In May 1660, James, Duke of York, the King's brother, came ashore at Dover from Lawson's flagship, the *London*. Revengeful Cavaliers in the new Parliament would have dismissed the Vice-Admiral and taken away his pension, but Charles and his brother were all too aware and appreciative of the enormous debt they owed him. Lawson was knighted, his pension of £500 a year restored, and to his salary was added a gift of £1000 from the sale of old Navy stores.

But Lawson was not allowed to retire on his laurels: for the next four summers he commanded the Mediterranean squadron. The Vice-Admiral was given two principal objectives—to crush the Barbary corsairs who preyed on shipping in the Straits from Tunis, Tripoli and Algiers, and to secure Tangier, England's first naval base in the area. Both tasks proved impossible, though Lawson's energy, audacity and determination were prodigious. Time and time again he cleared the seas of pirate ships and forced the local rulers to sign peace treaties only to see them broken as soon as his squadron had sailed out of sight. As he wrote to Sir Richard Fanshaw, England's ambassador to Spain and Portugal, in March 1664:

> We have a war with Algiers. They are more perfidious every day, and the most treacherous people ... but till it please God they feel some smart, no peace can be made with them.

Tangier, on the North African coast of the Atlantic, had been part of the dowry of the Portuguese princess, Catherine of Braganza, when she was married to Charles II. The Portuguese were glad to be rid of a place

111

that was defenceless against the Atlantic ocean on one side and the Moors on the other. However, in the face of Spanish, French and Dutch hostility, not to mention Barbary pirates, if the English were ever to become a naval and commercial force in this strategic area they had to have a safe harbour of their own. No one understood better than Lawson the crucial importance of Tangier; and it was he who persuaded the government in London to appoint Hugh Cholmley, son of his old enemy of the same name, as surveyor-general and chief architect of a great pier or mole that was to be built on the north side of the bay. The Tangier mole was 'the greatest engineering work as yet undertaken by Englishmen', and unfortunately it proved too great for their resources and their imagination.

Lawson was recalled to England when the Second Dutch War was about to start: his experience of naval warfare was indispensable and unrivalled. The Duke of York, who now commanded the battle fleet of over 100 warships, made Sir John second in his leading Red Division, while Prince Rupert was admiral of the White and the Earl of Sandwich led the Blue. In this fighting formation the English met the Dutch war fleet off Lowestoft in June 1665. The general mêlée that followed initial manoeuvring turned into a rout of the Dutch after the Duke and Lawson smashed a corridor through the enemy's line. The Dutch admiral Opdam was killed when his flagship blew up, and his fleet scattered and ran homewards. At least 26 Dutch men-of-war were destroyed or captured and as many as 8000 of their men perished or were taken captive. English losses were one ship and no more than 500 seamen. The battle of Lowestoft was one of the most decisive of England's many naval victories.

The most serious loss on the English side was Sir John Lawson. In the final stages of the battle, as his ship the *Royal Oak* pursued the fleeing Dutch, the Vice-Admiral received a stray musket bullet in the knee. A fortnight later when he was brought to Greenwich, the wound was not considered 'very bad'. However, when the King went down to see him the following day, Lawson's condition had worsened: 'he had a fever, a thrush and a hiccough, all three together', which Samuel Pepys regarded as ominous symptoms. A week later Lawson was dead.

Late on Saturday night, 1 July 1665, with only Admiralty officials present, Lawson was buried in the church of St Dunstan-in-the-East, next to the grave of his daughter Abigail. According to Pepys's prejudiced account, Sir John had died in disgrace for acting recklessly at the battle of Lowestoft; but the truth was that his burial coincided with the great plague when hundreds of Londoners died daily and were commonly buried at night. Still, it was an unfitting funeral for a national hero.

Sir John Lawson's last service to his native town was a gift of £100 to its poorest people. At first, his widow, Lady Lawson, was unwilling to carry out the terms of her husband's will unless she had a guarantee from Scarborough Corporation that the bequest would indeed go to those who needed it most. Eventually, in 1667, she accepted an assurance that six percent interest or six pounds a year would be doled out as charity 'until such time as their (sic) can be a conveneient piece of ground found out to be purchased with the said £100'. Even so the money was not handed over until 1669, and Lady Lawson's suspicions were justified: Lawson's legacy was initially used to pay for part of the costs of re-building St Mary's church tower which had fallen down ten years earlier. This was the last of many ironies in Lawson's life: that the old baptist should unwittingly finance the renovation of his parish church.

St Mary's new steeple was finally finished in 1672, but it was another decade still before Scarborough Council bought land on the south side of St Sepulchre Street for exactly £100 on which the Society of Owners, Masters and Mariners could at last erect their almshouse or hospital. When Ralph Thoresby passed through Scarborough in 1682 he was able to admire the newly-built Trinity House, accommodating 27 ancient seamen and widows of seamen.

Little has survived of Lawson in today's Scarborough. By 1832 Trinity House was so decayed and inadequate that it had to be almost entirely rebuilt: only the lower courses of the original massive stone walls remain. The house where Lawson and his family lived, 4 West Sandgate, was sold by one of his daughters, Anne, and later demolished to make way for a gas works. The last of the Lawson properties in Scarborough was sold by a grand-daughter in 1698.

We do not even know what Lawson looked like. The illustration drawn in Baker's *History* is entirely imaginary and anachronistic: nobody could be fooled into thinking it a likeness. Even the portrait of him by Sir Peter Lely, which belongs to Queen Elizabeth II and hangs in the Admirals' Gallery at Greenwich, was painted a year after his death on the orders of his most grateful patron, the Duke of York.

John Lawson put 'gent.' after his name but he was never accepted by London's high society as a true gentleman. For a man without ancestry, education or a fortune he went as far as it was then possible to go. Macaulay, the historian, probably had Admiral Lawson in mind when he wrote: 'There were gentlemen and there were seamen in the navy of Charles the Second. But the seamen were not gentlemen; and the gentlemen were not seamen.' The cruel joke at the royal court was that Sir John would be raised to the peerage when Nell Gwynn became a countess. The truth was that however much he might achieve he could never aspire to be more than a 'tarpaulin' admiral. Still, if Lawson was not the greatest of men, he was one of our greatest seamen.

15. George Fox, Peter Hodgson and Scarborough's Quakers

In 1651 George Fox came to Scarborough. Eight years earlier at the age of nineteen, he had abandoned his home and family in Leicestershire and given up his trade as a shoemaker to become a wandering preacher. His outspoken denunciation of clergymen, who lived on tithes, and their churches, which he dismissed contemptuously as 'steeple-houses', had soon incurred the wrath and punishment of authority. Most of the year 1650 he had spent in the correction house at Derby. After physical expulsion from York Minster, he had travelled north into Cleveland and then back southwards down the coast, passing through Staithes and Whitby before reaching Scarborough. There, according to favoured tradition, Fox stayed as a guest at the home of Peter Hodgson.

Hodgson is not an uncommon name in Scarborough: there are today more than two hundred Hodgsons in the local telephone directory. As early as 1519 a 'Robert Hogeson' was elected to be one of the town's bailiffs. Yet of all the many Hodgsons who have lived and died in Scarborough Peter Hodgson, father and founder of its Quaker family, was probably the most influential and heroic of that name. Nevertheless, though J.S. Fletcher included him as one of a dozen outstanding *Yorkshiremen of the Restoration* (1921), otherwise he has been unfairly neglected by historians.

Peter Hodgson's name first appears in Scarborough's Corporation records in November 1642. When Sir Hugh Cholmley, then Parliament's governor, asked the town's ruling body to raise and pay for a company of dragoons, 'Pet Hodghon' contributed thirty shillings. Of the Common Hall's 44 members he was then placed 21st in the Second Twelve. Altogether the town's leading men offered Cholmley £55 15s. 4d., five horses and four riders for them. Clearly, Peter Hodgson was already one of Scarborough's oligarchy, though not yet high enough to qualify for a senior post in its government.

When Cholmley changed sides in March 1643 some committed Parliamentarians left the town, some committed Royalists won promotion and office, but the majority of burgesses, like Hodgson, hung on, presumably hoping that they could still evade such commitments. In

October 1643, Peter 'Hodghson' was placed 14th in the Second Twelve and, a year later, 13th. As yet he was outside the golden circle of the First Twelve, but now poised on its perimeter.

However, Hodgson's persistent absence from Common Hall meetings during the summer of 1644 might indicate a growing disillusionment with or distancing from Cholmley's failing Royalist cause. Alternatively, since Peter was a master mariner, ship owner and corn merchant, he might simply have been following his trade at sea. Still he could not have been regarded as a Royalist 'delinquent' by Scarborough's self-styled 'well-affected' Parliamentary party otherwise he would not have been promoted to 10th in the First Twelve when the next elections were held in September 1645. For the next five years his name was listed in the town's First Twelve, though still as plain 'Peter Hodgson' and not yet elevated to the title of 'Mister'.

During these years of revolutionary ferment Hodgson seems to have been engaged more with business than politics. From the Corporation's record of indentures of apprentices we learn that between 1645 and 1653 he and his wife, Eleanor or Ellen, took at least four boys into their care to learn 'the art and mystery of mariners'. On Christmas day 1645 William Jackson joined the Hodgson household; four years later, he was followed by John Huntres, the son of a Fylingdales tailor, and Titus Coulson of Scarborough. In February 1651, William Ribye, son of a farmer at Irton, bound himself apprentice to Peter and Eleanor, and in June 1653, Henry Pearson from Pickering did the same. The absence of Eleanor's name from this last indenture suggests that Peter had become a widower by that date.

If Peter Hodgson spent so much time at sea and abroad from Scarborough this might explain his poor attendance record at Common Hall meetings, and his failure or unwillingness to secure any post in the borough's government. For instance, between June and September 1650, the Common Hall met seven times but Hodgson was marked present only twice, in June and August. Moreover, perhaps this absenteeism alone is sufficient to account for his relegation at Michaelmas 1650 from 11th in the First Twelve down to 14th in the Second, and even more remarkably his disappearance altogether from all Common Hall lists of members in 1651 and 1652. On the other hand, Peter's absence from Sandside might have had more to do with his religion than his commerce.

Peter Hodgson had a substantial house on the west side of Cargate (now Cross Street) on land which had once been occupied by Scarborough's Black Friars. According to Quaker tradition, in the autumn of 1651 George Fox preached to an assembly there from an upper floor gallery, and the event was recorded with an inscription carved on the wooden balustrade. However, it would be surprising if Hodgson had not already become one of the Friends of Truth, as they then called themselves, before Fox came to Scarborough. Why else would he have invited him into his house and allowed him to preach there? Just one entry among St Mary's churchwardens' disbursements for 1650-1 also suggests that Hodgson's conversion pre-dated Fox's visit: it records that sixpence was paid out 'for pulling up Peter Hodgshon pew'. Presumably, this was the family pew which he had bought in 1635 when the seats in St Mary's were first allotted; rated at £1 18s. it was not the most expensive, which cost £2 13s. 4d., but it was well positioned in the centre of the nave.

In 1651 the Quakers were not yet a persecuted sect: on the contrary, like many other contemporary radical religious groups such as Ranters, Anabaptists and Familists which had sprang up in the fertile ground of Civil War, the republican government regarded them as natural allies against Royalists. Particularly in the north of England, which was distrusted in London as potentially rebellious, the Commonwealth's military and civil authorities gave protection to Fox and his like. One of Fox's earliest converts was Durand Hotham (1619-91), of Fyling Old Hall and Cranswick, younger brother of the late 'Captain' John Hotham, who had served as Scarborough's Member of Parliament and then lost his head in 1645 for going over to the King. Durand was justice of the peace in the North and East Ridings. So was Luke Robinson, Scarborough's senior Member of Parliament and, during the 1650s, the most powerful political figure in north-east Yorkshire. Yet when Fox visited Robinson at his lodgings in Pickering, the justice met him 'at his chamber door', listened attentively and respectfully to what he had to say, and did not intervene even when his own favourite preacher was converted to the Friends. Throughout 1651 and 1652 Fox was allowed to travel freely throughout Yorkshire and Lancashire where he drew in many new followers.

In these circumstances, it is no surprise therefore to find that when Peter returned to the Common Hall at Scarborough after the elections of Michaelmas 1653 he had become junior of the two bailiffs. His senior partner was William Foord. As his lengthy will of 1663 reveals, Mr Foord, gentleman, was one of the wealthiest of Scarborough's burgesses. Besides his woollen draper's shop in Newborough, he owned several houses, kilns, stables and extensive ground called 'Frieridge', dozens of closes of meadow and arable land scattered over Scarborough's and Falsgrave's fields, a water mill at Cloughton, and part shares in five ships.

When he died he left £10 to one of his grandchildren and forty shillings to the poor people of the town. By 1653 William Foord was a veteran of the Common Hall: he had already served as junior bailiff in 1630-1, 1636-7 and 1640-1 and had sat in the First Twelve for a quarter of a century. Whereas his election was predictable, in contrast, Peter Hodgson had never previously occupied any municipal office.

In fact, Foord and Hodgson were much more than partners in office: as surviving letters of May, June and July 1654 indicate, they were also close business associates and friends, so that Hodgson's election probably owed something to Foord's patronage. Writing to Peter at his lodgings at the King's Head, in London's Tower Street, William assured his 'kind partner' that all his family were well and that he was pleased to hear that Peter would soon 'procure' his 'vessell againe'. As the correspondence continued it becomes clear that Hodgson's main purpose at London was to secure payment from the government for Scarborough's expenses in caring for the Navy's sick and wounded who had been brought ashore there. At this time the First Dutch War was raging in the North Sea and there were many casualties on both sides. Hodgson had carried a bill—which included the cost of a 'chirurgion'—for £36, but seems to have been delayed in the capital up to two months before it was settled. Foord was impatient for his return though not, he hoped, without a pair of spectacles for his 'ancient sight'.

While Hodgson was absent in London on the town's business, in July 1654 Scarborough's Common Hall elected John Wildman as its one Member in the first Parliament of Cromwell's new Protectorate. Wildman was an amazing choice for a borough which so recently had been reputed Royalist: he was a notorious Leveller, an outspoken critic of Cromwell and his government, who had already been defeated by Cromwell's intervention against him in the Westminster constituency. His adoption by Scarborough's forty-four electors was testimony to the prevailing influence there of the radicals—in particular, the two John Harrisons, father and son, master mariners Thomas Gill, William Nesfield and Henry Nicholson, and the even greater authority now wielded by the town's own Vice-Admiral, John Lawson. Lawson probably promoted Wildman's candidature as a gesture of opposition to Cromwell, but the Council of State quickly retaliated by declaring his election void on the grounds that he was not a person 'of known integrity, fearing God, and of good conversation'.

For the next two years the radicals ran Scarborough. Despite his 'many infirmityes, and weaknesses of bodye', in September 1654, Mr

John Harrison, senior, was persuaded to serve as bailiff for the eighth time in his long public career. Messrs Foord and Hodgson stood down as bailiffs only to become coroners during the forthcoming year. At Michaelmas 1655 when the elections in the Common Hall came round again, Mr John Harrison stayed on as coroner, his son was promoted into the First Twelve, and Mr Peter Hodgson occupied seventh place on that august bench.

All this changed abruptly and permanently in 1656. In February Vice-Admiral Lawson resigned his commission and for his intrigues against the Protectorate he was subsequently banished to Scarborough. The following September one of Lawson's rebellious captains, John Best of the *Adventurer*, was court-martialled. Of the many charges against him, one was that when his ship had been at Scarborough he had visited the Harrisons in their home there, and all three were found guilty of possessing and publicising subversive literature. When the new Common Hall assembled on Sandside in October 1656 there were no places in it for Lawson, the Harrisons or Peter Hodgson.

Official persecution of the Quakers had already begun in 1655. Whereas the Instrument of Government of December 1653, which provided the constitution for the Protectorate, had offered freedom of worship to all Protestants who professed 'faith in God by Jesus Christ', less than two years later Ranters and Quakers were excepted from toleration. Cromwell continued to receive Fox personally, but he and his followers, as they grew in numbers and militancy, attracted increasingly harsh persecution. The most scandalous case was that of James Nayler, another of Fox's converted Yorkshiremen, who in October 1656 rode into Bristol on a donkey with Quaker women strewing 'palms' before him. For his 'horrid blasphemies' the House of Commons ordered him to be whipped, pilloried, branded on the forehead with the letter B, and his tongue bored. After these punishments were carried out in London and again in Bristol, he was to spend the rest of his life in solitary imprisonment.

Significantly, John Lawson was one of the signatories of a petition for clemency on behalf of James Nayler. Though the Vice-Admiral was never himself a member of the Friends at Scarborough, it is evident that he shared some of their views, such as their hatred of church tithes. On the other hand, there is no extant evidence that either he or any of the Scarborough Quakers were persecuted, officially or unofficially, during the remaining life of the republic. Indeed, on the downfall of Richard Cromwell in May 1659, Lawson was called out of exile to become Vice-

Admiral of the Channel fleet—a position of the utmost power and responsibility. Clearly, Lawson's loyalty to the Commonwealth was regarded as unimpeachable and, given the growing paranoia about Quakers, he was not regarded as one of their number. At Michaelmas 1659, after his exclusion from the oligarchy for the past three years, Mr John Harrison, junior, was elected to the town's highest office of senior bailiff. At the same time, Mr William Nesfield and Henry Nicholson moved back into the First Twelve. It seemed that the radicals had returned.

However, fear of the alarming growth in the number and extremism of the Quakers is thought by historians to have been one of the principal factors in bringing about the restoration of the monarchy in 1660: it was the one obsession that united Presbyterians, Baptists, Independents, Anglicans and Catholics. At this point it is essential to appreciate that Quakers were not yet pacifists: their first declaration of non-violence was not made until January 1661. Many of their members were soldiers, seamen and former servicemen. They outraged other congregations and ministers of all denominations by public attacks on them during services and sermons. They defied traditional social norms by refusing to doff their hats in the presence of 'superiors', addressing everyone as 'thou' instead of 'you', and treating women as equals. They refused to pay tithes, swear oaths or acknowledge the validity of any sacraments. Even the Bible they regarded as superfluous. By 1660 there might have been as many as 60,000 Friends in England.

Consequently, despite the tolerance towards them of Charles II, his ministers and Parliament soon directed a campaign of savage persecution against the Friends. Whereas the King would have absolved them from swearing oaths—even oaths of allegiance—his Parliament passed an Act to punish anyone who refused them. Even the meetings of Quakers were to be punished by fines, imprisonment or transportation at the third offence.

In January 1661 Scarborough's bailiffs were reminded of the prohibition lately proclaimed against 'all unlawfull and seditious meetings and conventicles under pretence of religious worshipp', and charged to issue constables' warrants to search out illegal gatherings of 'Anabaptists, Quakers or Fifth Monarchy men'. However, before the bailiffs had time to act, the new governor of the castle, Sir Jordan Crosland, had already sent his spies down into the town. The following statement, dated Monday, 11 January, was made by one of them and corroborated by a second:

> Christopher Walton, being a corporal in the garrison of the Castle of Scarbroughe, upon his corporal oathe, saithe that yesterday he did see thirty people or thereabouts, men and women, meet together in the house of Mr Peter Hodgson ... and that there was a woman speaking amongst them, who gave over speaking as he came in...

A month later, Thomas Beswick, John Graham, William Gradell, James Mason, Henry Sedgefield, John Hodgson, Christopher Sheppard, William Hodgson, John Storr, Robert Mellow, William Stevenson and Thomas Pennell were brought before Scarborough's magistrates. All twelve were charged with meeting at Peter Hodgson's house on Sunday, 10 January, though William Gradell was excused because he had 'tabled and lodged' at the house for the past two months and was therefore judged to be one of the family. What happened to the other eleven and to Peter Hodgson is not recorded, but we know that nine men were imprisoned at Scarborough in 1661 'for refusing to take oaths'. As the chief offender, Peter was almost certainly one of the nine. Not that the Friends were any safer elsewhere: in the first two months of 1661 alone, over 500 of them were locked up in York castle.

As in other places in the kingdom, the severity of persecution depended to a great extent on the action or inaction of the local justices. During the year following Michaelmas 1661, when William Thompson and Timothy Foord, eldest son of William Foord, were bailiffs, there is no record of arrests, but after they were succeeded by John Hickson and John Kay, Scarborough's Friends were soon in trouble again. On Sunday, 30 November 1662, the constables invaded the house of 'William Gradell and Ellinor (said to be his wife)' to find there nineteen men 'with divers others & many women' who had 'mett together ... upon pretence of joynge in a religious worshipp'. At least five of the men—Mr Peter Hodgson, William Gradell (probably Hodgson's former lodger or guest), John Storr, William Hodgson and Christopher Sheppard—had been in Peter's house in January 1661, but all nineteen were fined from 20 shillings levied on Peter Hodgson, Thomas Sedman and Francis Beswick down to five shillings demanded from Nathaniel Wrench and John Carey. On this occasion, as usual, some of the Friends refused to pay the fines and the bailiffs had to issue a warrant for the appraisal and distraint of goods belonging to those who had not come forward with the money within the week allowed.

When George Fox returned to Scarborough in 1663, thanks to the faith and fortitude of Peter Hodgson, he found there a well-established congregation of Quakers. Where Fox preached during his second visit he did not say, but it is more than likely that he was a welcome guest at the Hodgson home in Cargate.

Peter Hodgson was imprisoned again in 1664. This time he had been tried in an ecclesiastical court for persistent and wilful absence from public worship in St Mary's parish church. According to one source he spent five and a half years of incarceration in York castle. While he was there George Fox came back to Scarborough for a third time, but now he too was a prisoner. For sixteen months, from May 1665 until September 1666, he was shut up in Scarborough castle.

Sir Jordan Crosland was still governor of Scarborough castle when Fox was brought there under guard from Lancaster. At first, Fox was given a cell which had both hearth and chimney, but when his fire's smoke blew back instead of going up the chimney he had to pay fifty shillings to have the flue unblocked and his room ventilated. However, when he complained to Sir Jordan that his living quarters were no more comfortable than purgatory, the Catholic governor found the comparison unamusing. Fox was moved to the upper floor of the most exposed tower in the castle curtain wall where there was neither hearth nor chimney. The tower openings had no shutters and the rain drenched him and his bed. He had only a plate to bail out the water. He was soon numb with cold and damp. The soldiers in the garrison stole his bread and beer. Fellow Quakers were denied access to him. He was treated like some exotic, caged animal.

Nevertheless, Fox was more than a match for any of his inquisitive visitors: those who came to gloat and mock sometimes left in frustration or even admiration, and all of them were amazed by his courage, faith and learning. For example, Dr Robert Wittie, Scarborough's spa-season physician, described sarcastically by Fox in his *Journal* as 'the great doctor of physic', rebuked him for refusing to take the oath of allegiance to Charles II. Fox's rejoinder was crushing. Since Wittie was well known to have been once 'a great Presbyterian' then at one time he must have sworn oaths renouncing the monarchy and accepting the Scottish Covenant only to have sworn the opposite more recently. In other words, any hypocritical, self-regarding rascal could swear an oath; true merit and loyalty were to be expressed in deeds not empty words and false promises. Wittie tried once more. This time Fox told the Calvinist that Jesus had died for all mankind, and especially for sinners. This so infuriated the doctor that he went away and never again visited Fox.

Crosland himself tried every method on his prisoner from indoctrination to intimidation. Catholics, Presbyterians, Anglicans and several different kinds of Protestant dissenters were invited up to the castle to argue with Fox, but all of them came away vanquished or enraged or both. The deputy governor threatened to hang him from the walls of the castle 'to keep the people down'. However, even Sir Jordan gradually came round to respect his famous prisoner. Finally, when he received an order from the King to release Fox, he did so gladly.

Though Crosland remained governor of Scarborough castle and a Catholic until his death in 1670, after his experience of Fox he took no further part in the persecution of the town's Quakers. When Fox made his fourth and last visit to Scarborough in 1669, Sir Jordan asked him to come up to the castle and there treated him with courtesy and kindness as an honoured guest.

Peter Hodgson came home to Scarborough in 1670, yet it was soon evident that whatever his sufferings at York his faith remained unshaken. In that year warrants issued by bailiffs Sir John Legard and William Lawson included a distraint on the goods of Peter Hodgson, senior, to the value of £26 14s. 'for a Meeting at his house'. Other names on the list of victims included familiar Scarborough Friends such as William Hodgson, John Storr, and Elizabeth, widow of John, Graham. Though most converts stuck by their convictions and Scarborough's congregation remained stable or even grew a little, persistent persecution took its toll of a few of the more faint-hearted. For instance, Francis Beswick had attended the meeting at Gradell's house in 1662 but in 1671 he had his son John, who was sixteen, and his daughter Mary, who was thirteen, baptised at St Mary's parish church. He had conformed.

One Scarborough Quaker who suffered exceptionally for his faith and yet kept it was Richard Sellers. In 1665, during the Second Dutch War, he was taken by force out of his fishing coble in Scarborough harbour and put on board the warship *Royal Prince*. When he refused to work at the capstan or even eat the Royal Navy's food, the boatswain flogged him, and sent him to the captain who then assaulted him. On the orders of Admiral Sir Edward Spragge he was put in irons and banished below decks to the 'bilboes'. Sellers would have been hanged from the mizzen yard-arm if the Admiral had not intervened at the last moment to prevent it. Though the 'Quakerly dog', as they called him, still refused to work or fight, he did consent to act as the pilot's look-out when battle was joined with the Dutch fleet. In this role Sellers twice saved the *Royal Prince*, first from running on to a sandbank and then from collision with an enemy fire-ship. Finally, as a just reward for his bravery and service, Admiral Spragge signed a certificate for his release from the Navy. Richard Sellers was a native of Kilnsea, but after his ordeal as a 'pressed' seaman he made his home in Scarborough and joined the Quaker congregation there. As late as 1684 he and his wife 'Prisseley' appeared on a list of Friends accused of attending one of Scarborough's weekly meetings.

By that year, again thanks to Peter Hodgson, Scarborough's Quakers had a meeting-house of their own. Evidently, Hodgson had not been bankrupted by fines, distraints and imprisonment: by 1676 when the new house 'for the publique meetings of the lord's people' was finished and opened altogether it had cost him £150 13s. 4d. Now there were nearly sixty names on the list of local Quakers—forty-one of them living in Scarborough and seventeen from neighbouring villages such as Hackness, Burniston and Staintondale. Scarborough's first meeting-house was built in Low Conduit Street close to Farrer's Hospital. Since there was no room there for a burial ground, Hodgson bought the Friends a plot on the south side of Bull Lane (now Westover Road) in Falsgrave.

Even now Scarborough's Friends were still not free of persecution. In the last years of the reign of Charles II there was a final assault made on their freedom to worship. Ironically, it was Timothy Foord, eldest son and principal heir of William Foord, Peter Hodgson's former partner, who led the attack when he was senior bailiff in 1682-3. Foord and Nicholas Saunders, the junior bailiff, came down to Low Conduit Street one Sunday and locked the Friends out of their meeting-house. When the Friends gathered outside the doors the bailiffs ordered the constables to disperse them by force. On this occasion at least a dozen local Quakers had their goods distrained.

The following year six men were presented before the town's general sessions 'for opening their shops on Christmas day last past'. At least three of the accused, William Slee, Thomas Buck and Joseph Wetherill, the shoemaker, are known to have been Quakers. Later that year they were reported for attendance at 'a conventicle' on three consecutive Sundays. Altogether thirty-four people attended these three Sunday meetings, thirteen of them women. Peter Hodgson's name occurred on all three lists, though only once as 'Peter Hodgson sen.'; on the other two Sundays the Peter Hodgson named might have been his son, also a master mariner. What penalties were incurred by these thirty-four Friends are not recorded in detail, but a subsequent entry states that several of them were delivered to York castle in December 1684 for failure to pay fines or give security for appearance at the next quarter sessions.

Finally, in the very month and year, March 1689, of the passage of the Toleration Act which granted Quakers freedom of worship, forty of Scarborough's Friends put their names to a marriage certificate. The previous December, William Stonehouse and Sarah Breckon, both of Scarborough, had 'promised love and faithfulness to each other' in the town's meeting-house. One of the forty witnesses was Peter Hodgson senior.

Almost nothing now survives of Peter Hodgson. His meeting-house in Low Conduit Street served the Friends well: it was not demolished and replaced by a new one in St Sepulchre Street until 1801. Since this new house also had spacious grounds for burials Hodgson's old cemetery on what became Westover Road was eventually abandoned; today it is an unmarked grass plot where local residents 'exercise' their dogs. Scarborough's Quakers have recently moved into their fourth meeting-house; the second is a neglected ruin and the third was destroyed to make way for a shopping centre. Ironically, the founding father of Scarborough's Friends has left behind only a money token; the coin is dated 1667 when he was a prisoner at York and presumably his son was trading corn in his name. At that time many Scarborough merchants issued their own money tokens since the town was notoriously 'a wicked place for clipping and coyninge'; and a Quaker's coin could always be trusted.

16. Robert Wittie and the Doctors

Mrs Thomasin Farrer might have been the first to discover the mineral spring waters at the foot of South Cliff—or Driple Cotes as it was then called—but there is little evidence to suggest that within her remaining lifetime the discovery was of very much benefit to Scarborough. Scarborough was the last place any sensible person would have chosen to visit for his health or pleasure during the 1640s and the 1650s. During the former decade the town endured bombardment, siege, street-fighting, martial law, forced army billeting and food rationing; and during the latter, the Puritan regime of men like Luke Robinson and Edward Carleton, vicar of St Mary's, was a discouragement to anyone in search of entertainment in Scarborough.

Nevertheless, it is certain that local residents and others outside the town were drinking its spa waters long before the Restoration in 1660. In his *History of Scarbrough-Spaw*, published in 1679, Dr William Simpson related how during 'the late Wars when the Garrison which was kept by Sir Hugh Chomly in the Castle ... were most of them fallen into Scurvy' many of the survivors of the siege were 'perfectly and speedily cured' when they 'drank of the Spaw water'. That at the surrender many of Cholmley's soldiers were weak and dying from the scurvy is undoubtedly true; that they were cured of it merely by drinking spa water is extremely doubtful; but the event described by Dr Simpson must have taken place in the summer of 1645.

Even before the Restoration, going over to Scarborough and staying there during 'the season' seems to have been the custom of at least some of Yorkshire's gentry. For example, Colonel Charles Fairfax, uncle of the more famous General, Thomas Lord Fairfax, had recently become military governor of Hull when he wrote from there to General George Monck on 11 May 1660. The purpose of his letter was to reassure Monck that he had carried out his duties at Hull with diligence and faithfulness. 'I have never been a stonecast from the works here', he wrote, 'save for a journey at the season of the year to Scarbrough Spaw.' In other words, Scarborough was already identified as a spa town and a visit there 'at the season' needed no further explanation.

However, if Mrs Farrer has to be credited with the discovery of 'Scarbrough Spaw', then Dr Robert Wittie deserves even more credit for being its first publicist in print. The very day of 'His Majesties most happy restauration', 29 May 1660, coincided with the date of the completion of that doctor's *Scarbrough Spaw, or A Description of the*

Nature and Vertues of the Spaw at Scarbrough in Yorkshire. The book was printed at York and in London and, early in October, advertised in two of the capital's weeklies, *Parliamentary Intelligencer* and *Mercurius Publicus*. In retrospect, Dr Wittie's pioneer work can be seen to have marked a new and vital stage in the history of Scarborough as a seaside resort.

Robert Wittie's earlier life is shrouded in mystery, probably because after he became a public figure he preferred to conceal a potentially embarrassing past. Nevertheless, some facts about him seem incontrovertible. He was the son of George Wittie, sometime mayor of Beverley, and baptised at St Mary's there on 14 November 1613. He was a pupil at Beverley Grammar School. From there he went to King's College, Cambridge where he graduated with the degree of Bachelor of Arts in 1632. Subsequently, he claimed to have acquired doctorates in medicine at both Cambridge and Oxford. At first, it seemed that he might become a schoolmaster: in January 1635 he was serving as usher, or deputy headmaster, at Hull Grammar School. But his interests were medical, not pedagogic: in 1641, on the eve of the Civil Wars, Wittie took out a licence to practise medicine.

Wittie covered the tracks of his Civil War career very well. Possibly he was commissioned in Parliament's army and served as an officer in the defence of Hull against the Royalist sieges of 1642 and 1643, but there are no surviving records of his war service until 1648. In July of that year, significantly at the time of 'the spa season', Captain Robert Wittie was in Scarborough. Whether he was in the town as a physician or as an army officer or as both is not made clear. However, whatever his role at the time, Wittie was invited up to the castle by Parliament's military governor, Colonel Matthew Boynton, who told him that he had received a letter from the Prince of Wales, who was then at Yarmouth with twelve warships. The Prince had written that he intended to sail north to Scarborough. Why Boynton should have confided in Wittie is suspicious, but if he believed the doctor might also turn Royalist and betray his commission he was mistaken. Two days later, when Boynton declared for the King 'by hanging out a red flag over the [castle] walls', Wittie left Scarborough hurriedly, rode to Beverley, and from there immediately wrote two letters of warning—one to Colonel Overton, Hull's military governor, the other to William Dobson, then Hull's mayor. Wittie's letters were the first to alert Parliament to Boynton's defection and the intentions of the Prince of Wales.

Sometime during the 1650s Wittie moved from Hull to York. By

1658 he was described as a 'doctor in physic at York'. However, wherever his home, Wittie's patients were scattered throughout Yorkshire and many of them were recommended by him to cure their ills with Scarborough's waters. As he explained in the second edition of his *Scarbrough Spaw*, he was 'usually wont every year to step to Scarborough', particularly when he was notified of 'any considerable success by the waters'.

Surprisingly, Wittie's first work of 1660 actually said very little about Scarborough's medicinal waters. It began with a wordy lecture on temperance, extolling the virtues of water and denigrating the vices of beer and wine. Wittie argued that before Noah discovered wine men had often lived a thousand years, but afterwards life-expectancy had fallen to a mere three score and ten. He then provided his readers with an unscientific analysis of the many different kinds of water to be found in rain, hail, snow, sea, lakes, rivers and springs, before finally reaching the extraordinary qualities of the water to be found at Scarborough. According to Wittie's professional opinion there was no known disease or disability that Scarborough water could not cure or ameliorate, but his prescription was particularly appropriate for those unfortunates who suffered from excessive wind and 'frequent Fluxes of the belly'. The water was a sovereign remedy for chronic constipation. The good doctor gave no credit in this respect to fresh fruit, vegetables, herbs or 'sallets' (salads). Patients who endured the consequences of an excess of meat and a deficiency of exercise would find no better purge than that on offer at Scarborough.

Wittie recommended Scarborough's waters from May to September, not because these were the warmest months, but because during the winter and spring the waters were diluted by rainfall. After his journey to Scarborough the patient ought to rest for several days before starting the treatment. He should begin with only two or three half-pints and then gradually increase the daily intake until it reached an optimum of four or five pints. It was essential that he should rise from his bed early enough to arrive at the spring by six and take the full dosage during the next three or four hours. This would allow the water to pass through him before midday dinner. It was not recommended to eat meat on a stomach still full of water which would then be 'washed down into the bowells unconcocted'.

In 1660 Dr Wittie had claimed that Scarborough spa waters were already well known in Hull, York and other parts of Yorkshire, and that some visitors had travelled a hundred miles to drink them; but we have only his doubtful word for it. Seven years later, however, he was able to address his second edition of *Scarbrough Spaw* to Lord John Roos, son and heir of the Earl of Rutland, and to the Earl of Suffolk, two notables who were witnesses to the efficacy of its waters. Roos had long been troubled by 'Hypochondriack Wind'; several physicians had been of no help so he had come to Scarborough from his home in Leicestershire. As a result, after three successive seasons, Lord John now enjoyed 'a constant state of health' and had become 'much more lively and fleshly than formerly'.

By 1667 Wittie was able to cite many other cases of almost instant and permanent remedy. Sir John Anderson was cured of gout, of scurvy, and of other troublesome indispositions. On one occasion he had consumed eight pints of spa water, and then passed eleven pints of urine, thus relieving himself of three pints of surplus 'humours of the body'. Though Christopher Keld lived only a few miles distant at Newby he was so pained with stones that he had sent for bottles of Scarborough water. After only two or three quarts and within less than half an hour he had rid himself of 'several stones besides much gravel'.

On the strength of his long experience, Dr Wittie was now in a position to recommend Scarborough water for a rich variety of afflictions—'diseases of the head, as the Apoplexy, Epilepsie, Catalepsie, Vertigo'; diseases of the nerves, lungs and stomach; besides asthma and scurvy, it also cured 'the Jaunders, both yellow and black, the leprosie'; and of course it had frequently proved to be a sure remedy for 'Hypochondriack Melancholly and Windiness'. It was true, the doctor continued, that the water had some known effectiveness when taken out of bottles at a distance, but he thought it much better when drunk at Scarborough.

In 1667 Dr Wittie made one other gift to Scarborough of immeasurable future value: on the basis of his own personal experience, to gout-sufferers he recommended bathing in cold, sea water. Drinking spa waters had been fashionable and commonplace for the well-to-do for several past generations. By 1667, Bath, Bristol, Tunbridge Wells, Epsom, Buxton and Harrogate were all well-established spa resorts offering mineral drinking waters to their aristocratic and gentry visitors. Bath and Buxton were also famous for their hot, mineral bathing springs. Yet all of these places were inland, and nowhere in the whole country, or perhaps even in Europe, at that time was cold sea water bathing taken as a cure or even as an exercise. Nevertheless, Wittie had convinced himself that plunging naked into the coldest sea waters around the British Isles followed by 'a sweat in a warm bed' was a certain remedy for the common complaint of gout. In his own small way, Wittie was a true pioneer, as bold and innovative as Columbus or da Gama.

Historically, the sea was feared and shunned. In Genesis it was the great abyss out of which God had created land and human forms to live on it. There was no sea in the Garden of Eden. The Flood was the instrument of God's punishment of mankind: the vast oceans were surviving remnants of this appalling catastrophe and continued to threaten the world with destruction. Even as late as the seventeenth century most people believed the sea harboured devilish monsters. In his *Anatomy of Melancholy*, published in 1621, Robert Burton had broken long-standing convention by suggesting that for their health gentlemen should learn to swim. Hitherto bathing in rivers and lakes was considered an immoral activity, better left to the uncouth lower classes. Burton's book was widely read, had a great influence on the behaviour of the English aristocracy and gentry and might be said to have started their practice of therapeutic bathing or hydrotherapy. However, though Burton acknowledged the purity of sea air and the pleasantness of coastal vistas, he did not recommend the seaside for holidays or the sea for bathing: such a recipe for vigorous health was left to Dr Wittie.

It would be some years yet before sea-bathing at Scarborough became an organised and recognised activity for visitors, but there can be no doubt that this new form of hydrotherapy was pioneered there long before it was introduced at southern resorts such as Brighton, Bournemouth and Weymouth. Of course Wittie was not entirely responsible: he did not invent the sea. Scarborough had all the natural advantages soon to be recommended by physicians: high cliffs that gave shelter from cold, northerly winds; a bay which offered magnificent views of coast and open sea; and, above all, a firm, flat, clean, sandy beach where bathers could walk in safety, ride in carriages or even gallop their horses. Moreover, at Scarborough the sea was perfect for the purposes of the doctors: because it was cold, salty and rough it had the most invigorating affect on bathers. Finally, nature had contrived to place mineral spring waters at the foot of coastal cliffs next to this ideal beach and lively sea—a unique combination that, with Wittie's publicity, made Scarborough into Britain's first seaside holiday resort.

Wittie's reign was short-lived, however. If Scarborough's growing fame attracted an increasing number of wealthy nobility and gentry, it was also sure to bring other physicians with them. Two years after Wittie's second edition, there appeared Dr William Simpson's

Hydrologia Chymica, a deliberate, spiteful attack on it. After pouring scorn on Wittie's ignorance of chemistry and his amateur analysis of Scarborough's waters, Simpson then proceeded to examine their therapeutic claims. He agreed that they were good for 'Scurvy, Dropsie, Stone or Strangury [painful, difficult passing of urine], Jaundise, Hypochondriack Melancholy, Cachexia's [chronic mental or physical debility], and Women's Diseases', but rejected them as remedies for 'Pestilential Diseases, Plurisies, Prunellas's [inflammation of the tonsils or abscessed throat], Poysons taken in or inbred ... Leprosie, French Disease [venereal syphilis], Morphew [leprous or scurfy skin eruptions], Cancer, Falling Sickness .... Apoplexie, Palsie or Asthma'.

Simpson also suggested sensibly that fresh air, physical exercise, wholesome food and abstinence might have had more to do with curing many of Wittie's patients than Scarborough waters. He accepted that Scarborough's spa was best visited during the summer months for the reasons given by Wittie, but argued that if boiled off 'the Essence of Scarbrough-Spaw' could be taken anywhere at any time with any fluid and would still act as a gentle and effective laxative. Finally, to undermine further Wittie's and Scarborough's reputations, Simpson contended that the air of Knaresborough, 'being upon high heathy common', was superior to that on the coast.

It was soon transparent that Wittie and Simpson were old enemies, personal as well as professional. Within months of the publication of *Hydrologia Chymica*, came Dr Wittie's rude reply, *Pyrologia Mimica*, a non-stop stream of invective and insult. . It seems that four or five years earlier Simpson had already questioned Wittie's medical competence in his practice at York. According to 'Sir Simpson', as Wittie mockingly addressed him, the latter's methods were out of date and his knowledge unscientific. However, Wittie had no intention of giving way to 'late Upstarts'; he compared Simpson, thirty years his junior, to 'a Cockerell ... newly hatched out of his shell' which had now begun 'to crow fiercely'. He was much better qualified as well as much more experienced. Simpson was a 'bare Batchelour of Arts' whereas Wittie was a 'Doctor in Physic in both Universities', and had taken his Master of Arts before Simpson was even born. Never one to silence his own trumpet, Wittie claimed that he was curing diseases before Simpson had learned what their Latin names were. As for being more modern, scientific and rational than Wittie, Simpson was in fact a notorious mountebank who had offered 'his Amulet for the Plague to sale, posting up his Bills on every corner of the streets' of York.

The newly-founded Royal Society soon became aware of this literary and medical controversy, but could find nothing fundamental to separate Wittie and Simpson. Consequently, the Society's reviewer of *Hydrologia Chymica* and *Pyrologia Mimica* pleaded with their authors to 'lay aside animosities, personal Reflextions, and private considerations'. However, if such 'animosities' clearly brought no credit to the professional reputations of contemporary physicians, their polemical works extended the fame of Scarborough spa ever wider amongst 'persons of quality'.

A third doctor, George Tunstall of Newcastle, was soon making his contribution to the heated debate. After visiting Harrogate in 1667, he had come to Scarborough for the first time in 1668, and returned there the following summer. In *Scarbrough Spaw Spagyrically Anatomised* (1670), he claimed that the waters there had given him 'a Fit of the Stone' within a fortnight, and gout in the joint of his big toe within a month. Even more damaging, Tunstall also alleged that Lord Irwin of Temple Newsam had been seized by jaundice after taking Scarborough waters and soon afterwards died of it. Tunstall's explanation was that the spa there contained 'stone powder' which had a devastating affect on the kidneys.

Wittie regarded such criticism as unpardonable betrayal. In *Pyrologia Mimica* he had described Tunstall flatteringly as an 'Eminent Physician and Chymist'. In 1668 Tunstall had brought his wife to see Wittie at Scarborough; after childbirth her 'belly' had refused to flatten and her husband 'with all his Art' had not been able to 'take it down'. Generously, Wittie had prescribed some of his 'preparations' and within a few days she had closed 'her boddice'. Yet there was not a word of this in Tunstall's ungrateful book. Wittie had a short temper at the best of times but Tunstall drove him into a literary frenzy. He dismissed the embarrassing story about the fate of Lord Irwin on the grounds that he had killed himself with too much wine, and concluded that Tunstall had denigrated the waters at Scarborough only because he had lately taken up residence and practice at Harrogate.

As if Tunstall was not enough, Wittie had also to contend with another broadside from Simpson. In *Hydrological Essayes* (1670) Simpson not only repeated his earlier calumnies but challenged Wittie to a medical competition: whoever of the two lost a patient-curing trial would 'depart thence as vanquished'.

Needless to say, Wittie ignored Simpson's gauntlet and preferred to pursue the quarrel in print. In 1672 he attacked both Tunstall and Simpson with his customary abuse: if his book was not superior to theirs, he retorted, 'it is fit only for Bum-fother'.

Tunstall's response from Harrogate plumbed similar depths of vulgarity. He dismissed Simpson, as Wittie had done, as an inexperienced novice, and described his work as 'Green Fruit', which had been plucked prematurely from the tree. But his principal target was Wittie: *A New-Year's Gift for Dr Witty* was not intended to please the recipient. Here were yet more aspersions cast on the therapeutic claims made for Scarborough spa and their chief propagandist, Dr Wittie, whom he called 'the Crackfart of Scarbrough Spaw'.

After that stinging rebuff Dr Wittie seems to have lost interest or heart. Perhaps by now he was beginning to feel the debilitating effects of sixty years of age. Though he lived on until October 1684 his last years were spent at York and London, not Scarborough. As a result, the final word was left, by default, to William Simpson, his old protagonist. In 1679 there appeared *The History of Scarbrough-Spaw*, the most literate, lucid and informative account up to that date. Now that Wittie was out of the way, Simpson could afford to be less acrimonious and more objective. Simpson's *History* consisted largely of more than seventy case studies of successful treatments of patients at Scarborough, many of them under Wittie's professional care.

The Marquess of Winchester, Simpson's most elevated patient, had been fully cured of 'Hypochondriacal wind', thanks to his recent stay at Scarborough, albeit 'at the latest season of the year'. Other patients were of lower social standing but had more serious complaints. Lady Legard of Ganton was relieved of jaundice; Mr Watson of Throxenby got rid of his many worms; and Mr Roger's daughter, a local girl, found a remedy at the spa for her 'Scorbutick Elephantiasis'. Mr and Mrs Thomas St Quintin of Flamborough had good reasons to be thankful to Scarborough's fortifying spring: they had been married for more than seven years without managing to produce an heir, yet after they came to Scarborough for the season she conceived within a month and subsequently gave birth to a son. Four years later the same miracle brought forth a daughter. On the other hand, for those who needed it for this purpose, not least of the spa's merits was its efficacy with venereal diseases, such as gonorrhoea or the clap. Even mental illnesses were known to succumb to the power of Scarborough's remedial waters. Mrs Granville, daughter of a bishop and wife of the dean of Durham, had suffered from periodic fits of overexcitement. After a succession of annual visits to Scarborough, however, she appeared to have found a complete and permanent tranquillity.

Not even at the peak of its popularity in the 1730s and 1740s would

Scarborough challenge the leadership of Bath or Brighton as England's hospitals and playgrounds for the rich and idle; by road or by sea it was too far way from London where most of them lived during the winter. Nevertheless, when during the season of 1733 the town had 1,053 visitors, who included two dukes, one marquess, seven earls, three barons, nineteen baronets and six knights, nearly all accompanied by their families, this remarkable level of aristocratic favour was a late tribute to the professional and polemical efforts of Drs Wittie, Simpson and Tunstall.

17. Alice Thornton

One of Dr Wittie's most valued and profitable patients was Mrs Alice Thornton. Though she was neither native nor permanent resident of Scarborough, and her connections with the town were therefore tenuous, her fascinating autobiography reveals such a remarkable life story that it deserves to be better known.

Alice was born in February 1627, the third daughter and fifth child of Christopher Wandesford and his wife Alice, née Osborne. The Wandesfords lived at Kirklington Hall in the North Riding of Yorkshire, about half way between Ripon and Thirsk. The Hall was then a fine Elizabethan house, built about 1570 by Sir Christopher Wandesford, Alice's great grandfather. However, after the death of Sir Christopher in 1590, the house and estate were neglected and the family fortunes squandered by Sir George, Alice's grandfather. When Sir George died in 1612 his twenty-year-old heir, Christopher, was faced with a colossal debt and an inadequate income to service it. Fortunately for the future of the family, Alice's father was a highly intelligent and prudent man. By the time she was born he had rescued the estate from bankruptcy, first by marrying Alice Osborne, sister of Sir Edward Osborne, with a dowry of £2,000, and then by running a frugal household, keeping careful accounts, and managing his landed inheritance with exceptional skill and foresight.

The Osborne relationship served the Wandesfords well, but it was far less important and fruitful than that forged by the young Christopher with Thomas Wentworth. Christopher was only a year older than Thomas, and as young boys they attended the same school of Dr Higgins, dean of Ripon, in his house at Well. Both of them then went up to Cambridge University, Wentworth to St John's College, and Wandesford to Clare Hall. Their friendship remained close and lifelong.

While Christopher Wandesford busied himself with the mundane matters of rents, leases and field crops, Thomas Wentworth went into politics. In 1621 he was returned as one of Yorkshire's two knights of the shire to the House of Commons, and retained his seat in the bitterly fought election of 1625. However, Wentworth's outspoken opposition to the King's favourite, the Duke of Buckingham, earned him the doubtful honour and certain burdens of sheriff of the county, an office which effectively disqualified him from renewing his place in Parliament. Nevertheless, Wentworth proved himself to be such a formidable opponent that King Charles preferred him as an ally rather than as an enemy: in 1628 he was created Viscount Wentworth and soon afterwards made Lord President of the Council in the North at York. For the next four years he was the King's stern governor of the northern parts of his kingdom, and such was his talent for administration that in 1632 Charles appointed him Lord Deputy in Ireland. While he was in Ireland, Alice's uncle, Sir Edward Osborne, the Vice-President of the Council, served as his deputy at York.

Having risen so high and so speedily Wentworth was not the kind of man to forget his old friend and confidant. Christopher Wandesford was given the lucrative post of Master of the Rolls and a seat on the Irish Council at Dublin. Also, when a new Irish parliament was summoned in 1634 he sat in it as member for Kildare. When Wentworth spent time in Yorkshire or London Wandesford acted in his place, and when Wentworth became the Earl of Strafford and returned permanently to England, Wandesford succeeded him as Lord Deputy in Ireland. However, both men had little time left to enjoy their power and newly-acquired wealth. A few weeks after Strafford was imprisoned in the Tower, his old friend and replacement fell ill and died in Dublin. Six months later, condemned by Parliament's Act of Attainder, Strafford was executed on Tower Hill.

Very few of these dramatic and tragic events were related by Alice Thornton in her autobiography, though they were to have momentous consequences for her personally as well as the kingdom generally. Her description of a childhood spent in Yorkshire and Dublin is one mainly of survival—of miraculous deliverance by the hand of God from a succession of diseases and accidents. She thanked God for her health and strength in infancy: unlike many of her age she never suffered from rickets and its deforming results. In retrospect she was very conscious of her good fortune in avoiding the many perils of childhood, such as 'evill accidents', 'evill persons', 'neglects and brutishness of nursses', 'infinitt hazards of overlaying', 'badnes of there food and evil milk', and, worst of all, the 'dreadfull malise of Satan'. Thanks to her 'guardian Angell' and 'the Providence of God', she had been protected from most of these potentially fatal hazards. Nevertheless, at the age of three, she had cut open her forehead with a fall on the corner stone of a hearth and might have bled to death but for her 'deare mother's skill' in tending the wound. A little later, she might have died 'of eating some beefe which was not boiled'. On this occasion, early and violent vomiting probably saved her life. At five she had measles, and soon afterwards survived small pox. Whether they disfigured her permanently she neglected to say, but her youngest brother John was marked for life by smallpox.

The dangers of sea voyages were also described and experienced by Alice. She and her mother had to wait a week at Neston on Deeside while a storm 'cast five ships upon the shore before our eyes'. When they finally sailed from there to Dublin in one of his majesty's newly-built warships, another gale drove them on to the Irish shore. They were all saved from drowning by local fishermen and 'through the infinitt mercys of our great and powerfull Lord God'.

Alice's father was not so fortunate. She believed that he had died of overwork which had damaged his heart. When his body was embalmed 'all the noble parts' were found to be very 'sound and perfect, saving the heart, which was decaied of one side'. She was proud of the fact that he was the only Lord Deputy of Ireland who had not been murdered or executed but had died 'untouched or peacebly in theire beds'.

Christopher Wandesford was buried at great expense in Christ's Church, Dublin. The funeral cost £1,300, an enormous sum by contemporary standards. The sudden and premature death of her father at the age of 48, and the disgrace and execution of his great patron and friend, the Earl of Strafford, were followed by a third catastrophe: in October 1641 there was a violent Irish Catholic uprising against English Protestant rule. What Alice subsequently called 'that horrid rebellion and massacre of the poore English protestants' forced the Wandesford family to return to Yorkshire, having lost everything in Ireland.

It took more than two years for the wandering Wandesfords to get home to Kirklington. Having just escaped a massacre in Ireland they sailed straight into a civil war in England. Given their known and close association with Strafford, the Wandesfords were bound to be Royalist supporters and their journey across the north of England was repeatedly delayed and diverted by the movement and presence of hostile Parliamentary soldiers. They were in Royalist Chester in July 1643 when Sir William Brereton's Roundhead cannon bombarded it. Then, passing through Warrington and war-damaged Wigan, they finally crossed the Pennines to reach Snape castle the following September. There, a few miles from Kirklington, they spent the winter of 1643-4 with Alice's elder sister, Catherine, who had married another Royalist, Sir Thomas Danby.

Thomas Danby had been brought up at Kirklington Hall as a ward of Christopher Wandesford and had eventually married his guardian's eldest daughter. Like Wandesford he was a relation and a friend of Wentworth: in 1637-8 he was Yorkshire's high sheriff and a conscientious collector of Ship Money. As a nominee of Strafford he sat for Richmond in the Long Parliament, and was one of only six Yorkshire

MPs to vote against Strafford's attainder. When the Civil War began he joined the King's side.

Catherine Danby was only 28-years-old but already worn out by childbearing when the Wandesfords came to stay with her. When she died in September 1645, as a result of a long and painful delivery, it was her sixteenth pregnancy, and six of the sixteen had been stillborn. No doubt Alice, who was 18-years-old at the time, must have been aware that a similar fate might be in store for her.

In July 1644 the Royalist cause in the north of England sustained a mortal blow on the battlefield of Marston Moor. As Alice later described the disaster: 'the battaile of Hessom Moore, when the blessed King Charles had by treachery lost the field, and his two generalls, Prince Rupert and Lord of Newcastle, exposed all the brave white cots foote that stood the last man till they were murthered and destroyed'. Even 25 years later, Alice still felt angry and bitter about the massacre of the Royalist Whitecoat regiment when they refused to surrender in the final stage of the battle.

Parliament's overwhelming triumph on Marston Moor now meant that its Scottish allies were free to accommodate themselves in Yorkshire without fear of Royalist resistance. Though the Wandesfords sought shelter and obscurity at their second home at Hipswell near Richmond, there was no safe haven from the Scots. Rather than have them live in her house, Alice's mother paid them each a double billeting rate of 1s. 6d. a week. But there was more at stake than money or household furniture: young Alice's virtue was put at risk. A Scottish captain called Innis took a strong fancy to her.

Once the captain had set eyes on Alice he was resolved to have her for his wife. Innis offered Alice's aunt three or four thousand pounds if she could procure her niece for him. In fear of abduction by this 'soe wild & bloody looked man', Alice fled into Richmond and hid herself in the house of one of the Wandesford's tenants until it was thought safe for her return to Hipswell.

Innis was determined to have his revenge, even if he could not have Alice; his lust had turned into hatred. One Sunday morning he brought his company of soldiers up to Hipswell and, when his demand for 'duble money' was refused, he threatened 'to break the house and dores'. When he saw young Alice at the chamber window, he cursed her violently and 'wished the deale [devil] blaw [her] blind and into the ayre [air]'. She had been a thorn in his heel, but he would be a thorn in her side. After his 'most vile and crewell' oaths, he and his men drove off Mrs

Wandesford's herd of 'delecate cattell of her owne breed' to their quarters at Richmond. In the end, General Leslie, the Scottish commander, made sure the cattle were returned to Hipswell, apologised to the Wandesfords for his captain's 'rudeness', and promised to punish him for it. In her autobiography, Alice subsequently praised God for her 'deliverance from this beast, from being destroyed and defloired by him'.

Alice also remembered that she and her family were fortunate to be spared from the plague which depopulated Richmond in the summer of 1645. Those who could, abandoned the town, those who were infected by the sickness were confined in their homes, and Richmond was sealed off from the outside country. At Hipswell, Alice's mother was generous to refugees with 'meate and monny', even though the 'malice of beggars was great to have don harme'.

At Hipswell Mrs Alice Wandesford ran a household very much on the same Puritan lines as Lady Margaret Hoby had at Hackness. There were family prayers three times a day at six and ten in the morning and nine in the evening. Before breakfast Alice assembled her children, heard them pray and read psalms or chapters of the Bible and then gave each of them her blessing as they knelt before her.

On Easter Monday, 31 March 1651, the Wandesford family suffered another grievous loss: Alice's eldest brother, George, was drowned while attempting to cross the swollen River Swale on horseback. The horse swam to the other bank. George was only 27-years-old.

Later that same year, in December, at the age of 24, Alice married William Thornton of East Newton in Ryedale. It was a marriage forced on her and her impoverished family by circumstances. In better times she might have expected a more prosperous and promising husband. Though William was of sound Puritan stock—his mother was the daughter of Sir Richard Darley of Buttercrambe and Elizabeth Gates of Seamer—he proved to be weak-willed, sickly and improvident.

The honeymoon was brief and its consequences were soon apparent: within seven weeks Alice conceived. Her first child, a daughter, was born in August 1652 but died within half an hour before she could be baptized. A second daughter, christened Alice, but usually called 'Naly', was born in January 1654. She was almost suffocated by a careless nurse who went to sleep on top of her. Betty, Alice's third, born in February 1655, died of rickets and consumption eighteen months later. Catherine, or 'Kate', her fourth daughter, was delivered in June 1656.

After four daughters in less than five years, Alice finally gave birth to her first son in December 1657. Unfortunately, she had fallen heavily in the sixth month of her pregnancy and she was convinced that this explained why he was delivered feet first and lived only half an hour. Number six was William, born in April 1660; he lived only long enough to be baptized. His tiny body was covered with red spots the size of half pennies. Robert, or 'Robin', her seventh, was born in September 1662. Alice suffered appalling agonies during her pregnancy and his delivery, but miraculously both survived. Joyce was next: born in September 1665; she was dead in January 1666, also covered with red spots. Finally, and mercifully, there was only one more. Number nine, Christopher, lasted only three weeks at the end of 1667. He too had red spots, convulsions and diarrhoea; his mother had breast gangrene.

Though still only 40-years-old Alice was now exhausted and chronically ill, but relief came with the death of her husband in 1668. There could be no more pregnancies. She was left a widow with three surviving children, 'Naly', 'Kate' and 'Robin', and spent the next year writing her autobiography, presumably expecting that she would soon join William. Amazingly, she lived on until she was nearly 80. Her only son Robert, who had caused her so much pain to bring into this world, did well: he became a Fellow of Magdalen College, Oxford and rector of the parish church of Boldon in County Durham, but died and was buried in the Nine Altars in Durham cathedral before his thirtieth birthday. Her eldest daughter married Thomas Comber, who subsequently became dean of Durham and rector of Stonegrave. Thomas also died before his mother-in-law, but his eldest surviving son, Alice's grandson, inherited East Newton.

Given her record of almost perpetual pregnancy and her husband's history of chronic illness, both Alice and William Thornton were frequently compelled to seek medical counsel, and they received it for many years from Dr Robert Wittie. Perhaps Wittie was already attending the Thornton family at East Newton before Alice married William, since her first reference to the doctor occurred as early as 1651 when he recommended that William should be bled. Dr Wittie was an enthusiast for bleeding his patients: he told Alice during her first pregnancy that she would fall into a fever if she did not cool her blood by drawing some of it away. When her third child, Betty, had rickets, Wittie prescribed St Mungo's well at Knaresborough; he said that the child should be immersed in the water there five, seven or nine times. Betty died. During and after her many pregnancies Alice endured severe reactions: she recalled how she had a 'shaking ague' which gave her fits twice a day; the hair on her head fell out; the nails on her fingers and toes dropped off; her teeth turned black and came loose. Several times she had jaundice. Alice first travelled to Scarborough in August 1659 on Wittie's advice to treat her haemorrhoids. She stayed there a month, drank the spa waters, was cured and conceived William. After that she and Mr Thornton, together and separately, regularly took the spa waters at Scarborough during the season. Dr Wittie attended her for all her pregnancies and deliveries and her husband for his 'melancholicke humour' and 'greivous distemper of the palsy'.[1]

From November 1666 until August 1667 Dr Wittie attended Mr Thornton: 'allmost each month [we] fetched to him when he relapsed', wrote Alice. The doctor suggested Scarborough spa 'where he had bin other yeares with good successe'. Accordingly, the Thorntons set out by coach from East Newton bound for Scarborough, but when she fell ill at Malton, Alice had to turn back. William went on to Scarborough with Dr Wittie in attendance, stayed there a month and seemed much recovered on his return to East Newton on horseback.

The following year, in September 1668, Alice again had to call in Dr Wittie when William had a relapse at Malton. Wittie assured her that her husband would soon make a recovery, but he died shortly afterwards. Wittie was at William's deathbed and at his funeral the next day at Stonegrave. A letter of comfort and condolence from 'good Dr Wittie' was greatly appreciated by Mrs Thornton.

Alice Thornton's autobiography is a rare and precious survival. Many Yorkshire gentlemen of her time left writings—Sir Hugh Cholmley wrote his family memoirs; Sir Henry Slingsby kept a diary; several others kept what they called commonplace books; and Alice's own father, Christopher Wandesford, wrote a 'Book of Instructions' for the benefit of his son which was edited and published by his great-great-grandson, Thomas Comber (1722-78), in 1777. But anything at all written by a Yorkshire woman of the seventeenth century would be hard to find. Only the fragment of the diary of Lady Margaret Hoby of Hackness comes to mind. It is of the greatest good fortune therefore that of Mrs Thornton we have more than the mere inscription on her tombstone in Stonegrave churchyard—'Alice Thornton 1706'.

---

[1] Recent medical research has identified a certain link between identical twins and the incidence of cerebral palsy. William Thornton was a twin. Richard the other twin died in 1656 aged 31.

18. Dicky Dickinson

Mrs Thomasin Farrer found Scarborough's spa waters, Dr Robert Wittie publicised their medical effectiveness, but it was Richard Dickinson, entrepreneur extraordinary and self-styled 'Governor of the Spaw', who first grasped and exploited their commercial potential. What Beau Nash was to Brighton, Dicky Dickinson was to Scarborough.

Scarborough Corporation was very slow to appreciate that it owned a source of liquid gold at the foot of South Cliff, or Driple Cotes as it was then called. Far from developing the site as a health resort, in 1645 the Corporation built there a pesthouse for local victims of the bubonic plague. There is no reference in the Corporation records to the spa well until as late as 1684, and even this betrays a certain lack of understanding and regulation. The Common Hall ruled that the spa water was to be sold commercially at only 6d. an 'anker' (approximately 64 pints or 36 litres), but any measure less than half an 'anker' was to be given away free of charge. According to this minute, the spring water was drawn off by 'women' (later called 'dippers'), and the proceeds of sale were 'for the poors use'. Seven years later the charges were doubled: from now on an 'anker' was to cost one shilling. Even so if a certificate of proof signed by a churchwarden or clergyman claimed that the water was exclusively for sick persons who were unable to visit the well, the 'dippers' were not to make any charge. As yet there was no question of the town deriving profit from illness and distress: the well at Driple Cotes was regarded locally as 'a gift from Heaven' which ought to be freely available to all who needed its therapy.

When Celia Fiennes came to Scarborough just over three hundred years ago she found 'a very pretty sea-port town' that had hardly yet begun to develop as a seaside health and pleasure resort. Still there were compensations for this lack of popularity: in Scarborough she discovered 'good accommodation and on very reasonable terms', whereas in fashionable Buxton during the season there were up to four beds in a room and sometimes three to a bed! Celia complained that no peace could be found in such dormitories when there was always someone going to or coming from the toilet. In contrast, at Scarborough, the best lodgings were to be had in the private houses of Quakers, who provided fixed meals at fixed prices and no doubt kept clean rooms for their guests. On the other hand, there was no accommodation whatsoever at 'the Spaw Well'. Twice a day at the ebb-tide drinkers had to cross 400 yards of smooth, firm, flat sand to reach the well from the town. When they arrived there, on foot or by carriage, they would find only the women drawers: there was neither shelter from the weather nor toilet provision for those expected to imbibe gallons of the mineral, brackish water and thereby purge their sluggish bowels. Perhaps it is wiser not to allow the imagination too much freedom in this matter.

Two years after Celia Fiennes's visit to Scarborough, the Corporation finally decided to make 'a large seasteron [cistern] ... for keeping the Spaw water'. This would bring a number of benefits and improvements: first of all, the well could be covered and locked to prevent unauthorised users from getting their water without paying for it. Only the bailiffs had the key and a night watch was in future to be kept 'to prevent [the cistern] being break up ...' Secondly, the water could be stored instead of allowing it to pour wastefully into the sea. And, thirdly, the well head could be protected from high tides which made the water too salty. The following year the Common Hall anticipated that profit from the well would be sufficient to maintain the town's paupers.

There is an undocumented tradition that Richard Dickinson became a tenant at will of the Corporation for the parcel of Driple Cotes which contained the spa well in 1700. The original lease was probably for a period of seven years and the annual rent one pound. Scarborough's councillors had at last woken up to the fact that the waters needed a full-time guardian. What they did not foresee was the enterprise and ingenuity of their new tenant.

Dicky banked on a growing custom of well-to-do visitors to the spa and understood that to attract them there and bring them back time and time again he had to offer much more than the drinking water. According to a traveller who passed through Scarborough in 1703, 'most of the gentry in the North of England and Scotland resort hither in the season of the year'. Perhaps this assertion was more propagandist than factual, but it does convey the truth that Scarborough's fame was spreading.

What Dicky had done to the site of Scarborough spa by 1715 was drawn by Francis Place of York in that year. The artist sketched and identified three buildings at the foot of the cliff immediately behind the well head. Set back from the other two was a simple, single-storey structure labelled 'the Ladeys House'. A second, similar building, at the top of a flight of wooden steps leading up from the sands, was described as 'Another house for the Gent[s]'. And between the two, a more substantial dwelling was said to be 'Dickies House'. All three buildings were now protected from the sea on a natural raised platform buttressed by a staith of stones and upright timbers. The well itself was shown to be covered by a stone table which served as a counter or bar for the women dippers.

Though one visitor of 1714 wrote that 'there is very good accommodation for those that drink the waters' at Scarborough, this was not the agreed verdict of all who came there. Sarah, duchess of Marlborough, spent six weeks in Scarborough in 1732. She conceded that the waters there were beneficial for scurvy and constipation, but she found everything else, especially 'the Ladyes House', most disagreeable:

> There is a room for the ladies assembly which you go up a steep pair of stairs into, on the outside of the house, like a ladder. In that room there is nothing but hard narrow benches, which is a punishment to sit upon. When the waters begin to operate, there is a room within it, where there is above twenty holes with drawers under them to take out, and the ladies go in together and see one another round the room, when they are in that agreeable posture, and at the door there is a great heap of leaves which the ladies take in with them ... I came home as fast as I could for fear of being forced into that assembly.

In other words, this was one duchess who did not defecate in public however genteel the company. Compared with Bath or Tunbridge she found Scarborough 'very dirty', its spa 'so extremely steep and disagreeable to get to either in a coach or chair', and in every part of it 'vast poverty'. To be fair, Sarah was 72-years-old; she had had to endure six days in a coach to get to Scarborough from St Albans; and the spa waters did nothing for her excruciating gout. Even if she had been aware of Dr Wittie's 'sovereign remedy' of cold sea-bathing, it is most unlikely that she would have risked such a desperate and hazardous cure. She had seen the duchess of Manchester bathe in the sea, but she was a much younger woman. Finally, to add to her trials, Sarah was kept awake in the night 'with the barkings and howlings of dogs and hounds which is kept all around me for the entertainment of fine gentlemen in this place'.

Another illustration of the failure of the Corporation to encourage visitors to come to Scarborough is that it was again left to personal enterprise and initiative to improve access to the spa well. After severe storms had damaged staithes and properties along the foreshore in 1720, an arrangement was made by John Bland and his business associates with the bailiffs: he would build a new coach road from Carr Street directly down to the sands and the Corporation would subsidise its construction. By 1723, at a cost to the Corporation of £85, the 'horse-way' was finished. Though to the duchess of Marlborough, who must have descended it, Bland's Cliff was still frighteningly steep, it was a great improvement on previous routes down to the shore of South Bay. John Cossins's 'New and Exact Plan of Scarborough', dated 1725, shows 'Dickey's House', the 'Spaw Well', and the new 'Coach Road to the Spaw' zigzagging down from Carr Street to the foreshore. A more direct way to the spa from St Nicholas Cliff down into Ramsdale was not made into a proper footpath until 1735. In May of that year the Corporation approved the work 'for the commodiousness of the spawers' on the condition that it was paid for entirely out of receipts from the spa.

By that time Dicky Dickinson had signed a new contract with the town's authorities. Only in this lease of 1727 is it made clear that he, and not the Corporation, had built the staith and the houses behind it under Driple Cotes. This would explain why the rent demanded was only £1 a year for the next seven years: the Corporation had title only to the land and well. By building substantially on the land Dicky had hoped that he could establish legal title to ownership of it, but the Corporation had no intention of granting him freehold rights.

In the lease of April 1727 Dickinson was described as 'a yeoman': there is no hint there of his extraordinary appearance and personality which so intrigued visitors to 'his' spa. Indeed, very little is known for certain about Scarborough's first and most famous 'Governor of the Spaw'. Two daughters of a Richard Dickinson were baptized at St Mary's in 1690 and 1699, but there is no way of determining who their father was. It is not even certain that he was married: the Mrs Anne Dickinson recorded in the Corporation accounts of 1738 might not have been his widow. We know only that for many years he lived with 'Peggy' in the 'Spaw House' and that she was not his legal wife.

What we know about Dicky Dickinson personally is derived almost entirely from observations drawn in one year. Writing to his brother, the vicar of Tunstall, from his lodgings in Scarborough in July 1733, Edmund Withers then described Dicky as 'a remarkable creature ... who for symetry and proportion, I mean for want of both, is perhaps the most singular deformity in the king's dominions'. Only a few months later, the anonymous author of *A Journey from London to Scarborough* provided further details. According to his account, Dicky was 'one of the most deformed pieces of mortality I ever saw, and of most uncouth manner of speech; however, with Aesop's deformity, he has some of his wit'. After explaining that Dicky rented the spa well from the Corporation at a small rent, had built two houses on the site for the convenience of gentlemen and ladies, and charged five shillings for a season's use of these 'retirements', the author then subsided into pretentious doggerel:

> Behold the Governor of Scarborough Spaw,
> The strangest phiz[1] and form you ever saw;
> Yet, when you view the beauties of his mind,
> In him a second Aesop[2] you may find.
> Samos[3] unenvy'd boasts her Aesop gone,
> And France may glory in her late Scaron[4]
> While England has a living Dickinson.

An even longer 'poem' in praise of Dicky, 'sovereign of the Spa', explained that because he could not straighten either his back or his knees he had the shape of a letter Z and 'a posture fit to shite'. Drawings of Dicky of the time and later depict varying degrees of his deformity. His left arm appears permanently bent at the elbow and his left hand misshapen and useless. His feet are splayed outwards at 'a quarter-to-three' and his legs are crooked and stiff. Usually he displays a mischievous grin on his face as if to say, 'I know I'm ugly but that's part of my fascination'. At least one of the surviving portraits of him, and perhaps the most flattering, dated 1725, shows him with a monkey and a fox, both chained to the chest which contains his subscription takings. He

---

[1] 'Phiz' means face, a colloquial archaism derived from 'physiognomy' and shortened from 'phizog'.

[2] By tradition, Aesop was thought to have been physically deformed.

[3] Aesop was born on the Greek Aegean island of Samos.

[4] Paul Scarron (1610-60) was the French novelist crippled by rheumatism at the age of 30.

sits before a table with quill pen and ink pot ready to enter another name in his book and take another five shillings from a 'spawer'.

In the background to George Vertue's engraving of this 1725 portrait Dicky's house is drawn as a fine mansion dwelling of two storeys with roof turrets. This view may well have been as flattering as the drawing of Dicky himself, but other depictions of his house by John Setterington in 1735 and John Haynes, probably in the same year, also suggest additions and improvements compared with his house as drawn by Place twenty years earlier.

There is no doubt that, by the 1720s, the spa and Dicky were doing well. A Corporation order of 1729 repeated the earlier charge of a shilling an anker and added that bottled waters were to cost 6d. a dozen, most of which went to the bailiffs. Income from the spa was now sufficient to pay for the town's new 'House of Correction, a Workhouse and a Gaol'! When Dicky's seven-year lease came up for renewal in 1734, his annual rent was raised from one to forty pounds.

A detailed indication of the profitable success of Dicky's spa is to be found in the 'list of the nobility, quality and gentry' who came to Scarborough during the season of 1733. Their names were recorded as subscribers to the spa, the Long Room, the bookshop and the coffee house. Altogether the names of 695 gentlemen and 360 ladies were entered in these subscription books. Of the gentlemen, there were two dukes, of Argyle and Rutland; the marquess of Lothian; seven earls, of Anglesey, Cholmondley, Huntingdon, Carlisle, Stair, Chesterfield and Marchmont; three barons, of Coleraine, Carmichael and Langdale; and five Yorkshire knights, Francis Boynton, Henry Slingsby, William Strickland, George Cayley and Charles Hotham. Colley Cibber, the poet laureate, was at Scarborough that summer; and so was Nicholas Hawskmoor, the architect, no doubt enjoying a rest after his great labours at Castle Howard, Blenheim Palace, All Souls' College, Oxford, and planning the completion of his next work—the west towers of Westminster Abbey. The female gathering was not quite so distinguished, but it did include ladies representing some of the leading aristocratic families in Scotland and England with names such as Campbell, Cecil, Howard and Wentworth. Not all gentlemen brought their wives and families; not all ladies were accompanied by their husbands: this was one of the attractions of this pleasure resort.

Such a constellation of stars and garters did not come to Scarborough merely to drink its waters, laugh at or with Dicky Dickinson, and pay five shillings for the season's use of his convenient 'retirements':

as Setterington's 'Perspective Draught' of 1735 shows, sea-bathing had by then become an organised, normal activity in South Bay. Some bathers walked into the sea, some flung themselves into it out of rowing boats, and a growing number of less robust or less reckless, or perhaps just more modest, swimmers preferred to enter it from Scarborough's new invention—the bathing machine. Significantly, the world's first, wheeled, bathing hut was drawn by Setterington on the edge of the sea immediately opposite the spa well and Dicky's houses. One day, though not in Dicky's time, sea-bathing at Scarborough would become more common than spa-drinking.

Finally, Dicky Dickinson's spectacular success owed much to the belated but necessary investment of the residents of Scarborough in their 'up-market' tourist trade. By 1725, the town had at least two assembly rooms, one in Low Westgate (now numbers 11 and 11A Princess Street), and a second, which eventually became the Royal Hotel, in St Nicholas or Long Room Street. By 1733, during the season, Mr Vipont, master of the Long Room at Hampstead, had taken over the Long Room in St Nicholas Street. He provided balls every evening, dinners every day prepared by poulterers and cooks from London, and every kind of indoor game and gambling from billiards to dice and cards. The company could spend their afternoons at the new theatre, on one of the two outdoor bowling greens, at the bookshop or in the coffee house. Since Celia Fiennes had visited the town the number of beds for guests and stable places for horses had doubled. The New Inn, New Globe, Blacksmith's Arms, and the Crown and Sceptre now offered accommodation to add to that of the Old Globe.

To ensure that 'the quality' kept their feet and skirts clean and dry, the streets of 'the politer parts' of Scarborough had been paved. Public subscription had paid for stone paving flags and posts along Long Room Street, which had lately become 'the Pall Mall of Scarborough'. Thanks to a donation of £100 from the duke of Leeds and £50 more from John Hill, Newborough had received the same treatment, whereas the whole town had contributed to expensive repairs to the surfaces of Merchant Row, King Street, Castlegate and Longwestgate.

Clearly, by the 1730s, going to Scarborough for the season was no longer an imposition on the invalid: visitors were now more likely to be in search of pleasures than cures. They came for cheap spirits and contraband wines, for a wide range of entertainments and diversions, and for the easy informality and intimacy of the company where social conventions and moral standards were relaxed, or even ignored. Therapy was more likely to be an alibi than a genuine motive for risking the hazards of a journey to Scarborough. They came for a good time.

Dicky Dickinson's demise was sudden and totally unexpected: literally, the world fell down upon him. On the morning of 28 December 1737 the first crack appeared and was heard in the cellar of Dicky's spa house. During the next 24 hours about an acre of land on the cliff above the spa slowly subsided 50 feet and the ground along the base of the cliff, where Dicky's houses stood, rose up 20 or 30 feet. Two entirely new terraces were created. By the middle of the afternoon of 29 December, with most of the population of Scarborough watching, all the spa houses, the staith and the well were buried beneath hundreds of tons of clay and sand. Dicky lost everything, even his household goods and furniture. Six weeks later he was dead.

Richard Dickinson proved to be the first and the last of his kind. Whereas he had been a private tenant running the spa as his own business and for his own livelihood, all his successors were merely salaried employees of the Corporation. Captain William Tymperton, master of Wills coffee house in London, 'a man well known and respected for his comical facetious disposition', the second governor, received 20 guineas a year. The Corporation, now fully alive to the indispensable value of the spa, lost no time in digging out the waters. Two new springs were discovered almost at once. Dr Shaw, 'the residentiary physician' at Scarborough, was delighted to declare that their waters were better than ever. By May 1738 the Ladies' Room was already built with brick walls and chimneys, timber roof, double front doors, four large windows and 'wainscotted throughout' its interior. According to the *London Daily Post*, a similar room for gentlemen would be erected within the next ten days. All this was at the expense of the Corporation, which had woken up, at long last, to the realisation that Scarborough had become a leading health and pleasure resort for the rich, sick and idle.

19. Thomas Hinderwell

Thomas Hinderwell was born on 17 November 1744 in a house on St Nicholas Cliff, 'next in line with Donner's Hotel', and died at his home in Newborough, only a hundred yards or so from his birthplace, on 22 October 1825. On the face of it, during those 81 years, Thomas had not travelled far, but in fact his life was one of colossal and varied achievement.

Thomas was the elder son of Thomas and Rebekah Hinderwell: he had a younger brother, Francis, who was later drowned at sea, and two sisters. His earliest education was in Scarborough and afterwards he was sent as a boarder to the grammar school at Coxwold, where he studied classics under the Reverend Robert Midgley. It was the custom at Coxwold for leavers to present a book to the school: Hinderwell's gift was a beautiful copy of Xenophon. He was still only eleven years old.

The next stage in his education was spent at sea: he was apprenticed to the master mariner Robert Burn, 'a man of correct moral feelings and considerable nautical information'. For the next twenty years Thomas gathered experience and knowledge, and not a little money, as a merchant seaman, master mariner and eventually shipowner. At first hand he knew most of the ports of Europe and the Mediterranean. In 1773 he took supplies to St Petersburg during Russia's war with Turkey. Two years later, he was master mariner of his own ship the 240 ton *Nancy* with a crew of twelve. She was his last ship: at the age of 31 he was rich enough to retire and settle permanently ashore in Scarborough.

After 20 years at sea he spent the next 40 years as a member of Scarborough's ruling body, the Common Hall. His father had been elected junior bailiff in 1775, but the younger Thomas was junior in 1781, and senior in that post in 1784-5, 1790-1 and 1799-1800. According to his biographer, John Cole, he remained a member of the First Twelve until his retirement as 'father of the house' in 1816 at the age of 72.

Thomas had an unrequited and unconsummated 'attachment' to Elizabeth Woodall, who died in 1801 at the age of 51, and he remained a life-long bachelor. His mother died in 1797, and his father a year later, at the age of 92. Without a family of his own, but with sufficient income from his shipping interests to live independently, Thomas was driven by piety and humanitarian zeal into a multitude of charitable pursuits.

As a master mariner and shipowner Hinderwell was a long-serving member, warden and twice President of Scarborough's Trinity House. This Society of Owners, Masters and Mariners had been founded in 1602 to provide succour for the widows and orphans of seamen and 'broken seafarers', though it was not until nearly 80 years later that the Society was able to build its own House or Hospital. By Hinderwell's time the Hospital in St Sepulchre Street was far too small and decayed to fulfil its intended purposes, and he was at the forefront of an appeal for its reconstruction. In the event, nothing happened in his lifetime, but the £100 he left in his will to Trinity House constituted the first subscription to the new building which was finished eight years after his death at a cost of £1,600. Thomas was also a leading member and benefactor of Trinity House's sister charity in Scarborough, the Merchant Seamen's Society, which had its own hospital. During the year 1791-2 he was President of that hospital, and in 1811 he is credited with a gift of £100 to its trust fund.

Another of Hinderwell's many good causes was Scarborough's Amicable Society. Founded in 1729 by Robert North, one of the town's most eccentric and benevolent gentlemen, this Anglican organisation provided clothing and schooling for children of the poor. By 1811 the Society had 265 members who made weekly donations to add to the Sunday collections made in St Mary's, so that by 1817 it was able to move its 60 children out of a room in Trinity House to a purpose-built school costing £1,200 in Duesbury Walk (now North Terrace). Hinderwell was a veteran trustee of the Amicable Society, served as its President in 1784-5, and left £50 to it in his will. The purpose and success of the Amicable School was no better described than in Hinderwell's own words:

> Experience has confirmed the utility of this establishment, in preserving the children from the contagion of vicious examples, and leading them into the paths of holiness and social duty. Instead of falling victims to profligacy, many of them have filled useful occupations in life, with credit and advantage.

He was particularly pleased to record that many of the boys had later gone to sea to qualify as mates and masters, and some had 'fought the naval battles of their country' in the Royal Navy. In 1804 Hinderwell was the author of the rules of Scarborough's Amicable Society; and on leaving the school every boy received a copy of 'a judicious tract' also written by him.

Hinderwell's concern for the education and moral welfare of the town's poor children extended beyond his patronage and support of the Church of England's Amicable Society: in his will he left £20 to the Lancasterian School and the same sum to Scarborough's School of Industry. Thomas was an Anglican but this did not prevent him from associating with the town's many Nonconformists whose voluntary subscriptions eventually in 1810 paid for a school for 400 children. The Lancasterian School—so-called because it employed the monitorial system of teaching favoured by Joseph Lancaster—was built in a field on the north side of the Rope Walk (now Rutland Terrace fronting Castle Road). Nor was Hinderwell attentive to the educational needs of boys only. The School of Industry was founded in 1808, under the patronage of the ladies of Scarborough, who, in Hinderwell's words, were 'impressed with sentiments of the tenderest sympathy for the delicate and destitute situation of their sex in the lower classes of life'. About 100 of Scarborough's poorest girls were given free moral instruction and taught practical domestic skills.

One of Hinderwell's most beneficial and lasting achievements was his successful campaign to provide Scarborough with its first lifeboat. For many years past there had been meetings at, and private discussions in, Trinity House about the need for Scarborough to have a special boat for the sole purpose of saving lives at sea. But it was Thomas Hinderwell who originally launched a public appeal for a lifeboat fund, and it was he who chaired the Lifeboat Committee when it first met in December 1800. In fact, the first appeal raised only £212 1s. 6d., whereas the bill for building the boat alone came to £129 5s., and after a year the Lifeboat Fund was in deficit. A second appeal had to be made in 1802, and later £100 borrowed from the local bankers, Messrs Woodall and Company.

Nevertheless, the lifeboat, designed by Henry Greathead of South Shields, was built in Christopher Smith's yard on Sandside, and a house for it put up on the east side of the old pier. Within its first year of operation Scarborough's lifeboat, the second in Britain, had saved the lives of the crews of the brig *Aurora*, the sloop *Isabella*, and the brigs *Assistance* and *Experiment*. At the end of 1801, the *London Sun* published a graphic account of the rescue of the crew of the *Aurora* written by Thomas Hinderwell. Also, when the claims of Henry Greathead to be rewarded for his invention were examined by a House of Commons committee, it was Hinderwell who appeared before it on his behalf. Apparently, the committee was most favourably impressed by his convincing advocacy. That Scarborough was the second lifeboat station in the country after Tynemouth therefore owes much to the initiative and dogged persistence of Thomas Hinderwell. A year before his death the town acquired a second lifeboat.

When shipwrecked mariners were brought ashore invariably they needed food, clothing and accommodation. Another of Hinderwell's numerous acts of thoughtful charity was to found in 1822 Scarborough's Humane Society which had a Receiving House on South Bay beach to provide these basic necessities.

As an evangelical Anglican Hinderwell was also active in several other religious causes. The 'bleak and exposed situation of St Mary's church', its inconvenient hill-top location, and its insufficient accommodation for a rapidly growing parish population, meant that Scarborough's Anglicans had long felt the need for an additional building. Hinderwell was one of the signatories to a petition presented in 1821 to the commissioners appointed by Parliament for building new churches. Unfortunately, Thomas did not live long enough to see Christ Church: its foundation stone was not laid until a year after his death. However, his generous donation of £70 to its costs was equal to that of the Speaker of the Commons, Charles Manners, and exceeded only by noblemen such as the earl of Mulgrave and the duke of Rutland, and the richest townsmen, such as John Tindall, shipowner and principal shipbuilder.

Not least of Hinderwell's successes was his foundation in 1812 of Scarborough's Auxiliary Bible Society. This was a local branch of the British and Foreign Bible Society. Appropriately, Hinderwell was the Society's first president. At the inauguration of the branch and on its anniversaries in 1813 and 1814 he delivered exemplary speeches outlining its objectives. For him the Bible united all Christians of whatever denomination; without its light man would exist 'in a deplorable state of darkness and imbecility—ignorant, depraved, helpless ...' He also said that in his view the grand purpose of the British and Foreign Bible Society was 'to civilise and evangelise the world, by the universal diffusion of the pure word of God'.

Hinderwell was dead before Parliament abolished slavery throughout the British Empire in 1833, but he did have the satisfaction of witnessing the ban on the slave trade which came into force in 1807. Delighted with the success of William Wilberforce, his old friend, in 1811 Hinderwell dedicated the second edition of his *History of Scarborough* to him. Hinderwell's dedication and tribute read:

> To William Wilberforce, Esq., Member of Parliament for the County of York, as a memorial of long and disinterested attachment, resulting from the purest regard for his private virtues, and the unsullied patriotism and exalted humanity of his public life.

Hinderwell was the author of several tracts and pamphlets on subjects dear to him such as shipwrecks and Sunday observance; but he is best known and most valued today for his *History and Antiquities of Scarborough and the Vicinity*, first published in August 1798. Only five hundred copies of this first edition were printed by William Blanchard at York and sold for half a guinea each. Hinderwell dedicated it to 'The Magistrates of the Borough of Scarborough, the Burgesses and Inhabitants at large'.

Hinderwell's *History* broke new ground. Thomas Gent had written and published histories of York in 1730, of Ripon in 1733 and of Hull in 1735, and had intended to add Scarborough to the list, but never did. His only contribution to a history of the town were notes published as an addenda to his *History of Hull*. James Schofield, the Scarborough bookseller, has claim to being the town's earliest historian, yet his *Historical and Descriptive Guide* of 1787 was a better introduction to the contemporary visitors' scene than an historical explanation of it. The second edition of 1796, titled simply, *The Scarborough Guide*, contained even less history. Additional material introduced on plants and fossils was written by William Travis, the surgeon, and that on the spa waters, by Scarborough's leading, resident physician, Dr Belcombe. Moreover, whereas Schofield had invited readers of the first edition to send him corrections, additions and improvements, which would 'render a subsequent edition more compleat', he disclaimed all responsibility for the second, 'he having seen the copy only since it was printed'.

Contemporary readers were soon appreciative of the extraordinary merits of Hinderwell's *History*. William Hutton, who, a few years later, brought out his *Tour to Scarborough* (1803), was in Scarborough when Hinderwell's work first appeared. Since he was leaving for home the following day, he walked to the bookshop as soon as it opened, offered the bookseller 'a shilling for the loan of the book for two hours, and a deposit of a guinea for security'. However, before the two hours expired, he was back at the shop to buy the book outright.

In his *History and Topography of Yorkshire*, published in 1812,

John Bigland wrote that Hinderwell's *History* was 'one of the most accurate and interesting of all the topographical works relating to this, or any other part of England: it ought to have a place in every library, and to be a companion to everyone who visits the romantic scenery of Scarborough'; and no one at the time was better qualified than Bigland to pass such a complimentary judgement.

A dozen years later, in his *Historic Sketch of the Parish Church, Wakefield*, the Reverend J.L. Sisson concluded, rather pompously:

> In the course of my excursions from home I have collected several volumes on these subjects [local histories], but I can safely say there is not one amongst them of more intrinsic value than Mr H's *History and Antiquities of Scarborough*. I had the opportunity of comparing the statements of Mr H. with conclusions drawn from my own personal observations and researches: and it is hardly necessary to add that I invariably found these statements correct.

Not only Hinderwell's contemporaries were indebted to Hinderwell: as his biographer, John Cole, wrote a year after his death, the publication of his *History* 'conferred a lasting obligation upon his native town'. Hinderwell had recruited the services of the two contributors to Schofield's *Guide*—William Travis and Dr Belcombe—but otherwise the remainder of the book was essentially his own.

In its time and place Hinderwell's *History* was a masterpiece. Though he lived long before history became a rigorous and scholarly discipline, Hinderwell was never knowingly inventive and rarely inaccurate when reporting events that happened after 1066. His book is still a model of judicious balance: comprehensive, without being overloaded with tedious, trivial or irrelevant detail; interesting, but never frivolous; critical, but never facetious or superior. As a historian, he was twice-blessed: Hinderwell was a local man with valuable local contacts and steeped in local knowledge, yet he was also well-educated, widely read and extensively travelled. It would be grossly unjust to dismiss his book as merely antiquarian.

In contemporary terms Hinderwell's sources were impressive. As a classical scholar, he was able to quote from Ptolemy, Horace and Tacitus; as a man deeply involved in public affairs, he referred, for instance, to Leatham's report of 1794 on the agriculture of the East Riding. He might not have had direct access to many primary sources of evidence, but he had a surprisingly wide appreciation of secondary authorities in print. For example, for the Civil Wars of the 1640s in which Scarborough was much engaged and damaged, Hinderwell consulted almost every source then available, from the histories of Rushworth and Whitelocke to the Journal of the House of Commons and some contemporary newsbooks, both Royalist and Parliamentarian. As for state papers, which were then entirely in manuscript, Hinderwell freely acknowledged his dependence on the Reverend Daniel Lysons 'for his laborious researches in the Tower [of London], and the British Museum'. In Hinderwell's day there was no Public Record Office. Neither were there County Record Offices at Northallerton and Beverley, though as senior bailiff and veteran burgess of the Common Hall, Hinderwell had privileged access to the town's Corporation archive.

Hinderwell's scepticism, modesty and caution are refreshingly unusual for the time he was writing. Commenting on the suggestion that the borough of Scarborough might have had pre-Conquest origins, he said that he regarded such speculation as unproductive since there were no 'authentic records of that period' known to him. Of church memorials, he wrote that 'coloured' as they were by 'the partial pencil of affection', they should not be accepted as faithful descriptions of the dead. He considered that future chemists might well blush at the feeble and inflated attempts of his contemporaries to analyse the properties of Scarborough's spa waters. He could not swallow the exaggeration claims of local mineral water enthusiasts, adding, wisely, 'to superstition commonly succeeds scepticism'.

It is a backhanded compliment to Hinderwell that even some of his few errors were repeated by many successors and took a long time to correct. The author of his third, posthumous edition of 1832, and later Joseph Brogden Baker, who published a history of Scarborough in 1882, both followed him blindly in giving the date of Stafford's abortive coup as 1554, instead of 1557. Several authors of local histories have given the start of the Civil-War siege of Scarborough as February 1644, when it should have been February 1645. They forgot, as Hinderwell did, that by the Old Style calendar the new year began on Lady Day, 25 March, not 1 January. Hinderwell's belief that the Cistercians had an abbey on St Mary's hill was not finally discredited until Hamilton Thompson wrote his chapter in Rowntree's *History* of 1931.

On the other hand, Hinderwell avoided traps that others later fell into. He knew that however Oliver's Mount got its misleading name, Oliver Cromwell never set foot in Scarborough. Unlike Professor Grant in Rowntree's *History*, he did not confuse Seamer fair with Seamer market, or Guiseley with Guisborough; and it was Grant in 1931 and Gordon Forster in 1966, not Hinderwell, who wrongly thought that the Royalists surrendered Scarborough castle as well as Scarborough town in September 1648.

No one knew and reported the contemporary scene better than Hinderwell. To him we owe a detailed description of Scarborough and its hinterland two centuries ago. He noted the transformation of the eastern end of the Vale of Pickering brought about by the recent construction of the Scalby cut overflow which had drained off the Derwent's flood waters into North Bay. He saw Weaponness before it was enclosed and its earthworks destroyed. He saw the foundations of the Franciscan friary buildings long before they were built over by the Scarborough School Board. His town maps of 1798 and 1811 reveal a Scarborough that was still essentially medieval in area and had only just begun to grow out of its old wall and ditch enclosure.

Hinderwell had none of the archaeological and few of the manuscript revelations now available to modern local historians. Nevertheless, his *History* remains required reading for anyone seriously interested in Scarborough's rich and eventful past, not merely for its own sake, but also as a particular illustration of national experience. Both the broad sweep and the in-depth inquiry are to be found in his work, since Hinderwell was careful to consult not just the local historians such as Drake and Charlton but also the national authorities such as Smollett, Hume and Robertson. Finally, and not of least importance, Hinderwell's *History* illustrates that though historical investigation does not make men wise, wise men make the best historians.

Perhaps the depth, if not the extent, of Hinderwell's philanthropy has been exaggerated. In a sermon preached only a week after his death, his friend, Samuel Bottomley, Scarborough's Presbyterian minister, spoke only the truth when he said of him:

> I have never known an undertaking in the town, in which charity was concerned, whether in feeding the hungry, clothing the naked, instructing the ignorant, visiting the afflicted, or saving the drowning, but Mr Hinderwell took an active and principal part in it.

However, in his own time and town, Thomas was a very rich bachelor, and in today's terms, a millionaire. His gifts of £100 to Trinity House, £50 to the Amicable Society, £20 each to the Girls' School of Industry and the Lancasterian School look less than bountiful when measured against his overall wealth and his final bequests. Out of landed and property estate valued at nearly £16,000, Hinderwell left £15,600 to be divided between his married sister Alice and his numerous nephews and nieces. To his servant, Ann Johnson, 'for her kind attention and service in my last illness', he gave only £10. His final charitable gesture was an instruction to his executors 'to avoid the ostentation of a public funeral' and instead distribute £50-worth of bread to the poor people of Scarborough. To put these sums into perspective, in 1825 the average income per head of the English population was about £30 a year.

Even Hinderwell's best remembered bequest—that of all his 'books, manuscripts, pictures, collections of pebbles, fossils and other curiosities' and what he called 'my museum'—went to his nephew, Thomas Duesbery; and it was he, not his uncle, who later gave the collection to Scarborough Philosophical Society to form the basis of their new Rotunda Museum when it opened in 1828.

In the place that he loved so much, little of Hinderwell has survived. A drinking fountain, erected as late as 1860, 'to the memory of Thomas Hinderwell by some who knew and loved him' has long since disappeared. Granby House, where he was born, was demolished in 1899, and the site has remained empty, without benefit of even a wall plaque to record its association. Very few of the crowds of visitors to the last resting place of Ann Bronte in St Mary's graveyard are even aware of the Hinderwell family's simple, horizontal tombstone only yards away. Here, close to the wall of Farrer's Aisle, Thomas was buried in the same grave as his mother, father, sister Ann and brother-in-law, William Duesbery.

Scarborough's own remembrance of Hinderwell has been late and minimal. After the First World War, when the borough council built its first housing estate at what it chose to call Edgehill, one of the new streets became Hinderwell Road. A decade later, in 1932, the same council's new primary school, opened to accommodate the children of the estate, was given the historian's name. However, recognition of Hinderwell's outstanding merit had by that time become national: in 1891 he was given a whole column in the *Dictionary of National Biography*, a distinction then awarded to only one other native Scarborian, Admiral Sir John Lawson.

As early as 1810, the Yorkshire antiquarian, John Bigland, had written of Hinderwell's *History*: 'Mr Hinderwell's work ought to have a place in every nobleman's and gentleman's library.' Nearly two centuries later, all Thomas Hinderwell's work, not just his *History*, deserves better public appreciation.

20. John Hatfield

Of all the many criminals who came to Scarborough to prey on its wealthy and often gullible visitors none became more notorious in the land than John Hatfield. However, by the late eighteenth century, Scarborough's innkeepers had much experience of dishonest guests and William Stephens, who had the New Inn in Newborough Street, was no exception; on 25 April 1792, for failure to pay his outstanding hotel bill, 'Major' Hatfield was lodged in the debtors' prison in nearby Newborough Bar.

Though it was as yet unknown to Scarborians, 'Major' John Hatfield already had a long record of fraud and deceit. He was born about 1758 at Mottram in Longdendale in the county of Cheshire, one of the eight children of a poor estate woodsman. His mother, the daughter of a schoolteacher, gave him lessons in reading and writing, but he had no formal education. After the imprisonment of his father for theft and the death of his mother, John was apprenticed to a Chester linen draper for whom he became a travelling salesman. At the tender age of fifteen he showed remarkable ingenuity and boldness by seducing and marrying the natural daughter of the very rich Lord Robert Manners, who presented him with a bankers' draft for £1,500 as her dowry.

Hatfield took his young bride and draft to London, rented a house in fashionable Mayfair, and lived there in extravagant style. Exploiting his Manners connection, he soon ran up heavy debts which Lord Robert agreed to settle on condition the couple left the capital. The Hatfields emigrated to the American colonies, but by 1782 John was back in London, having deserted his wife and their three children. She, it is said, died penniless of a broken heart.

The accumulation of more unpaid bills landed Hatfield in London's King's Bench prison, but again he was bailed out by Lord Robert. When Manners, now the Duke of Rutland, was posted to Dublin as Ireland's Lord Lieutenant in 1784, Hatfield followed him there. Another unpaid account put him in the Dublin Marshalsea until once more he was rescued by Rutland and then escorted to the packet boat bound for Holyhead.

Back in England, Hatfield toured the south coast resorts practising his arts of deception before making his way north in 1792 to Scarborough. One of the borough's two parliamentary seats was in the pocket of the Rutland interest and Hatfield, who had now adopted the military rank of major, claimed falsely to have the duke's backing for his candidature in the next election. However, this scheme also misfired when he ran out of money and credit and failed to dupe the worldly Mr Stephens. Nevertheless, though now confined indefinitely to Newborough Bar's debtors' prison, he still contrived to make his prolonged stay there uniquely comfortable and even profitable. His quick wit, ready tongue and skilful flattery soon persuaded Miss Grant, the otherwise stern wardress, to allow him and other debtors free movement within the prison. Even more impressive testimony to his talents was his success in publishing 'several amusing sketches' and *A New Scarborough Guide*, the latter impudently dedicated without his permission 'to his Grace, John, Duke of Rutland'.

Hatfield's *Guide*, written anonymously by 'A Gentleman', was published in 1797, and offered at one shilling a copy. Its 52 pages contain a wonderful mixture of useful information and hypocritical special pleading, and provide one of the few insights into Hatfield's contradictory and complex character. That he was able to gather so much local intelligence on Scarborough's 'customs, amusements, lodging-houses etc.' a year before Hinderwell's *History* came out and while he was still locked up is further proof of his remarkable powers of persuasion and the exceptional freedom allowed him by Miss Grant.

Hatfield took three full pages to denounce the evils of ladies' 'cosmeticks' and deplore the weakness of women who were 'the infatuated dupes of false colours'. Rouges, cerises and bismuth, he declared, would only damage their natural, smooth, healthy skin and destroy their looks. No doubt drawing on his personal experience, Hatfield reminded his 'respectable readers' of the 50,000 'unhappy females of London whose trade requires every adventitious aid to repair the ravages of disease and excess'. Coming from someone who had made a full-time career out of wearing 'false colours' and duping all and sundry this warning was another example of his colossal hypocrisy.

In contrast, Hatfield's advice on diet was commendably sensible, if rather vague. He recommended to his readers that they should eat what they enjoyed in moderation; and that they should take less solid food and drink more. A healthy diet was balanced and natural; only the sick or obese need alter their regime. Presumably Hatfield had Scarborough's over-weight and invalid 'spawers' in mind when he wrote that 'temperance' was 'the basis of health'.

After praising the homes and occupants of the local gentry and aristocracy at Wykeham, Brompton, Scampston, Castle Howard and Duncombe Park, and noting that Hutton Buscel was 'the residence of lovely widowhood', Hatfield went on to condemn Scarborough's gaol, without even a hint that he was one of its inmates. Externally, the building was 'a public nuisance' which spoiled the entrance to the town; internally, its government was 'a disgrace to the country'. Debtors were locked into their cells day and night; the best rooms were reserved for the gaolers; and the exercise yard was exclusively for the female keepers who used it to wash the linen of 'strangers who came to the spa'. With customary effrontery, Hatfield hoped that 'for the honour of humanity' a remedy would soon be found 'for such gross violation of every decent principle'.

Should his readers conclude that he had only negative thoughts about the town, Hatfield ended his *Guide* with what was intended to be a compliment to Scarborough. This was a year of exceptional social misery and political instability. The war with revolutionary France was going badly for Britain; ruined harvests had led to shortages of grain and starvation bread prices; and there was even a mutiny in the Royal Navy. In these circumstances there was fear of both foreign invasion and domestic rebellion. However, Hatfield assured his readers that scandalous rumours concerning the disaffection of the local Volunteer militia were totally untrue: Scarborough was a loyal and law-abiding town.

How many copies of Hatfield's *Guide* were printed, circulated, sold and read it is impossible to say. Presumably his little paperback was soon superseded the following year by the first edition of Thomas Hinderwell's magisterial *History*. Perhaps Hatfield's outraged outburst led to more humanitarian treatment for the debtors in Newborough Bar, but it did not earn him enough money to pay his debts or persuade anyone to settle them and thereby secure his release. 'Major' Hatfield remained a prisoner for another three years.

According to the archdiocese of York's register of marriage licences, John Hatfield, aged 40 of Scarborough, was married to Michilli Nathon (sic), aged 23 of Scarborough, on 14 September 1800. St Mary's parish register gives the same date for their wedding, adding only that Hatfield was a widower and correcting his bride's name to Michelli Nation. The great impostor had at last regained his freedom, but only by taking another wife.

Though there are different versions of how this extraordinary event came about, all agree that Miss Nation, a well-to-do lady from Devonshire, had been living with her mother in a lodging-house opposite Newborough prison. Though the two had never exchanged words, Hatfield had eventually captured the sympathy of this rich, young gentlewoman 'by exhibiting himself in full regimental dress and shedding tears' for her to see from across the street. According to one account,

161

Michelli was moved to visit his prison cell and agreed to pay all his bills; according to another, after more than six years of gazing at each other across Newborough, she had never spoken a word to him until he was released and they were married the next morning. Soon afterwards the newly-weds left Scarborough to live together in the second Mrs Hatfield's own home in Tiverton.

In effect the marriage lasted only eighteen months. During that time John resumed his old ways—spending extravagantly, cheating business partners, and gaining money by false pretences. Running out of local credit and credibility, he abandoned his pregnant wife and baby daughter without a penny and returned to the fleshpots of London. Here, in another attempt to gain immunity from creditors by becoming a member of Parliament, he tried unsuccessfully to win a seat for the rotten borough of Queenborough.

Having failed to become a member of Parliament for either Scarborough or Queenborough, Hatfield then decided to pose as one. In July 1802 he arrived at Keswick in a splendid carriage claiming to be the Honourable Colonel Alexander Augustus Hope, younger brother of the Earl of Hopetoun, and member for the Scottish constituency of Linlithgow. He had learned his new role with such thoroughness and he carried it off with such bravado that the whole neighbourhood accepted him without question. At Grasmere he duped John Crump, a wealthy Liverpool merchant, into advancing him money; and his plan to marry Miss D'Arcy, a very rich heiress, was frustrated only by her guardian's cautious insistence that he provided proof of identity.

Undaunted, 'Colonel Hope' then courted Mary Robinson, only daughter of the landlord of the Fish Inn at Buttermere. Mary was famed throughout the Lake District as 'the Maid of Buttermere', an incomparable young beauty who spent her days on the neighbouring fells shepherding her sheep. Not surprisingly, Joseph Robinson was all too pleased to give his daughter in marriage to a member of the aristocracy and the wedding took place by special licence on 2 October 1802 in the parish church of Lorton.

The marriage of an innkeeper's daughter to an earl's brother excited widespread public interest. Under the heading 'The Romantic Marriage', Samuel Coleridge, who then lived at Keswick, described the event for the London *Morning Post*. The effect of this publicity was to demolish Hatfield's cover and expose him as a bigamist as well as a lying impostor. Coleridge's report was brought to the notice of the real Augustus Hope, who denounced Hatfield in a letter to the *Morning Post*, and it was also seen by George Hardinge, a senior Welsh justice and a personal friend of the colonel.

On his way home from Edinburgh to South Wales, Hardinge sought out the new bridegroom at Keswick. When confronted and challenged, Hatfield changed his story: he had been misrepresented; he was Charles, not Alexander, Hope, MP for Dumfries, not Linlithgow.

After the real Charles Hope's open letter to the national press and Hardinge's exposure, Hatfield's infamy was all too evident. Nevertheless, he cleverly eluded arrest by taking a 'fishing trip' on Lake Buttermere which became a successful flight from the district. However, letters of his left behind in an old trunk and discovered by his distraught, deserted bride revealed Hatfield as a bigamist as well as a criminal swindler and forger. Hearing of these letters Coleridge rushed off a second article to the *Morning Post*. What had previously been 'The Romantic Marriage' now became 'The Fraudulent Marriage'.

A few days later a police notice appeared in the *Daily Advertiser*, offering a reward of £50 for information leading to the arrest of the 'notorious impostor, swindler and felon' called John Hatfield, who had 'lately married a young woman, commonly called the Beauty of Buttermere, under an assumed name'. Hatfield was then described in considerable detail as five foot ten inches tall, aged about 44, with long, thick, light, greying hair tied up in a club, powerfully built with old duelling wounds on his cheek and two fingers of his left hand. His conversation was fluent and elegant but not to be trusted particularly by females since he was 'very fond of compliments ... and likely to insinuate himself where there are young ladies'.

By the time that Hatfield was cornered and apprehended in south Wales at the beginning of December 1802 his notoriety was national news. Coleridge had become Mary's champion: 'The Keswick Impostor I', his third article in the *Morning Post*, was soon followed by 'The Keswick Impostor II'. Both were heartfelt defences of Mary's innocence and virtue and denunciations of a bold, bad man who had seduced her. Consequently, even though neither Michelli nor Mary would testify against him in or out of court on a charge of bigamy, Hatfield was already guilty in the public view long before he was questioned in London by Bow Street magistrates and then sent for trial at Carlisle assizes.

'The Great Seducer', as Hatfield was now widely known, was finally brought before judge Sir Alexander Thomson at the Carlisle court on Monday, 15 August 1803. He was faced with three charges of false impersonation and forgery, capital crimes. However, during the nine days he had spent in the county gaol before the trial, Hatfield had won over everyone who had come into contact with him. As he gave convincing proof of repentance, generosity and deep religious conviction, revulsion turned upside down into reverence. When his escorted post-chaise passed from the prison to the Town Hall he was applauded by a huge crowd of sympathetic and admiring bystanders.

None the less, whatever favourable impression Hatfield had made on others, including the reporters on the *Carlisle Herald*, he did not fool Judge Thomson. The jury was instructed to return a verdict of guilty. The next day Hatfield was sentenced to be hanged, and the execution took place on Saturday, 3 September before an enormous crowd. With unfailing audacity, he had asked to be buried at Burgh-by-Sands where king Edward I had his grave, but his corpse was interred without ceremony or clergyman present in the local ground reserved for the criminal dead.

Hatfield's 'widow', Mary Robinson, had won the sympathy and support of the whole country, not least the poet William Wordsworth. Later, in *The Prelude*, he wrote of her as 'a virtuous wife' and 'artless daughter of the hills' who had been 'wedded ... in cruel mockery' then 'deserted and deceived'. Four years after Hatfield's death and her child by him, Mary married Richard Harrison, a prosperous farmer. They lived at Caldbeck in Cumberland and had four children. The death of 'the Beauty of Buttermere' at the age of 59 in 1837 was considered noteworthy enough to be announced in the *Annual Register*. On the other hand, of the fate of Michelli Hatfield and her two young children nothing is known. It is possible that all three perished on the road to Carlisle in the blizzards of April 1803.

John Hatfield, alias 'Major' Hatfield, alias 'Colonel Hope', was an accomplished liar, constantly on the run ahead of creditors, law officers and victims of his deceits. So many conflicting stories were written by and about him that it is now impossible to disentangle fact from fiction and to be sure of his movements and exploits. The last word goes to the *Annual Register* of 1803 which after his trial commented that his 'extraordinary career' was 'veiled in mystery' and would 'most likely remain so'.

21. Sir George Cayley

Whether Sir George Cayley eventually arrived in paradise is not yet known, but he was certainly born in Paradise House in Scarborough on 27 December 1773. His parents had taken the house only for the winter so that at the age of two months George was brought home to the family home at Brompton, seven miles inland from Scarborough.

George was the only son and heir of Thomas, who himself was heir to old Sir George Cayley, the fourth baronet. The Cayleys were descendants of a Norman knight, Osborne de Cailly, one of Duke William's followers in 1066. Edward Cayley had bought the Brompton estate in 1622, and his son, Sir William, was rewarded by Charles II with a baronetcy in 1661 for the family's sacrificial services to the crown during the Civil Wars and Interregnum.

As is so often the case, young George owed his precocious intellectual development to his mother, Isabella, a gifted, liberal-minded lady. She encouraged her only son in his drawing, to keep a daily record of his observations and experiments, and to mix freely and profitably with the people of the village, especially with the local watchmaker and blacksmith. By the age of 15 George was making notes on the locomotion of hares, how fish used their fins to propel themselves through water, and the flight of different birds. One of his early notes read: 'the downward beat of a crow's wing—by my stopwatch—is 2.647 per second'. About the same time he observed that it took exactly one hundred days for his thumbnail to grow half an inch.

Isabella also made sure that her exceptional son had an exceptional education. Instead of wasting his brain on Latin and Greek grammar at one of the local boarding schools for the gentry, George was sent to Nottingham to become the private pupil of the Reverend George Walker. Walker was a Unitarian minister with advanced political views, but he was also a fellow of the Royal Society and eventually president of the Manchester Literary and Philosophical Society. Walker taught his young apprentice mathematics as well as radical politics.

When George became dangerously friendly with his tutor's daughter, Sarah, after two years at Nottingham, his mother sent him further south to Hackney College in London. Hackney was another academy of scientific learning and left-wing politics; its principal, George Cadogan Morgan, was another Unitarian minister. These were the heady days of the early French Revolution and young George was naturally much affected by the extraordinary excitement and optimism of the times. At one point he even insisted on being called 'Citizen Cayley', though his mother refused to address him as such.

George's grandfather had died in 1791 and Thomas then succeeded him as fifth baronet. However, young George's father had never enjoyed any better health or luck than intelligence, and followed his father to the family's burial vault only a year later. So George was only nineteen years old in 1792 when he inherited the Cayley titles and lands. After another year in London he returned to Brompton Hall to take over management of the estate from his widowed mother.

In 1795, still only twenty-one, George displeased his mother by announcing his engagement and forthcoming marriage to Sarah Walker, daughter of his former tutor. Isabella thought her son too young to marry, and Sarah too headstrong, volatile and eccentric for Brompton. Soon after the marriage Sarah was outraging the Cayley tenants as much as her Methodist mother-in-law. Like any common gypsy woman, Sarah smoked a clay pipe in public; and, unlike any gentle lady, she rode to hounds astride of her horse. Even her husband, who was as open-minded as anyone, disliked her addiction to field blood sports. Sarah was too 'liberated' for her time and place.

Meanwhile Sir George's new responsibilities were not permitted to frustrate his zeal for scientific inquiry and experiment. His special interest in aerial flight had begun at an early age. Before his nineteenth birthday he had built a working toy helicopter from two corks, eight bird feathers, a wooden shaft and a whalebone. Soon afterwards he was considering the possibility of devising an engine 'which possesses the power of a horse with less weight than a man' which might propel an heavier-than-air structure. In 1804, Sir George wrote in his notebook: 'I am well convinced that Aerial Navigation will form a most prominent feature in the progress of civilization during the succeeding century.' Already he was a man of extraordinary imagination and vision, as well as scientific knowledge.

At an early date, Sir George applied his scientific and practical skills to the mundane problems of land reclamation. In 1800 he drew up a petition to Parliament for 'an Act for draining, embanking and preserving divers tracts of land within the township of Muston, in the parish of Hunmanby, and also within other parishes adjoining, or near to the rivers Derwent and Harford [Hertford]'. The petition was signed by other leading, interested landowners in the locality, principally Digby Legard of Ganton and Sir Christopher Sykes of Sledmere.

Cayley's project was to canalise and embank the two rivers named which every winter flooded an area of more than 10,000 acres at the eastern end of the Vale of Pickering. Thanks mainly to the persistence of Sir George, within six months the Act was passed. He became the chairman of the directors of the Muston Drainage Company, a post which he held for the next half century. Cayley engaged the expert services of his friend, William Chapman, a Newcastle engineer, and together they devised a drainage scheme which still works effectively two hundred years later. Instead of trying to run off all the surplus surface water into the existing river beds, ditches were dug parallel to the main river channels. As a result, land which had been virtually useless and worthless was sown with cereals or became permanent grassland for pasture.

As the paternal squire, Sir George had regard not just for his own pocket, but as a matter of priority for the welfare of his tenants and servants. During the Napoleonic wars, at a time of exceptional suffering and privation for most ordinary people, he saw to it that his own tenants did not starve. In 1805 he started a cottage allotment scheme in Brompton whereby every householder there was allowed at least half an acre of land to grow his own vegetables and fruit and keep his own poultry and pigs.

Sir George's concern for his tenants was expressed in another way: when the son of one of them, George Douseland, lost his right hand when working at the water-mill, Cayley set about designing and making an artificial replacement in his workshop. In 1845, after he had described his latest invention in the *Mechanics' Magazine*, Douseland was presented to Prince Albert at the Royal Society's annual soiree. The Prince was reported to have shook George 'by his iron hand and expressed himself much pleased with the ingenuity of its movements'. The Duke of Wellington, who was also present, was said to have been greatly impressed by Cayley's work.

However, Sir George, always the perfectionist, was far from satisfied: for many years he continued to work on improvements to his original design. Whereas earlier hand substitutes were little better than hooks or crude pincers for seamen and labourers, Cayley wanted to build a hand that could perform nearly all the functions of its flesh and blood predecessor. His later models, though never patented, gave the wearer the means to write with a pen, use a knife, fork or spoon, and even to pick up objects as small as a pin.

About the same time that he was granting allotments to his cottage tenants, Sir George was engaged in a series of outdoor experiments at Scarborough. During the winter of 1804-5, as Napoleon prepared to cross the Channel with an invading army, Lord Mulgrave, military governor of Scarborough castle and master-general of the ordnance, allowed Cayley to take one of the army's six-pounder cannon and gunpowder from the castle's arsenal. The ammunition, in the form of several original types of shell and shot, was designed and made by Sir George in his workshop.

Cayley's concern was aeronautical rather than ballistic, but he was curious to discover whether the range of a missile could be significantly increased and its accuracy much improved by its shape and form. The shots were fired into a calm sea beyond the harbour and their distance noted by 'an artilleryman conveniently placed for the purpose'. What the people of Scarborough and in particular its seagoing community thought of Cayley's alarming and noisy experiments is not recorded in his notebook.

As so often was the case, nothing practical came from these experiments. For nearly forty years neither the War Office nor the Admiralty showed any interest in Cayley's work and even then were not prepared to pay his expenses. Nevertheless, Sir George had proved to his satisfaction that with the same powder charge a bullet-shaped shell offered less air resistance and would travel much further than round shot; and that if given fins which spun it in flight a shell would find its target with greater accuracy and consistency. Finally, during the Crimean War, when Sir George was in his eighties, he sent designs of a breech-loading rifle to the War Office, and they too were ignored.

In 1808 Cayley wrote in his notebook that he believed a 'new mode' of making a lightweight wheel might be tried: instead of a thick, heavy wooden or metal spoke to carry the load, he suggested that 'a light strong cording' would be sufficient to strengthen the rim. The rim itself might be of cast iron. In the notebook he sketched a detailed description in words and drawings of how such a new kind of wheel could be made and maintained. Cayley's light wheel was intended by him to be used for flying machines, but the principle of his 'tension wheel' was later applied successfully to the design of the modern bicycle wheel.

In January 1826 Sir George published details and drawings in the *Mechanics' Magazine* of what he called 'the universal railway', his latest invention. The purpose of this mechanism, he wrote, was to allow locomotive vehicles to overcome 'the impediments and resistances of every sort of road, land, morass or water'. Instead of running on wheels touching the ground, such a vehicle would have a continuous rail, train or chain placed under and revolving around its wheels. Nothing came of Cayley's patent 5260 until its principles were later employed to construct the caterpillar tractor and the military tank nearly a century later.

Sir George's welfare concerns were not confined to his own tenants and employees: every reported human tragedy and all forms of public distress aroused his sincere sympathy and sometimes prompted his inventive genius. For example, when a lifeboat capsized in the mouth of the river Tyne, he went to his drawing-board to design a new model that would be unsinkable and self-righting.

Not surprisingly, Sir George was an enthusiast of steam railway locomotion. He was one of the first to recommend a new line to link Scarborough with York and plotted most of its eventual course a dozen years before it was actually built. However, as a witness to the death of Huskisson on the Manchester—Liverpool railway in 1830, he was greatly worried by the dangers of the new railways to their passengers and crews as well as curious bystanders.

As someone who had spent many years studying the dynamics of weight and speed he was alarmed by the fragility of passenger coaches and the poor protection they had against accident and collision. With safety matters in mind, Cayley recommended new designs for more effective buffers, padded cushion seats for all, not just first-class, travellers, and 'a broad, padded belt to be placed in front of each passenger'. On this last recommendation, he added, 'How John Bull may relish this sort of strait-waistcoat I do not know; but perhaps some modification of it for his own safety may be tolerated.' These words of wisdom were published in 1831; having recognised the necessity of safety seat belts in aeroplanes, motor cars and coaches, 'John Bull' still declines them in his trains.

Of mechanical arrangements to increase railway safety he suggested an automatic braking system supervised and operated by a conductor, and a lamp-signalling system to prevent collisions between trains; but his pessimistic forecast was that accidents were bound to occur however great the precautions taken. Finally, he deplored the practice of placing second and third class carriages at the rear of trains 'to serve by being smashed up with the bones of their passengers as buffers to those of the first class'. The one Cayley recommendation for railways which was never adopted, fortunately, was the use of wooden tires for locomotive and carriage wheels.

As early as 1809 Sir George had published an essay on the mechanical principles of aeronautical flight in *Nicholson's Journal*; it was the fruit of many years of thought and experiment, but his first public statement on the subject that most enthralled him. Soon afterwards the essay was followed by two more. This triple paper was an epoch-making document: if its ideas, facts and suggestions had been acted upon the powered aeroplane would have been flying generations before Orville and Wilbur Wright took to the air almost a hundred years later. As Orville acknowledged in a letter: 'Sir George Cayley was a remarkable man. He knew more of the principles of aeronautics than any of his predecessors, and as much as any who followed him up to the end of the nineteenth century.'

Absorbed from youth by the dynamics of flight, as early as 1799 Cayley had jettisoned the impractical notion of using moveable wings in imitation of bird flight and devoted his time and ingenuity to designing a fixed-wing craft. The basic configuration of the modern aeroplane— streamlined fuselage, a tail unit with elevator and fin rudder for longitudinal and lateral stability and manoeuvre, and aerodynamic wings which afforded maximum lift and minimum drag—was designed and built by him by 1809.

However, the answer to how such a structure could be propelled through the air eluded him. Given the need for an engine of minimal weight but great power, Cayley soon rejected the idea of a steam-driven aeroplane, or even a steam-driven balloon. In his long search for an appropriate means of propulsion Sir George experimented with many different kinds of engine, but eventually found none to suit his purposes. In 1807 he found the gunpowder engine too unreliable and dangerous; and throughout the rest of his life he continued to design and test various types of hot-air engines. Despite his many disappointments he remained rightly convinced that such a power unit could be made and that it would consist of 'the sudden combustion of inflammable powders or fluids ... in close vessels'—a remarkable prediction of the internal combustion engine. In the absence of petroleum, for fuels he tried alcohol, spirit of tar, and carburetted hydrogen gas.

Cayley's design of the form of the modern aeroplane was no mere drawing-board sketch: by 1804 he had already flown the first of what were to be many successful model gliders. From time to time, between other inventions he returned to gliders, making full-scale boy or man-carrying versions in 1809, 1849 and 1853. Of all his many glider trials the best known and most successful was the last in 1853. The final flight of 500 yards down Brompton Dale has long since entered folklore and is now encrusted with anecdotal and doubtful additions. Whether Sir George's last glider was monoplane, biplane or even triplane is not certain, since he designed models of all three versions, but it seems likely that its occupant in 1853 was a Cayley groom or coachman. According to the popular account, after the glider had crash-landed, its shaken 'pilot' was heard to complain respectfully to its inventor: 'Please, Sir George, I wish to give notice. I was hired to drive, and not to fly.'

At the age of forty-seven, Sir George wrote down privately what in effect was his personal agenda for living: 'Inform myself of the useful branches of human learning—history, philosophy, political economy, political creed, practical arts, works of taste and genius. Apply knowledge in acting wisely, and with energy, in favour of one's country, one's family, one's self and of the general welfare of the human race, and others, the inferior creatures in man's care.' Besides being intensely paternal and patriotic Cayley was a deeply compassionate and caring man who greatly desired not only knowledge for himself but to make it accessible to as many others as possible. As well as pioneer and prophet he was a most successful publicist.

In 1821 Sir George was one of the original founders of the Yorkshire Philosophical Society whose declared aim was 'to promote science in the district by establishing a scientific library, scientific lectures and by providing scientific apparatus for original research'. Cayley remained an active member of the society all his life and for some years served as its vice-president. In 1831 he was also a founding member of Scarborough's own Philosophical Society. During the same year, when the British Association for the Advancement of Science held its inaugural meeting at York, Sir George was present to pay his life membership subscription.

But Cayley's educational work was not confined to Yorkshire: what was at first called the Royal Gallery of Arts and Sciences and eventually became London's Regent Street Polytechnic Institution also owed its birth to Sir George. The royal charter of 1839 was granted in his name, and he was chairman of the Institution's directors for the remainder of his life. The purpose of the Polytechnic was to exhibit working models of machinery, such as the printing press, power loom and rotary steam engine; to provide laboratories for experiments; and to introduce visitors to the marvels of contemporary engineering achievement. Evening classes were held for students of navigation, engineering and the principles of railway engine driving.

Three times Cayley tried to found an aeronautical society, and three times he failed because of lack of support. The Aeronautical Society of Great Britain, the world's oldest of its kind, was not set up until 1866, nine years after his death, by men who owed their interest and expertise in the subject to Sir George's pioneer work.

Sir George was never unwilling to share his knowledge and discoveries with fellow scientists and the general reading public. Throughout his long, busy life he contributed dozens of major papers and lengthy letters to a series of leading journals of the time—*Nicholson's Journal*, between 1807 and 1813, Tilloch's *Philosophical Magazine*, between 1816 and 1829, and the *Mechanics' Magazine*, from 1826 until 1856.

During his lifetime Cayley acquired a wide circle of distinguished friends, correspondents and fellow enthusiasts, not just in his own country but also on the Continent. For example, he helped Baron de Ferussac found the encyclopaedia, the *Bulletin Universalle*. Amongst Sir George's many outstanding colleagues and associates were Charles Babbage, Lucasian Professor of Mathematics at Cambridge, that 'implacable enemy of organ-grinders', who never delivered a professorial lecture at his university but who invented the automatic digital computer; Sir William Siemens, fellow inventor, metallurgist and electrical engineer; Dr P.M. Roget, secretary of the Royal Society, but best known for his *Thesaurus of English Words and Phrases*; I.K. Brunel, engineer extraordinary; Sir Joseph Banks, the botanist who as a young man sailed with Captain Cook; Lewis Carroll, a regular visitor to Regent Street; and George Stephenson, inventor of steam-engine locomotives.

Sir George was also involved in parliamentary politics. At the height of post-war repression and reaction, in 1818 Cayley published a lengthy pamphlet addressed to the radical Major John Cartwright setting out his views on the controversial subject of parliamentary reform. He accepted that ultimately there would have to be universal suffrage probably under a republic, but he warned his readers of the perils of extremism that had proved so catastrophic in France. In his youth he too had been inspired by the example of the French revolutionaries, yet now he counselled caution and recommended only moderate, gradual reform of the British parliament.

For many years Sir George had been chairman of the Whig Club at York, the most influential party political group in the north of England.

However, it was not until the Reform Bill of 1832 had been passed and the franchise widened that he finally consented to accept nomination for a parliamentary seat. He agreed to stand for one of Scarborough's two borough places.

On the eve of the Reform Act of 1832 Scarborough had a population of nearly 9,000 living in over 2,000 houses, but only the 44 members of the self-elected Common Hall had the parliamentary vote. For more than half a century the borough's two seats had been in the 'pockets' of two aristocratic families and their clients—the Manners, whose head was the duke of Rutland, and the Phipps, whose senior member was the earl of Mulgrave. However, whereas in the last contested election before 1832, held in 1802, only 33 votes were cast, the Act of 1832 had extended the vote to all £10 householders in the borough, who numbered 508. The Great Reform Act had brought about just the extent of modest, cautious change that Sir George had recommended.

On the eve of the poll, in front of Scarborough's Town Hall, Cayley declared to his audience: 'I had the honour to be born, fifty-eight years ago, within a hundred yards of this spot', and promised that, if returned, he would represent the interests of the whole of his native town, and not merely those of any political or sectional group. Along with his fellow Whig and neighbour, Sir John Johnstone of Hackness, who polled 285 votes, Sir George was elected with 255 votes. The Tory candidate, Sir Frederick Trench, backed by leading members of the Corporation and standing in the Rutland interest, came bottom of the poll with 145 votes.[*]

Sir George's parliamentary career was brief and relatively unrewarding. In 1834 his petition on behalf of Scarborough's shipowners sank without trace, though his support for municipal reform eventually bore fruit in the government's Municipal Corporations Act of 1835, which finally swept away all the corrupt borough oligarchies such as Scarborough's. A system of local administration which had persisted for 600 years finally came to an abrupt end: in future the Town Hall was to be run by councillors elected by all the borough's ratepayers.

By 1835, when the fall of the Whig government forced another parliamentary election, Cayley's disillusionment with politics was all too evident. He stood again for Scarborough only because no other suitable Whig candidate could be found at short notice, and the result was a relief and a release for him. This time Trench came top of the poll with 176 votes, Sir John Johnstone second with 161, and Sir George third, with

---

[*] In a two-member constituency each elector had two votes

122. Cayley had 'fought' and lost his second and last parliamentary election.

Sir George Cayley died at Brompton Hall twelve days before his 84th birthday, and was buried in the family vault under the chancel of Brompton parish church. His wife had died three years earlier. They had had ten children, seven girls and three boys, but only Digby of the boys survived to succeed his father as the seventh baronet. It was said that Sir George had been born in paradise but lived in purgatory on account of the hard time his wife had given him, yet he was far too tolerant and considerate a man to be hurt by Sarah's ill-temper and strange ways.

Recognition and appreciation of Cayley's great achievements have been long delayed, particularly in his own country. The first biographical article on Sir George to appear in print was published in New York; and the first historical work to acknowledge his greatness was originally published in Paris. He was a conspicuous absentee from the *Dictionary of National Biography*, and had to wait until 1993 before appearing in that Dictionary's *Missing Persons* volume. Only after the centenary of his death were plaques, recording their illustrious associations, placed on the outside walls of Paradise House and Cayley's workshop in the grounds of Brompton Hall.

None the less, Sir George was a visionary genius, an astonishing prodigy, who stands above all the other subjects in this collection. The range of his interests and activities, the depth of his knowledge, the originality and inventiveness of his intellect and the energy, stamina and compassion he brought to all his work were extraordinary. Few men anywhere have lived a life more worthy and productive and passed on benefits more valuable and enduring. If England has its Leonardo da Vinci his name would be Sir George Cayley.

22. Thomas Whittaker

Thomas Whittaker's start in life could hardly have been less promising: he was born to poor parents on a farmstead at Grindleton in August 1813. Grindleton is in Ribblesdale and until boundary revision in 1974 was in the West Riding of Yorkshire; now it is in the county of Lancashire. In the early seventeenth century the village had given its name to an extreme religious sect, the Grindletonians, but even today on the edge of the Forest of Bowland and overlooked by Pendle Hill it is still rather remote and inaccessible; in 1813 it must have been much more so.

As one of a family of eight boys and a girl there was no question of a formal education for Thomas; laboriously and patiently he taught himself to read and write. The only school he knew was a Sunday School. By the age of seven he was already working at the nearest textile mill, which meant setting out at five in the morning to walk there and not returning home until eight at night. He was paid half a crown (12½p.) a week.

When he was ten his parents moved the family down the valley to Preston and then over to Blackburn. These were hard times and work was not easy to find. However, Thomas was highly intelligent and skilful and was soon earning wages well above the average as an expert cotton 'dresser'. Nevertheless it was not long before he fell out with his employer and fellow workers. They found his constant denunciation of alcohol increasingly intolerable. A crisis came when he refused to collect his weekly wages, as was the custom, in the local public house. Thomas was sacked. After that he moved back to Preston where he met Joseph Livesey, the temperance advocate. It was there at Preston, in the Theatre Royal, in 1835, at the age of twenty-two, that before Livesey he took the pledge to abstain from alcohol for the rest of his life.

Preston was the starting place of a movement that was destined to have enormous consequences. Thomas was one of the original seven pledgers there; when he died nearly 65 years later the temperance societies in Great Britain claimed to have made seven million converts.

It was at a temperance meeting at Preston that the term 'teetotal' was first coined. A notorious tippler, Richard Tanner, nicknamed 'cockle Dicky' because he sold fish, cockles and mussels from a street handcart, had come forward to take the pledge in a state of alcoholic incoherence. As a result, 'total abstinence' came out of his mouth as 'tee-tee-to-total' abstinence. From then on all total abstainers called themselves teetotalers.

Thomas Whittaker was not content merely to take the pledge himself: from the age of twenty-two he devoted the remainder of his long life to the cause of temperance. Abandoning his trade and leaving his young family behind during lengthy absences, he set out on the road to preach abstinence throughout every town and village in the British Isles. Everywhere he met resistance, and in some places hostility and physical threats. Churches and chapels shut their doors in his face. He was refused lodgings and often slept under hedges. Since bellmen and town criers refused to advertise his outdoor lectures, one of his converts, a joiner, made a wooden rattle for him. Subsequently all his speeches, indoor as well as outdoor, were preceded by a noisy demonstration of the rattle's powers. Whittaker's wooden rattle became his talisman and his trademark; he kept it all his life.

Nevertheless, Thomas overcame all obstacles and opposition. As he once told a friend: 'You know that I cannot work in kid gloves. I like to roll up my shirt-sleeves, and hit with a sledge-hammer.' Hecklers were dealt with mercilessly; Thomas had a quick wit, a caustic tongue and an instinct for spotting an opponent's weakness.

Within two years Whittaker's reputation had grown so much that he was invited to address a gathering of the newly-founded British and Foreign Temperance Society at Exeter Hall in London. There were perhaps as many as 2,000 people at the rally. Later, Thomas wrote that he had never before spoken to so many 'well-dressed and respectable people'. Such an audience might have overawed a lesser speaker but Thomas was more than equal to the occasion. In his own words, 'I held them for forty-five minutes between my finger and thumb.' Afterwards he was asked to become one of the Society's full-time, paid agents, a post he occupied for the next twelve years.

Thomas Whittaker first came to Scarborough in 1839 at the invitation of the local Methodists who then met in their chapel on Church Stairs Street. Ten years later he decided to make a permanent home in the town where he bought a Temperance Hotel in Newborough. Though he was to be often away from home on extended lecture tours, including one as far as the United States, he soon made his presence felt in Scarborough.

As early as 1850 he was elected vice-president of the town's Temperance Society, whose members included such leading local Quaker families as the Tindalls and the Rowntrees. The Society's 13th report that year contained a tribute to 'Mr T. Whittaker (who has recently become a resident in Scarborough) for his gratuitous exertions, which have been of essential service to the Society'. The accounts of 1850 show that Thomas had already delivered a lecture and donated ten shillings to the Society.

On the other hand, when it came to combating the political and religious rulers of Scarborough, Whittaker found his patience and his persuasive powers stretched to the limit. Access to the local press was denied to him: he had to address the burgesses by handbills. None of the religious denominations accepted him wholeheartedly; even some Methodists objected to his vitriolic attacks on brewers, publicans and distillers. For a time Thomas was a lay preacher at Queen Street but he fell out with the Wesleyans there and never returned to full membership. He came to have most affinity with the Unitarians. His strongest opponents were Anglicans and Catholics.

On two town issues, however, Whittaker defeated the Anglican establishment and what he called 'the Londesborough clique'. By 1855 the people of Scarborough had run out of burial space. Until this time they had interred their dead in denominational plots: Anglicans, Quakers and Baptists were carefully segregated in their own graveyards. Dr Whiteside, vicar of St Mary's, wanted this segregation of the dead to continue in new ground. If he had had his way Anglicans would have had an exclusive cemetery entrance and been divided from others by a stone wall and high fence of iron railings. In the event, after a public poll, Whiteside lost and Whittaker won. What became known as Dean Road cemetery, run by an elected burial board, was to be non-denominational.

Ten years later, Whittaker made another valuable contribution to Scarborough's future. By the 1860s the rapid development of South Cliff had reached such a point that it was clear to all but the most reactionary that the valley separating it from the old town would have to be spanned by a carriage bridge. Subsequently, it was alleged by Whittaker's enemies that he had objected to a bridge on principle, whereas in fact he had objected only to the original Town Hall proposal which would have meant cutting down nearly all the trees in the Plantation and narrowing Valley Road to a mere footpath. The bridge that was finally opened in 1865 saved the trees and spanned a wide road underneath it. Fittingly, it was Alderman Sir Meredith Thompson Whittaker, Thomas's son, who presided over the opening of the new, widened Valley Bridge in 1928.

One event which had brought Thomas into the most public and controversial prominence in Scarborough took place in early March 1861. Whitby's lifeboat had been called out to rescue the crews of endangered ships during a tremendous storm. After four crews had been brought into harbour safely, the lifeboat was launched a second time to go out to a fifth ship. However, the lifeboat capsized and twelve of its thirteen men were drowned.

After the inquest, which revealed that some of the dead Whitby men had been given or had taken spirits, Whittaker wrote a famous letter to the local press. He contrasted the sobriety and success of the Hartlepool lifeboat, which had rescued the crews of 26 ships in 13 hours and whose men were fortified with 'hot coffee', with the calamity that had befallen the Whitby men:

> The sympathy of the nation is touched for those men and their families, and justly so; but there is a sequel to the sad scene. The men had from mistaken kindness been supplied, in some cases freely so, with spirits by which more than one of them had lost that self-control and sobriety essential to safety in such a storm.... Oh this devil drink! What blind humanity!! What miserable ignorance!! There are more tempests from the public house than from the winds and more destruction in the bottle than in the fury of the waves.

Whittaker's outspoken letter was taken as a disrespectful attack on the dead lifeboat men rather than a denunciation of drink. An effigy of him was swung from a ship's spar in Scarborough harbour for half a day, paraded through the town streets, flogged and smeared with red ochre before being burned. It was said that the demonstrators against Thomas numbered 3,000.

Yet, as Thomas himself put it, 'The effigy business did me a lot of good; it made me many friends.' Two years later he was elected to the Town Council at the head of the poll for South Ward. After the declaration of the result he was carried in a chair shoulder high around the streets of the borough. A fisherman who had played a forward role in the public riot of 1861 walked in front of the chair carrying a temperance banner. Thomas served the next twenty years on Scarborough's Town Council with a break between 1873 and 1876. In 1880 he was finally chosen to be mayor. As the mayoral chain was placed on his shoulders he swung his temperance rattle in triumph. At his mayoral banquet he broke all precedent by banning alcohol and admitting women.

During his mayoral year Whittaker was appointed a justice of the peace in the borough. From the magistrates' bench he preached temperance just as he did from the mayor's chair. However, though he was usually lenient with drunken offenders, he was invariably harsh on publicans, brewers and distillers who made profit out of human weakness and misery.

At this distance in time it is difficult to appreciate fully the importance of alcoholic drink in the social, religious and political life of Victorian Britain. For most working class men and women, in town and country, the public house was the only social centre they knew and drink their chief solace. During the first sixty years of the life of Thomas Whittaker consumption of alcohol rose steadily. By the 1870s there was a licensed place for every 200 people in the land, and consumption had reached its all-time peak at an annual average per throat of 10 pints of spirits and 275 pints of beer. Public houses were required to close only between 1 and 2 am, and there were no restrictions on the ages of customers. It was common practice to 'soothe' babies with gin or rum. Workmen were paid wages in beer; candidates bribed voters with drink; elections were orgies of drunkenness.

In these circumstances, largely promoted by religious groups, particularly Methodists and Quakers, a number of temperance organisations had come into being. Thomas Whittaker was just one of many so-called 'temperance lecturers' who toured the country to denounce the demon drink. Unfortunately for them the temperance workers were deeply divided amongst themselves. The moderates campaigned for restrictions on opening hours and tighter licensing laws; the radicals wanted every locality to have a free vote on whether they would keep their public houses or not, the so-called 'local option'; and the extremists would have closed down every drinking shop in the land and prohibited the making, selling and importing of any alcohol. Thomas Whittaker was a prohibitionist, the most extreme of all temperance advocates.

Whittaker's advocacy of prohibition was utterly sincere and passionate. Indeed, he was passionate about all the many causes he espoused. When once asked by a legal counsel at a trial at York whether he was 'a warm politician', Whittaker replied, 'Hot, sir, hot!'. Though by nature a genuinely devout man, his hostility to drunkenness was as much medical as it was moral. He would have agreed wholeheartedly with one of the most graphic anti-drink inscriptions of the 1860s still to be read on a vicarage wall in Sussex:

There is no sin which doth more deface God's image than drunkenness: it disguiseth a person and doth even unman him. Drunkenness makes him have the throat of a fish, the belly of a swine, and the head of an ass. Drunkenness is the shame of nature, the extinguisher of reason, the shipwreck of chastity, and the murderer of conscience. Drunkenness is hurtful to the body: the cup kills more than the cannon; it causes dropsies, catarrhs, apoplexies; it fills the eye with fire, and the legs with water, and turns the body into an hospital.

Even in his seventies it was one of Whittaker's bluffs to bet any publican that he could outrun him in a foot race; he claimed that any teetotaler was always fitter than an habitual drinker. No one is known to have accepted the wager.

By the 1850s the question of drink had become inextricably tangled with national party politics. In oversimplified terms, the Liberals favoured reform whereas the Tories were backed by the brewers. For this reason, therefore, though Whittaker was in many other respects conservative, his temperance advocacy put him in the Liberal camp. Before the secret ballot was introduced in 1872, Scarborough's poll books reveal that Thomas voted Whig/Liberal in the contested parliamentary elections of 1852, 1859 and 1868; in the first for the Earl of Mulgrave, in the second for John Dent, and in the third for Sir John Johnstone and John Dent.

However, though all these candidates were successful, the tide began to turn against temperance and the Liberals in the election of 1874. With some exaggeration—probably because he himself was defeated at Greenwich by a whisky distiller—the Liberal prime minister, William Gladstone, complained that his government had been swept out of office in 'a torrent of gin and beer'. His government's moderate Licensing Act of 1872, which forced public houses to close at midnight and not reopen until 5am and banned the sale of spirits to under sixteen-year-olds, outraged the prohibitionists and aroused the wrath of the brewers and publicans. One Anglican bishop declared that he preferred Englishmen to be free rather than sober. Much to the dismay of men like Whittaker, Disraeli's Tories won a landslide victory in 1874. In Scarborough, Sir Charles Legard, the Tory candidate, had come top of the poll, forcing out John Dent, Whittaker's preference, and leaving the radical reformer, Professor Thorold Rogers, holding up the bottom.

In municipal politics too the reaction against licensing reform was evident. In the local election of November 1873 Whittaker and Tugwell, his running mate in the South Ward, were subjected to a barrage of abuse and invective. As the *Scarborough Mercury* reported, 'Placards and squibs of the most offensive and in some cases the most slanderous character were posted and distributed about the town with a view to damaging the prospects of the retiring Councillors in this ward ... We are sorry to say that another feature of the election was the apparent facility with which beer could be obtained by the voters, particularly in the South Ward, and cab loads were seen driven to the doors of certain public houses ... a great amount of drunkenness was seen ... and we have heard of several cases where men boasted of the quantity of drink they had obtained without being asked for payment.' Whittaker and Tugwell were unseated. Not until 1883 was a Liberal government able to pass a law severely limiting the legal expenses of candidates in parliamentary and municipal elections.

'The effigy business' might have won Whittaker friends in the 1860s, but it was his entry into newspaper proprietorship which helped to rescue him and his fellow radicals from the debacles of 1873 and 1874. At that time the town had no fewer than three weekly newspapers—the *Scarborough Gazette*, founded in 1845; the *Scarborough Mercury*, dating from 1855, and bought by the printer and stationer, E.T.W. Dennis, in 1870; and the *Scarborough Express* started in 1865 by W. W. Coopland. When pressure was brought to bear on Coopland to deny Thomas Whittaker space for his letters and articles, the latter started up his own newspaper, which he called *The Watchman*, and had printed in Leeds. However, *The Watchman* survived only two years from 1867 until 1869.

Soon after Thomas returned from his American lecture tour in 1875 he joined a consortium of local Liberals and radicals to buy the *Mercury* from Dennis. Two years later he secured a controlling interest in the weekly. By that time he had won back his seat on the Town Council in a by-election. Encouraged by their recent parliamentary success but alarmed by the Liberal take-over of the *Mercury*, early in 1876 Scarborough's Conservatives launched the town's first daily newspaper; they called it *The Daily Post*. The party political battle lines were finally drawn in 1882 when the Whittakers set up their reply; the *Scarborough Evening News* was an offshoot of their weekly *Mercury*. By this time, though Thomas continued to contribute under his old nom de plume of The Watchman, the *Mercury* and *Evening News* were effectively run by his sons, Meredith Thompson and Thomas Palmer. Not until 1986, when Paul, great-great-grandson of Thomas, sold out to East Midlands Associated Press, did the Whittaker era in Scarborough finally come to an end. By then all the rivals of the Whittaker newspapers had been killed off or taken over.

Thomas Whittaker died at his home at 1 Belgrave Terrace on 20 November 1899; his burial service took place nearby at Westborough Wesleyan Methodist church; and, appropriately, his body was interred in Dean Road cemetery which he had done so much to establish. The principal address at his funeral was given by W.S. Caine, Liberal MP for the borough in 1880-5, and president of the British Temperance League.

The long life of Thomas Whittaker had been one of heroic achievement and perhaps greater disappointment. He had lived to see Sunday closing in Scotland, Ireland and Wales, but not in England. The local option had been adopted by a Liberal party that had been out of office for the past four years and would remain powerless in opposition for the next six. Chapel attendances were declining. Millions had taken the abstinence pledge, but many had broken it and millions more despised it. Babies were still dying of cirrhosis of the liver. No advance had been made on licensing restrictions since the Act of 1872. Alcohol consumption had fallen since its peak in the mid-seventies but this was probably as much the result of growing affluence and security as of temperance propaganda. The inscription on the handsome tombstone of Thomas Whittaker 'temperance advocate' describes his defiant frustration and anger:

> Tell me not what strong drink has been, nor what it is intended to be. I know what it is now. It is Britain's curse, it is the God of this nation.

23. Baron Albert and the Denisons

In the autumn of 1926 the archaeologist, F C Simpson, carried out a preliminary excavation of a prominent earth mound on the edge of Seamer Moor near the top of Row Brow overlooking Scarborough. Simpson had previously discovered and exposed a Roman signal station on the sea cliff of Scarborough castle headland; and on Seamer Moor he hoped to find another Roman relay tower which might have linked Scarborough's with the nearest inland military garrison at Malton, or Derventio as the Romans called it. Sure enough he uncovered a deep, V-shaped ditch, a wide berm inside it, and a circular stone work crowning the summit of the hill—all features suggestively Roman in character.

On Ordnance Survey maps the site excavated by Simpson is called Seamer Beacon, since long after the Roman occupation the hill was used as ground for bonfires lit to warn the locality of impending invasion or domestic disorder. However, from the middle of the nineteenth century local people called the mound and the folly tower that once stood on top of it Baron Albert's Tower.

Baron Albert, the first Lord Londesborough, was born on the very same day that Lord Nelson won his greatest and last naval victory over the French and Spanish fleets at Trafalgar—21 October 1805. He first saw the light of day at 8 Stanhope Street, Piccadilly, London. He was the third son of Elizabeth Denison and Henry, the first Marquess of Conyngham. After school at Eton he served briefly in the Royal Horse Guards, but soon found military life too strenuous for his delicate health and too undemanding on his intelligence. At the age of 19 he joined the diplomatic corps and was first posted as attaché in the British legation at Berlin. Subsequently, he saw further service as secretary in the embassies at Vienna and Florence.

In 1833 Albert left the diplomatic service and came home to marry Mary Henrietta, fourth daughter of Lord Forester. They had a son and heir, christened William Henry Forester, before Mary died in 1841. By this time Albert had gone into politics: in 1835 he was returned as Whig MP for Canterbury, a seat he occupied until 1841, and then again from 1847 until 1850. In the meantime he had taken a second wife, Ursula Lucy Grace. Altogether, by his two wives, Albert fathered twelve children.

By 1850 Albert had changed his name and become one of England's richest men. The previous August his maternal uncle, William Joseph Denison, had died at his palatial home in Pall Mall. William

Joseph had no children but he did have an immense fortune, said to be worth £2.3 million. Of this he gave £500 to charity and the rest to his sister's third son on condition that he adopted the name of Denison only and that his personal property was to be used to buy land entailed on three generations.

The founder of the Denison fortune was Joseph, William Joseph's father. Joseph was a native of Leeds who had walked from there to London as a penniless boy in search of riches and, unlike most who had trodden the same path, found them. According to a later admirer, 'by unabated industry and the most rigid frugality' Joseph amassed a colossal treasure in money, shares and property. When he died in 1806 to his two daughters, the Countess of Conyngham and Lady Lawley, he left £20,000 each, and to his only son, William Joseph, an income of £15,000 a year. By that time, William Joseph, born in 1770, was already an established figure: he sat as Whig MP for the Camelford seat from 1796 until 1802, and represented Kingston upon Hull in the year of his father's death. Two years later he was sheriff of Yorkshire. The bulk of the Denison landed estate was in Surrey, which William Joseph represented as its county Member of Parliament from 1818 until his death in 1849; but father and son were keen to buy land in Yorkshire.

Consequently, in 1787, when it came on to the market, the Denisons bought from the Duke of Leeds his extensive estate on the outskirts of Scarborough. Altogether they paid him nearly £200,000—£15,000 for Willerby, £38,000 for Staxton and Flixton, £36,000 for Osgodby, and £110,000 for Seamer, Irton and East Ayton. Thanks partly to the effective drainage of the hitherto swampy carrs and the high price of cereals which thrived on their rich soil, these lands became enormously productive and profitable during and after the French Wars.

Soon after his inheritance and in fulfilment of the terms of his uncle's will, Albert added further to the family's Yorkshire properties. Londesborough Hall, situated in the East Riding between Pocklington and Market Weighton, had long belonged to the Cavendish family. However, in 1819 they demolished it and re-used the stone to build a new wing to Chatsworth House, their main country residence in Derbyshire. Their Londesborough estate was eventually sold to George Hudson, the railway tycoon. He made sure the railway between Hull and York did not pass through his land, but could not prevent his own bankruptcy and ruin soon afterwards. Hudson's downfall was Albert Denison's opportunity: in 1849 he became the new owner of the whole Londesborough estate. His uncle had been offered a peerage more than once but rejected it; Albert had no such reservations: in March 1850 he chose the title of Baron Londesborough.

Baron Albert's appetite for Yorkshire's acres seemed insatiable and his means to buy them inexhaustible. In 1854, for about £270,000, he purchased the manor of Selby and other land from the widow of the Hon. R Petre. About the same time he bought the estate of Grimston Park, south of Tadcaster, from Lord Howden. Altogether, within ten years, he enlarged his uncle's original holding in Yorkshire to about 70,000 acres, which yielded a gross rental income of nearly £100,000 a year.

Though Baron Albert preferred to live at Grimston Park when he was in Yorkshire, to Scarborough people he was always associated with the name of Londesborough. His summer marine residence in Scarborough's Crescent is still known as Londesborough Lodge; the oldest route to Scarborough from his estate at Seamer was re-named Londesborough Road in his honour; and Scarborough's old theatre and music hall in Westborough, which later became a cinema, was called the Londesborough.

In the winter of 1859, to avoid London's fogs, Baron Albert went to St Leonard's-on-Sea, but finding his health no better there he returned to his London home, 8 Carlton House Terrace. There he died on 15 January 1860. He was still only 54-years-old. Though his association with Yorkshire had been short-lived, in only a decade he had made a great impact in the northern part of the county, and chose to be buried at Grimston Park.

His funeral on 24 January was a hugely attended gathering. The London North-Eastern Railway Company provided special trains for the mourners departing from Scarborough, Bridlington, Hull, Beverley, Market Weighton, Selby and York. Up to six hundred breakfasts were served to those who arrived at Grimston. In Scarborough the bells of the two main Anglican churches—St Mary's and Christ Church—tolled between one and two in the afternoon, the hour of Baron Albert's interment in the family vault. In 'accordance with nautical tradition', vessels berthed in Scarborough harbour hoisted their flags to half-mast height. For one who was not a native of the locality and had made his first appearance there less than ten years earlier as a complete outsider it all seemed an extraordinary, even exaggerated, tribute.

Cynics might say that the tribute was to Lord Londesborough's wealth and not to his work, but they would be only partly right and wholly unfair. True, most of those who attended his funeral were only tenants and servants, present out of duty and because their expenses were paid, yet many more who did not travel by train that day to Tadcaster had reason enough to admire and appreciate the achievements of Baron Albert.

The first Lord Londesborough was a man of many, varied interests. Though he suffered from pulmonary tuberculosis—which ultimately killed him—and was therefore unable to undertake strenuous physical exercise, he was still the most active and energetic of men. On doctor's orders he was obliged to spend entire winters in Greece, Italy or southern France, where he had a villa at Cannes. Even so, Albert kept a journal on his travels which formed the basis of his published book *Wanderings in Search of Health*—full of interesting, descriptive detail of the contemporary Mediterranean scene as well as many references to antiquities there.

Baron Albert's first enthusiasm was for archaeology. If he had been healthier he would have spent much time out-of-doors alongside the diggers; as it was he had to be content to pay and watch others excavate sites and then to publicise and publish their findings. To his regret, his archaeology was more 'armchair' than 'field-work'. He had first shown a curiosity about the remote past when he lived at Bourne Park near Canterbury. His accounts of excavations of the Saxon tumuli on Breach Downs nearby, published in *Archaeologia*, furnished much of the evidence then available on the customs, artefacts and arts of the Anglo-Saxons. In 1840 he was elected fellow of the Society of Antiquaries, and three years later he was one of the founders and first president of the British Archaeological Association. At the first congress of the Association held at Canterbury he entertained its members at his home at Bourne Park and conducted an excavation in their presence.

After Baron Albert moved up to Yorkshire in the early 1850s he became the patron and financier of numerous pioneering excavations on his own estates, particularly those on the Wolds and in the neighbourhood of Scarborough. By the time of his death he had unearthed, bought and collected one of the finest private museums of antique and medieval art at his house at Grimston. Especially admired was his unique collection of armour and of gold and silver coins and rings. The baron made sure that all his pieces were professionally preserved and meticulously catalogued.

In recognition of his services to archaeology and antique art the first Lord Londesborough was elected fellow and later president of the Royal Society. His other offices included the vice-presidency of the Archaeological Institute and the presidency of the Numismatic Society. Without too much exaggeration, an admiring obituarist wrote of him:

'Lord Londesborough must be regarded as having placed himself at the very head of antiquarian science in this country.'

But Baron Albert was no bookworm. Whenever he spent summer time in Scarborough he went sailing in one of his yachts which he kept in the harbour there. He loved the sea and sailing. One of his many titles was Vice-Admiral of the Yorkshire Coast—an undemanding office inherited by his son and grandson. Another of his outdoor sporting interests was horse-racing. As befitted a nobleman of such gigantic wealth he owned a stable of race-horses and was regarded as a great patron of the turf even though his own mounts seem to have had little success. He was often to be seen at the meetings at York, Doncaster and Beverley.

When Baron Albert first toured his Yorkshire estates in 1850 he was greeted and treated like a reigning monarch. Queen Victoria could not have had a more welcoming reception, though she preferred to visit stately houses such as Castle Howard. When he first arrived at Seamer station on the train from York the first Lord Londesborough was met there by 150 of his local tenants, who drew his carriage through Seamer village to the appropriately named Denison Arms. Again, such acclamation might be regarded as no more than the customary deference to the rich and powerful, but Baron Albert was genuinely respected everywhere for his generosity and charity. As one of his many friends wrote of him: 'his benevolence was as ample as his means were great'.

Though William Henry Forester Denison, the second Lord Londesborough, might have been less worthy and deserving than his father, he was no less popular, particularly in Scarborough. In the general election of 1859 he had stood as a Whig candidate for Scarborough borough and came top of the poll, ahead of Sir John Johnstone of Hackness and John Dent, the other Whigs, and George Cayley of Brompton, the Tory. However, the death of his father soon afterwards and his succession to the peerage ended his brief career in the House of Commons. Nevertheless, when in 1863 he brought his new bride, Lady Edith, daughter of the Duke of Beaufort, to Scarborough nearly the whole population of the town turned out to watch his cavalcade pass from Seamer station to Londesborough Lodge. They were given a nine-gun salute.

The second Lord Londesborough had much more enthusiasm for sport than for archaeology, or indeed any other intellectual interest. For instance, it was noticed that whereas Baron Albert had valued Seamer and Irton Moors for their enormously rich potential as prehistoric cemeteries, his son saw them only as recreational playgrounds.

Horse-races were first held on Seamer Moor as early as August 1758 but lack of financial support from Scarborough Corporation brought the annual meeting to an end thirty years later. By this time the new owner of the moor was Joseph Denison. Assured by Scarborough Corporation that no races would be held there again, Joseph ordered the ground to be planted with trees. For the next half century no races took place on Seamer Moor until a new company was formed in 1867 and the following year the annual race meetings were resumed. All this was made possible by 'the consent and liberal patronage of the Right Honourable Lord Londesborough'.

Perhaps even above horse-racing Lord Londesborough loved cricket. The origins of Scarborough's late summer annual cricket festival are to be found in the famous challenge match between Lord Londesborough's XI and C I Thornton's XI, played on Castle Hill in September 1871. Since the War Office insisted that no charge for admission to its property could be made, Londesborough footed the entire bill out of his own pocket. However, he also made it plain that he would not continue to subsidise such a fixture unless more appropriate facilities were provided for it; so that indirectly his initiative led eventually to Scarborough Cricket Club acquiring its North Marine ground. In 1873 Londesborough staged a North versus South match on the new field, and three years later the first nine-day cricket festival took place there. The club took gate receipts and Londesborough paid the players' expenses and entertained them at his Lodge and at the Grand Hotel. The *Leeds Mercury* described the occasion as 'Lord Londesborough's Cricket Week'.

Londesborough's patronage of cricket was not confined to Scarborough: he was a keen supporter of the Yorkshire county club. Most of the members of Londesborough's XI was made up of Yorkshire players and whenever the county played at Lord's he was there to greet them, having driven into the ground in his 'four-in-hand'. In 1876 he was elected president of the MCC.

Yorkshire county cricketers were not the only distinguished guests at Londesborough Lodge. In three consecutive years, 1869, 1870 and 1871, the Prince of Wales, the future King Edward VII, stayed at Londesborough's Scarborough marine residence. The prince and his host were well suited: both enjoyed horse-racing, shooting game birds and sailing in yachts; both entertained lavishly and loved the music hall. However, soon after his return to Sandringham at the end of October 1871, the prince fell dangerously ill with typhoid fever. For more than a month his life was threatened. His father, the Prince Consort, had died of the same fever just ten years earlier, and the whole nation waited anxiously for news from Sandringham. When the doctors declared that Edward had survived and was on the road to complete recovery there was a palpable sense of relief felt across the country. As the prince's biographer later wrote, 'an elemental upsurge of loyal emotion destroyed republicanism overnight as a significant factor in British radical politics'.

That the prince had been infected by the notoriously foul drains at Londesborough Lodge there can be little doubt. Another guest there, Lord Chesterfield, died of the same disease on 1 December. Significantly, the Prince of Wales never returned to Scarborough, though his friendship with the Londesboroughs remained undiminished. In 1887, the second Baron was created the first Earl of Londesborough and also took the title of Viscount Raincliffe. Perhaps Edward and his mother, Queen Victoria, were well aware that Londesborough's drains had helped to restore the nation's regard for the heir to the throne.

The first Earl of Londesborough died in 1900 at the age of 65 before Edward succeeded his mother. Though still a very rich man, his fortune, like most of those of the English landed aristocracy, was in decline. Death duties had already begun to erode entailed inheritances and the land no longer yielded the huge profits known to Baron Albert and his uncle. The golden age of English cereal farming had passed.

Scarborough's annual cricket festival survived and prospered, but only because commercial sponsorship was called in to take the place of aristocratic patronage. Londesborough Lodge also survives, but only incongruously as the office of Scarborough Borough's Tourism Department. Scarborough's Londesborough theatre was demolished in 1960. The names of Denison and Londesborough are better known now as public houses than as people. Lady Edith's Drive became a public highway used by motorists who do not know it was named after the first Earl's wife. Similarly, Lady Mildred's Ride and Lady Grace's Ride are also now open to the public who walk along Row Brow but are not likely to be aware that Mildred was the first Earl's youngest daughter and Grace his daughter-in-law. Even the earldom of Londesborough and the viscounty of Raincliffe became extinct when the fourth Denison to hold these titles died as long ago as 1937. The present Baron Londesborough, Richard John Denison, is the ninth with this title. Baron Albert's Tower now belongs to Scarborough Borough Council and most of Seamer and Irton Moors to the Ministry of Defence.

24. Sir George Sitwell

In the spring of 1900 the Sitwell family posed for their painting by the American artist, John Singer Sargent, in his London studio. Head of the group stood Sir George Reresby Sitwell, fourth baronet, a handsome, tall, slim, pale, blue-eyed man with a turned-up moustache. Lady Ida, his elegant and beautiful wife, also stood in the centre of the portrait, arranging flowers in a silver bowl. Sir George was then just forty-years- old and Lady Ida little more than thirty. Of their three children, Edith, the eldest, already tall at twelve, stood next to her father, his hand resting affectionately and protectively on her shoulder; while the two boys, Osbert, nearly eight, and Sacheverell, not yet three, played happily with their toys on the floor.

Sir George paid fifteen hundred pounds for the painting, and was well pleased with it. *Punch* poked gentle fun at it, but *The Illustrated London News* gave it both prominence and praise. Yet, in fact, in almost every sense, the portrait was a fake, deliberately devised by Sir George to convey only what he wanted the world to believe. Though now he rarely mounted a horse, Sir George's long riding boots were meant to refer to his sporting ancestry. Lady Ida was too highly bred to fasten her own shoelaces let alone pick and arrange flowers: that would have been the head gardener's job. The loving relationship between father and daughter and the carefree contentment of the two boys were also fantasies. Sir George had never forgiven his first-born for being a girl, for having an aquiline, not a Sitwell nose, and for not having naturally curly hair. As for the boys, Osbert was already a disappointment, and both he and his younger brother had far greater regard for the Sitwell servants than for their own parents. Edith's precocious arrogance and burning resentment were the two genuine characteristics that her father could not and Sargent would not conceal.

Even the background to Sargent's group portrait was at least in one sense a deliberate deception: under Sir George's detailed direction it had all been transported from Renishaw Hall, the Sitwell home in Derbyshire, to Sargent's studio in London. The enormous dark panel of Brussels tapestry was from the ballroom at Renishaw; and from the same place came other family heirlooms—the superb sideboard designed by Robert Adam and made by Chippendale; and even the silver flower bowl was a Sitwell racing cup won at the Chesterfield races in 1747. As usual, Sir George had stage-managed every item.

Sir George Reresby Sitwell was born in London on 27 January 1860. The Sitwells, or previously Cytewels, had been settled in Derbyshire since at least the end of the thirteenth century, and the first Renishaw Hall was built by an earlier George Sitwell in 1625. During the following generations a succession of Sitwells had added handsomely to the house, its contents and estate, but in 1846 the second baronet was ruined by bank failure, the collapse of land values and the dishonesty of a trusted brother. For many years after Renishaw was abandoned in favour of cheaper accommodation elsewhere.

Sir Reresby Sitwell, the third baronet, had occupied Renishaw briefly in 1857 with his new bride, but within five years, at the age of only forty-two he was dead. He left a widow, two young children, George and Florence, and an impoverished estate; so that young George never knew his father and inherited his title from him at the age of two.

The Sitwells had old connections with Scarborough. Francis Sitwell travelled there from Renishaw in the summer of 1736 in his new chaise which had cost him £31. He stayed at the New Inn in Newborough and did what all the other well-to-do visitors to Scarborough did in those days—walked over the sands to the spa house early in the morning, dined at one of the ordinaries for a shilling, spent the afternoons at the theatre or in the coffee-house, and in the evenings played billiards, cards or dice in the Long Room. The spa waters did him so much good, the following year he sent his servant to Scarborough for some bottles of it to thin his blood. From then on the pattern was set: the Sitwells drove over to Scarborough nearly every summer season in their carriage, took lodgings on St. Nicholas Cliff in one of the boarding houses there and enjoyed all the special treats that the resort had to offer visitors with money.

However, it was Sir Reresby's widow, George's mother, who first settled in Scarborough. Thanks partly to her good business sense but mostly to the fortunate discovery of rich coal seams below the southern fringes of Renishaw Park, the Sitwell finances were soon buoyant. In 1867 she built a fine house on Scarborough's South Cliff and called it Sunnyside. Later she bought number 5, Belvoir Terrace, Belvoir House, and Wood End, both in Scarborough's exclusive Crescent.

In those days the Crescent was the private demesne of the rich and titled. The centre ground was a private garden and croquet lawn

191

surrounded by iron railings to keep out non-residents and stray animals. On the north side, Belvoir Terrace and Crescent Terrace were occupied by retired bankers, industrialists and barristers, and on the south side, overlooking Ramsdale valley with views of South Bay, were four detached villas. Wood End, built in 1835, a fine classical house of brown ashlar, was the most westerly of them. So as a boy Scarborough was George's summer playground and the millionaire Denisons of Londesborough Lodge were his close neighbours.

From an early age young George displayed an air of aloof superiority. Asked who he was at the age of four, he replied, 'I am George Sitwell, baronet. I am four years old and the youngest baronet in England.' Brought up almost entirely by doting women who indulged his childish whims and fantasies, he found in later life that he could not tolerate contradiction or correction. He was always right; only others were capable of error.

Another characteristic of Sir George which did not endear him to his fellow mortals was an early reputation for cleverness. When he went up to Eton in 1874 he was placed in the highest form accessible to a new boy, and within a short time he had reached the 'first hundred', the intellectual cream of the college. At the age of sixteen he published anonymously a slender volume of satires and parodies. During one particularly hot summer he sat up for several nights running, his feet in a bowl of cold water and a wet towel wrapped round his head, 'swotting' for the upper school history prize. To his astonishment he failed to win the history prize and instead was awarded the school divinity prize, for which he had not intended to compete. Many years later he told a Scarborough newspaper reporter, 'Looking back, this seems characteristic of many things I have done since then.'

When Sir George went up to Christ Church, Oxford, at the age of nineteen in 1879, his credentials were exemplary: he carried recommendations and introductions from a dozen leading Oxford men. However, no doubt unknown to one of his referees, his great-uncle and ward, Archibald Campbell Tait, the archbishop of Canterbury, George was already a confirmed atheist, or, as his son Osbert later wrote: 'He was no mere agnostic.' Osbert's explanation was that his father's childhood and boyhood had been 'martyred by religion', and that his 'unbending atheism' was a reaction to this.

Not that Osbert had reason to complain about his father's lack of religious faith: on the contrary, on at least one occasion, he was very grateful for it. As a ten-year-old boy he had suffered from recurring nightmare fears of hell and damnation, and when his father was told of this he said to Osbert: 'My dear boy, if you go to hell, you'll certainly find all the people you most admire there already—Wellington, Nelson, and the Black Prince—and they'll discover a way of getting you out of it soon enough.' From then on, Osbert was permanently cured of his terrors.

Another, at the time sensational, outcome of Sir George's scepticism took place in 1880. When still an undergraduate at Oxford he was one of a group of young men who exposed the fraud of an exhibition of 'spiritualism' at the headquarters of the British National Association of Spiritualists. A 'spirit' of what was claimed to be 'Marie', a twelve-year-old dead girl, was seen by Sir George and the others to be none other than the thinly-disguised 'medium', who had changed her dress behind a curtain. According to Osbert, after this experience, for his father there were 'no spirits, no ghosts, neither angels nor devils, no God, nothing behind the scenes, as it were, but the Law of the Survival of the Fittest...'. For the remainder of his life Sir George regarded this exposure as one of his best achievements: it continued to be listed in *Who's Who* as 'captured a spirit at the headquarters of the Spiritualists, London, 1880'.

As for Sir George's later religious beliefs and practices, his daughter Edith disagreed with her brother Osbert. She wrote that her father was 'an agnostic by profession' who 'said his prayers every night on the chance of this being a good investment'.

Sir George had convinced himself that the Sitwells would one day produce a genius, and that he was to be his father. Consequently, it was with deliberate care that he chose his bride, the mother-to-be of this future prodigy. He rejected the daughter of a Yorkshire peer mainly because she had a pronounced aquiline nose; he was on the look out for a Grecian. In fact, he did not need to look far: the Honourable Ida Denison had a perfect nose and she lived only next door but one to Wood End at Londesborough Lodge. Moreover, it was seriously believed at the time that she had royal blood running through her veins. Her paternal grandfather, Baron Albert Conyngham, who had changed his name to Denison, was reputed to be the illegitimate son of George IV by his mistress, the Marchioness of Conyngham. There was no proof of this, but it appealed to Sir George's imagination and snobbery. Also, Ida's mother, Lady Edith Somerset, was daughter of the seventh Duke of Beaufort, and could therefore trace her ancestry back to John of Gaunt and the Plantagenet kings of England.

From the outset the marriage was doomed. Lady Ida was only seventeen and her groom just as inexperienced at the age of twenty-six.

According to their younger son's later account, they had met only twice at luncheon before the wedding day. After only a few days, horrified by her close encounters with George, Ida fled back to her parents, who immediately forced her to return to her husband. In order to achieve the optimum procreative result, Sir George first read a number of improving works before summoning his wife to his bed by declaring, 'Ida, I am ready now.'

Sir George and Lady Ida had not one interest or characteristic in common: they were perfectly incompatible. Whereas she could neither add up nor subtract figures, he kept meticulous and accurate household and estate accounts. She was extravagant, impulsive, self-indulgent, pleasure-seeking and gregarious; he was parsimonious, austere, withdrawn and solitary. She stayed in bed until noon, read French novels and played bridge obsessively; he was an insomniac who smoked 20 or 30 foul-smelling Egyptian cigarettes a day, kept notes on everything, and read scientific journals. Whereas Ida's Londesborough family were sporting philistines, spending recklessly on race-horses, mistresses, gambling and yachts, and shooting fantastic numbers of game birds; the Sitwells, by contrast, were pious and penny-pinching. Sir George's children called their maternal relatives 'The Golden Horde'. Lady Ida mocked her husband by announcing that a baronet was the lowest form of life. Even their tastes in flowers clashed: she adored sweet geraniums, lilies and tuberoses, the stronger in scent and colour the better; he liked only the pale greens and light blues.

As his many notebooks testified, Sir George's interests were wide-ranging and peculiar. Some of their titles included 'The Correct Use of Seaweed as an Article of Diet', 'Rotherham under Cromwell', and 'Court Formalities at Constantinople'. He seriously considered the publication of an illustrated pamphlet which would describe his experiments to combat insomnia; it was to be called 'The Twenty-Seven Postures of Sir George R. Sitwell'. He had a life-long enthusiasm for medieval history, and was an authority on the Crusades and the Black Death. At the age of 25 he had contributed to an academic work on the feudal history of Derbyshire. However, his greatest interest was the history of the Sitwells. In 1894, on his own press, he had published a biography of one of his ancestors, William Sacheverell. Though he spent much labour researching the history of the fork, unfortunately he never published his discoveries.

In some ways Lady Ida was hardly less eccentric than her husband. She kept a length of old rope twisted in a knot tied to the head of her bed. When Osbert's curiosity finally got the better of him, his mother explained that it was a piece of a hangman's rope which had cost her eight pounds but was so rare that it was well worth keeping as a talisman. What magic the rope was expected to work Lady Ida did not say. Since Sir George never entered his wife's bedroom it is doubtful that he knew of the rope's existence, though he would have begrudged the eight pounds wasted on it.

Sir George had hoped to make a career and a name for himself in politics. In the seven elections he stood as a Conservative candidate at Scarborough he won only twice and sat in the House of Commons in 1885-6 and 1892-5. He had no natural gift for public speaking or political intrigue—two necessary requirements for success. During four years in the Commons he spoke only four times. His election victories at Scarborough he owed to his control of the *Scarborough Post*, the town's first daily newspaper, and the backing he received from the anti-Liberal brewers and publicans. When he won in 1885 the opposition press denounced him as the candidate of bankrupts, 'drunken swearing blackguards' and 'fallen women', not to mention publicans and brothel-keepers.

Though the Liberal party lost heavily throughout the country in 1895 and again in 1900, Sir George failed to retain and recover Scarborough's seat for the Conservatives. After his defeat in 1900 his involvement in politics gave way to a passion for continental travel and landscape gardening. He divested himself of the *Post*, which had cost him heavily in money and aggravation, and in 1906, much to Lady Ida's disgust, declared himself a Liberal. Thereafter she said he was no better than a socialist. However, Sir George's defection from the Conservative party had nothing to do with any political views he might have held: he took revenge on a party that had failed to reward his services with a peerage.

After his surprising rejection by Scarborough's electors in 1900, Sir George suffered a series of illnesses—most of them imaginary—which culminated in what would later be called a nervous breakdown. He was sure he was dying. He could not sleep. Restlessly he moved from house to house—Renishaw, Belvoir House, Londesborough Lodge, Wood End—sometimes spending only one night in each. Osbert's first knowledge of his father's plight came when he overheard the governess telling his tutor at Wood End how extraordinary it was that a grown man should break down simply because he could not get his own way in everything.

Sir George consulted several doctors and in the end took the advice which pleased him most—he should travel abroad. For the next half dozen years he journeyed all over Europe until he found what he half knew he was looking for. In the autumn of 1909 his motor car broke down mid-way between Florence and Volterra in Tuscany in front of a gateway flanked by two stone lions. By a rough path the gateway led to a ramshackle, massive, medieval ruin once owned by a family whose crest, like that of the Sitwell's, was a lion rampant. By 1909 this huge, crumbling building without running water or sewage system was occupied by 297 Italian peasants who lived precariously by growing their own food and plaiting straw.

In this accidental way Sir George discovered the castle of Montegufoni, the hill of the screech owls. He found it irresistible and bought it for £4,000. From then on he spent more and more time in his hill-top castle until finally he withdrew there from the real world altogether.

When the First World War began in August 1914 Sir George decided that it would be safer to move his family from Derbyshire to Scarborough, so that he and Lady Ida were at Wood End when the German navy bombarded the town the following December. During the shelling the Swiss footman went up on to the roof to watch it; Lady Ida stayed in bed; and Sir George found shelter in the cellar. A piece of shell that had passed through the front door of the house was taken to London by train the next day by Lady Ida. Triumphantly, she presented the steel fragment to Osbert, who was about to leave for France. She explained that it was bound to bring him good luck there.

Still at Wood End, Sir George refused to believe that the bombardment was over; he expected the Germans would soon come ashore at Scarborough in order to take him hostage. To outwit the enemy he therefore made elaborate plans to hide himself in a little thatched hut on an island in the valley below Wood End. Here he would live out the war like Robinson Crusoe, his boredom alleviated by 'a few books' sent down to him from time to time from the London Library.

Within days of arriving on the Western Front and joining the Grenadier Guards in the line, Osbert received a letter from Sir George full of fatherly advice. Osbert was unlikely to experience 'the same weight of gunfire' his father and mother had just survived at Scarborough, but directly he heard the first German shells he should seek shelter. To endure a lengthy and intense barrage he should keep himself warm, eat plenty of nourishing food at regular intervals and, above all, take long rest periods. Sir George recommended an afternoon nap!

Sir George's inability either to understand or appreciate his three gifted children was further illustration of his loss of contact with reality or even reason. There is space here for only a few examples. In 1908, Sir George threw a twenty-first birthday party for Edith: it took two years to plan, involved extensive and expensive redecorations at Renishaw and, though Edith hated horse-racing, was timed to coincide with the Doncaster meeting. Of the thirty guests invited none of them knew another and only two were of Edith's age. Throughout his life Sir George never forgave his firstborn for being female with an aquiline nose who later made a career of literature and the arts.

Sir George insisted that his sons went to Eton. Osbert hated every minute of it there. Later he took some revenge by writing, 'I liked Eton, except in the following respects: for work and games, for boys and masters.' In *Who's Who* Osbert defined his education as 'during the holidays from Eton'. Sacheverell's housemaster at Eton, an Anglo-Irishman with a sporting obsession, was later described by him to Osbert as 'the second stupidest man in the world after father'.

On one occasion, as a practical joke, Osbert wrote to his mother deploring the fact that her husband was squandering money on 'the Scarlet Woman' while his children lived in poverty. When Sir George was allowed to see the letter he exploded with anger and told his son that to accuse anyone falsely, let alone a parent, of adultery was a crime punishable by life imprisonment. Osbert wrote back to his father apologising for his 'unwitting' offence. 'We had heard of adultery,' he explained, 'but when we asked the chaplain to explain to us the meaning of this, he told us it meant "being grown up".' Sir George accepted his son's apology, convinced of his naïve sincerity.

When Osbert left Eton in 1911—a failure in the eyes of his father as well as his teachers there—Sir George refused to consider him for Oxford. Instead he packed him off to a military crammers' school to prepare for entry to Sandhurst. Osbert was careful to fail the entrance examination, but his father still secured him a commission in the Hussars. After a breakdown and recuperation in Italy, Osbert was posted to the Grenadier Guards. At least this got him away from hateful Aldershot and boring horses and into the society of London. However, in 1914, impatient with his son's wasteful, aesthetic life in the capital, Sir George found him a job in the town clerk's office at Scarborough. Fortunately for Osbert and the Town Hall, within a month the First World War began and he was recalled to his regiment.

After the armistice of November 1918, Captain Osbert was given leave to stand as a candidate for Scarborough's parliamentary seat. As a

Liberal without the benefit of Lloyd George's infamous 'coupon', he had little hope of success: his one advantage was war service, his greatest liability was the potentially damaging interference of his father, who came over from Renishaw to Wood End to give Osbert his unwanted advice. Sir George reprimanded his son for referring in his speeches to the past war and a future League of Nations to prevent another; the voters, he said, did not want to be troubled by such problems, they liked only facts. Above all, he should always conclude a speech with a quotation, the longer the better, and best of all from Byron.

Osbert appealed to his mother for protection. Between them they planned to exploit Sir George's hypochondria. Lady Ida told her husband that a pain in his waist was a dangerous case of shingles and he should take to his bed at once. The only cure was prolonged rest and isolation in his own room. In this way Sir George was kept in bed until the very day of polling when Lady Ida hired a bathchair and sent him to vote for their son.

Sir George's hypochondria was both acute and chronic. He had a dread of disease. He would go to considerable inconvenience to avoid the presence of the ill. Even colds frightened him. When young Osbert at the age of eleven was dangerously sick and had to spend four months in bed, his father never came anywhere near him—not even to the bedroom door.

In 1925, at the age of 65, Sir George decided to emigrate to his beloved castle in Tuscany. He shut up Wood End and moved all its furniture to Renishaw. He was easily persuaded that permanent retirement to the Mediterranean would be good for his delicate health and would also allow him to escape death duties. Accordingly, he wrote letters to Winston Churchill, then Chancellor of the Exchequer, to inform him of the consequences for the Treasury, and to the archbishop of Canterbury, for reasons which are none too clear. Sir George also pleased himself with the thought that, like Charles V, he was renouncing the world in the sunset of his life. In truth, his three offspring were delighted to have him out of the country so that they could at last pursue their literary careers free of his infuriating obstruction.

One question that bothered Sir George on the eve of his departure was what he should wear in Italy. He decided that a revolver was a necessity in a region notorious for brigands who held up motor cars on remote mountain roads; and his sons had no difficulty persuading him that he should also hang a dagger on his belt.

The enormous Tuscan castle and its huge grounds suited the ageing Sitwells. The role of 'Il Barone' in his castello was exactly the romantic-gothic pose Sir George enjoyed. They entertained—or at least received—a continuous file of guests, often unaware of their identities. On D.H. Lawrence, for instance, Lady Ida wrote: 'Mr D.H. Lawrence came over the other day ... He says he is a writer.' According to her husband, they had been visited by a man with red hair who said his name was Lawrence. After luncheon Lawrence's wife had jumped on all the beds to test the mattresses for softness.

Though Sir George loved to show visitors round his houses and their gardens, he also insisted that they should be obedient and obliging. To all who stayed at his home he addressed the following command: 'I must ask anyone entering the house never to contradict me or differ from me in any way, as it interferes with the functioning of the gastric juices and prevents my sleeping at night.'

When Sir George once offered Osbert a proposed guest list for an artists' party, his son observed that Whistler, Degas, Renoir, Rodin and Sargent were all dead. Time had become a total mystery to Sir George: past, present and future were utterly confused. Frequently he wrote letters describing events which had occurred centuries earlier as though they were contemporary. He was so wrapped up in himself and his own thoughts and theories that he did not always immediately recognise members of his own family.

Lady Ida died in 1937, but Sir George continued to live alone in his castle on the hill of the screech owls. He refused to believe that Italy and England could ever be at war with each other. When Osbert asked his father what he would do if the unthinkable happened, he replied, 'Take to the mountains'. These were prophetic words. Sir George died in Switzerland in 1943, three years after he had been forced to take refuge there. He never saw England or his family again.

Sir George Reresby Sitwell is remembered, if at all, only as the father of Edith, Osbert and Sacheverell, his three brilliant children. Nevertheless, however much Scarborough ought to celebrate its distinguished natives (Edith was born at Wood End and 'Sachie' at Belvoir House in the Crescent), their father deserves a place amongst the town's more notable eccentrics.

25. Joshua Rowntree

Two young men were strolling along the foreshore sands in Scarborough's South Bay when they heard a child screaming in fear. A little boy was stranded on one of the movable gangplanks used to allow visitors to enter and leave the coble boats without getting their feet wet because now the landing end of the plank was under water. Immediately one of the young men ran into the sea knee-deep, put his arms around the child and carried him to the safety of the shore. The two men then continued their walk. Not a word had been spoken either between them or to the boatman whose negligence had endangered his infant passenger. The saviour of the boy was called Joshua Rowntree.

Joshua was the first son and fourth child of John and Jane Rowntree. He was born on 5 April 1844 in a five-storied house in Princess Street, Scarborough. Joshua's paternal grandfather, John, had founded a grocery business in the town, and Joshua's father, a second son, had a shop at the corner of the top of Bland's Cliff and what was then called Carr Street but later became the upper limit of Eastborough. Joshua's mother was Jane, the daughter of a Pickering corn miller, Joshua Priestman, and twenty years younger than his father, who died in 1845 before Joshua was one year old. After the birth of a posthumous fourth daughter six months later, Jane became a chronic invalid so that Joshua was brought up in Princess Street by a hired nurse and the family cook, Bessy Fletcher from Lastingham.

The Rowntrees were Quakers. Joshua's father had spoken at a meeting of the Friends in St Sepulchre Street the morning of his death. His home in Princess Street was the place where Scarborough's Quakers held their monthly meetings. At that time the Friends all still wore the plainest of clothes and were easily recognised when they went abroad; and they were still the victims of much persecution and ill-treatment, both legal and social.

Later Joshua recalled that as a boy he was called 'Quack, quack, quack' by 'street urchins'. His father had already done much in Scarborough as a Poor Law Guardian, a town councillor, founder of the

Lancasterian school and leading campaigner for the abolition of church rates to diminish discrimination against Nonconformists, but in 1845 there was still some way to go before they achieved equality with Anglicans.

At the age of eight Joshua was sent to Scarborough Grammar School which was then kept in a town house by a certain Mr James Sykes. According to Joshua's recollections, the headmaster 'believed much in dunce-caps and caning. I have seen five boys whacked and perched up at once.' Religious teaching there he described as 'very unedifying'. Within a year he was withdrawn and then sent to a 'venerable ex-Wesleyan minister at Falsgrave'. However, his teaching was 'very wooden' and within a short time Joshua became a boarder at the Friends' School at Bootham in York.

Because of his unusual size Joshua was soon dubbed 'elephant' by his fellow pupils at Bootham. He was top of his class in history but in no other subject came anywhere near such distinction. He volunteered to stoke the school boiler and fires for sixpence a week. Presumably he was thought to have the physique for such laborious employment. School games were unorganised and unsupervised but they suited Joshua because of his superior weight and height. From a teacher who lacked a sense of humour but not a taste for sadism he learned only a smattering of the German language.

After Bootham Joshua was articled for four and a half years to a firm in York of 'good Evangelical church solicitors'. There he learned little law but read a great deal of history and poetry. He was already deeply interested in politics. On most contemporary questions, such as the Game laws, land law, Nonconformist rights and American negro slavery, he took a radical position. As his diary reveals, he was a very serious young man. In 1863, at the age of nineteen, he was deploring his loss of temper, his idleness, and his outspoken extremism. He had 'foolishly' wasted time reading a novel; and he had allowed himself to lose self-control during a heated debate.

After a further year of law study in London, at the age of twenty-two, Joshua returned to Scarborough there to set up a solicitor's practice with Mr William Drawbridge. He and his mother and three surviving sisters moved from Princess Street in the old town to one of the three houses on Ramshill Road known as Rawdon Villas. Very soon Joshua was in the thick of local politics and controversy.

In 1868 Scarborough Borough Council decided to sell their Town Hall in St Nicholas Street to a bank and move their meetings to the

Justices' Court or Court House in Castle Road. Joshua agreed to become secretary to a committee which was set up to oppose this decision. When the Council refused to yield, the committee appealed directly to the Lords Commissioners of the Treasury who withheld their consent until after the forthcoming municipal elections. When Joshua's committee's candidates won both the North and South Ward seats on the Council, the sale was cancelled. The old Town Hall was then re-designed as a public room above shops on the ground floor. It was Joshua's first local success and it brought him into the limelight of municipal politics. Soon afterwards he and Drawbridge prevented the privatisation of a long flight of steps running down from the South Cliff to the Spa buildings; they were restored to full, free public use.

Joshua was a natural radical. Even as a boy on his jacket he had sported the orange rosette of the Whig-Liberals. He read all the works of John Stuart Mill, the libertarian, and regarded him as one of England's most gifted and noble authors. He was especially enthusiastic about Mill's championship of women's rights. He supported Josephine Butler and others in their campaign to repeal the Contagious Diseases Acts which had legalised prostitution in the 1850s. His political heroes were the Liberals, John Bright and William Gladstone.

However, Joshua soon found the Liberal party too conservative and complacent. After the Reform Act of 1867 had merely doubled the male electorate from one to two million and excluded all women on principle from the parliamentary franchise, he was told by John Dent, one of Scarborough's Members of Parliament, that no further reforms of the House of Commons were necessary. Consequently, when the next general election occurred in 1874, a committee of radical Liberals, chaired by Joshua, invited Professor Thorold Rogers to stand for one of Scarborough's two parliamentary seats. Since there were already two official Liberal party candidates, Sir Harcourt Johnstone and John Dent, and only one Conservative, Sir Charles Legard, the Tory vote went entirely to Sir Charles, who came top of the poll, whereas the opposition vote was split three ways. Professor Rogers came bottom but received enough votes to put Dent into third place and deprive him of his seat. Naturally, the Liberal leadership was greatly annoyed by Joshua and his meddling committee: John Bright, who admired John Dent, said that Rowntree should not be allowed out without a nursemaid.

Undeterred by initial defeat and the rebukes of the Liberal establishment, Joshua continued to support radical causes and radical candidates. In the next general election of 1880, he gave his backing to

W.S. Caine, a left-wing Liberal, who came second in the poll to Johnstone and beat both Tory candidates. Joshua's opening speech at the first meeting of the contest was judged by many to have been the most memorable and effective of the whole campaign.

In 1885 Joshua and John Woodall, the banker, toured the area speaking in favour of Gladstone's Third Reform Act. The Bill that had extended the vote to farm labourers was well received in the rural districts, but most Scarborians were outraged that in the redistribution of seats their borough had been deprived of one of its two representatives. As a result, in the general election of that year, Scarborough's one seat went to the Tory, Sir George Sitwell.

The following year, when the Liberal party was grievously split by Gladstone's Irish Home Rule Bill, Rowntree stood by the Prime Minister, even though no fewer than five former Liberal MPs of the borough joined with the Conservatives to oppose him and an Irish parliament. Though it meant giving up his office of town mayor before its term expired, paying a fine of £50, and facing the wrath of many former political allies, Joshua accepted the invitation to stand as a Home Rule candidate in the election of July 1886.

Joshua was confronted by the sitting Conservative, Sir George Sitwell, the anti-temperance lobby of brewers and publicans, anti-Irish and anti-Catholic bigotry and the implacable hostility of the Liberal Unionists, but he argued the case for Home Rule with such sincere conviction and persuasion that he won the seat by 102 votes. With only one exception, Scarborough was the only constituency in England to record a Liberal gain.

The rejection of Gladstone and his Home Rule cause by the British electorate meant that Joshua Rowntree spent the full-length Parliament of 1886-92 on the opposition benches. Yet despite the loss of many former friends it cost him, he continued to espouse the Irish cause. Fearlessly and prophetically, he condemned Conservative coercion of the Irish nationalists as foolish, immoral and ultimately self-defeating. After a tour of Ireland in the autumn of 1886 he was able to speak from first-hand experience as well as passionate belief of the appalling suffering of evicted tenants and imprisoned nationalists. One letter he wrote from Ireland to Scarborough concluded with the phrase, 'It makes one sick at heart'. Altogether, as a Member of Parliament, he visited Ireland seven times and struck up close friendships with several Irish Home Rule Party leaders such as William O'Brien, John Dillon and Tim Healy, though not, apparently, with Charles Stewart Parnell.

At a time when trade unionists were regarded generally as subversive or even criminal, Joshua was their sympathetic champion. It was always in his nature to take the side of the underdog. As a Member of Parliament he made it his duty to keep in touch with the trades council in Scarborough, attended many local union branch meetings, and fought against greedy and oppressive employers. When one of his Adult School pupils accused a Scarborough builder of using sweated labour and was sued for slander, Joshua investigated the allegations and found them to be entirely true. The slander writ was dropped on his insistence.

Throughout his long active public career Joshua also promoted the cause of women's rights. Though they were still denied the parliamentary franchise, he was the first candidate in Scarborough to hold election meetings for women only. Women were also not allowed to sit on juries, court benches or councils, but there were some public offices open to the most able, bold and ambitious. In 1870, Joshua persuaded Miss Florence Balgarnie, daughter of the Congregational minister, to contend for a place on Scarborough's new School Board, and helped to secure her election. Two years later, he sponsored the candidature of two ladies for places on Scarborough's Board of Poor Law Guardians. Only one of them was successful and even she was most reluctant to take her place as the sole female on the Board which hitherto had been exclusively male. However, Joshua persuaded her to take her rightful place, arguing that if she withdrew it would set back the cause of the advancement of women to act on public bodies.

Joshua had married Isabella Tindall of Kirby Misperton Hall, near Pickering, in 1880, the year of his mother's death. She was the daughter of Robert Tindall, who had been a Scarborough Quaker, along with his shipowning, shipbuilding brothers, William and James, until they were forced to arm their crews who refused to sail without weapons. The Tindalls had once been neighbours of the Rowntrees in Princess Street, but they were Tories and had always worn blue colours at election times. So when Joshua and Isabella were married at Ilkley, not in the Meeting House on St Sepulchre Street, or even in Scarborough or the bride's local church, their choice of location was intended to avoid any embarrassment their choice of partners might have caused. Nevertheless, after the honeymoon, Joshua brought his new wife back to Scarborough to live at Rawdon Villas. It was there that their only son, Maurice Lotherington Rowntree, was born in 1882. Whatever the religious and political handicaps to it, their marriage was to be long and happy.

In 1892 Joshua lost his parliamentary seat to his old enemy, Sir

George Sitwell. However, though he never made any further bid to sit in the House of Commons, Joshua's interest and involvement in politics, national and international, remained strong. Of the many worthy causes in which he engaged himself one was to suppress the opium trade between British India, its principal supplier, and China, its main market. A Royal Commission, set up in 1893, had investigated the scandal and produced seven large Blue Books of evidence. Rowntree read them all and for several years worked doggedly on what eventually became his *Imperial Drug Trade*, first published in 1905. After the return of a Liberal government with a huge majority in 1906 Joshua's hopes rose, but he had to wait until 1913 for the news that the export of opium had been finally prohibited.

Of all Joshua's many enthusiasms perhaps the one that he valued most dearly was adult education. Soon after his return to Scarborough from London in 1866 he had set about founding a school for adults in the town. Two painters, a bricklayer, and a labourer came to his Sunday class for a few weeks and then left, in his own words, 'for richer pastures'. Every week Joshua walked down Ramshill to the Valley, along the sands of the foreshore, up the Lifeboat then the Courting Steps to the improvised schoolroom above a fish warehouse in St Sepulchre Street, each time hoping that he would find there more not fewer 'scholars' in his class. Eventually, the word spread and Joshua's Sunday class prospered and expanded. He welcomed all, not just Quakers. He had a natural gift for teaching. However ignorant or foolish his pupils he never talked down to any of them. Whenever he was away from Scarborough he wrote long letters to his class telling them what he had seen and done and what his thoughts were. Two buildings that still stand in Scarborough owe their existence to Joshua's promotion of adult education. In 1875 a new Adult School was built in the garden behind the Friends' Meeting House; and in 1903 Joshua laid the foundation stone of a new centre for Scarborough Adult School—the Roscoe Rooms.*

Out of Joshua's Adult School came a rowing club which in time became Scarborough's Amateur Rowing Club; Joshua was its president until his death. As a boy he had watched the cargo ships and fishing boats coming into and leaving Scarborough harbour from his bedroom window in Princess Street, and it planted in him a lifelong love of the sea. He was never happier than when rowing a boat in South Bay or when sailing with

---

* Since these words were written, Rowntree's former Adult School in Springfield has been demolished.

and talking to Scarborough's fishermen. The 'East Enders' or 'old towners' were Joshua's most loyal constituents.

Joshua's earliest memory of his abhorrence of violence came during the Crimean War when he was about ten years old. Next door to his house in Princess Street there lived a retired ships' carpenter with whom the young Joshua spent many happy hours. The carpenter made for him a model of the schooner *Talitha* and together they sailed it in the Castle yard pond. One day when he was chopping firewood for the Rowntrees in their front cellar the old carpenter moved the block with his foot and said to Joshua, 'I wish this was the neck of Tsar Nicholas.' Joshua's reaction he recorded later with these words: 'As often in my life, I felt that there was something wrong in the utterance, but did not see how it was to be put right.'

As he grew older Joshua's pacifism grew stronger. He devoted more and more of his time and energy to the cause of peace. In his lectures, his diaries and his work peace was a continuing theme. As a Member of Parliament he had attended the third international peace congress, held in Rome in 1891. When the Boer War began in 1899, he was a natural choice as chairman of Scarborough's South African Conciliation Committee.

By March 1900 the war in South Africa was only six months old yet British forces there had already sustained heavy, humiliating defeats. Anti-Boer feeling in Britain was widespread and bitter. Nevertheless, Rowntree and his committee invited Cronwright Schreiner, a former member of the Cape Parliament, to speak in public at Scarborough. Schreiner's meetings in other towns had previously caused disturbances; his mere presence in Scarborough caused a riot.

Schreiner was to address a public gathering at the old Town Hall in St Nicholas Street on 13 March. Joshua invited guests to meet him the evening before at Rowntree's Cafe in Westborough between 8.30 and 10.30. By seven o'clock first tomatoes then stones were being thrown at the windows of the cafe by members of an increasingly large and angry street mob outside. The Chief Constable and the Chairman of the Watch Committee entered the cafe and advised Joshua to abandon his reception and leave by the back door.

Joshua himself was one of the last to depart and as he walked alone down Huntriss Row he was jeered and jostled by the crowd. His hat was knocked off his head and he was fortunate not to receive a blow from a stick aimed at him. He had to take sanctuary in a neighbouring house. When he finally reached his home in Ramshill he found that stones had been thrown through his drawing-room windows. Other members of the Rowntree family also had their houses and shops attacked. The mob remained in Westborough until ordered to disperse by Captain Fell who commanded the troops he had marched out from nearby Burniston Barracks.

Of the many letters of sympathy and support sent subsequently to Joshua one was from the leader of the Labour party, Keir Hardie. When Joshua issued a public statement on behalf of his family, declining to make any claim for compensation but deploring the attacks on freedom of speech as well as persons and property, he received further widespread endorsement from other political leaders and in the national press.

Nine months later, in December 1900, Joshua and Isabella sailed to Cape Town. Their mission was to examine at first-hand the rumours and reports of concentration camps, atrocities and other indignities and cruelties suffered by the Boers and their families in the aftermath of military defeat. What the Rowntrees found confirmed their worst fears. Joshua's description of the harrowing conditions of the concentration camps in Natal and Cape Colony (he was not allowed to enter the Orange Free State or Transvaal) was later quoted in the House of Commons. There, Lloyd George, the young Liberal radical, referred to Joshua as 'a former Member of this House—and everyone who knows him will be convinced of the accuracy of every statement he makes. His word is as good as his oath.'

The outbreak of the European war in August 1914 was a devastating blow to an ageing Joshua. For some years before he had been fearful of such a disaster and had tried to foster better relations with the Germans. For instance, in the summer of 1912, he had invited a party of German Friends from Frankfurt to stay in Scarborough and attend meetings and adult classes there. The following year he was president of the National Peace Congress held at Leeds. In his last public speech, made in the Friends' Meeting House at Manchester in September 1914, he regretted that European governments were now in the grip of army generals and admirals who were using 'the anarchic barbarism of war' to pursue their 'blind materialism'.

The German bombardment of Scarborough three months later must have grieved him sorely, not only for the destruction it caused but also for the jingoist hysteria it provoked in reply. Typically, however, he was never a dogmatic pacifist: for those Friends who now enlisted or joined the medical corps he expressed nothing but sympathy; he would not agree to their expulsion.

In 1912 Joshua and his son Maurice had bought a cottage by the site of the first Quaker Meeting House at Staintondale, a few miles north of Scarborough. They called the house 'Worfolk' in memory of a Staintondale Friend who had lived there in the seventeenth century. Increasing deafness and physical weakness now restricted Joshua's activities; he spent more of his time at 'Worfolk' and less at Rawdon Villas, now occupied by Maurice, his wife and their two daughters.

In June 1914 Joshua entertained members of the summer school, that year held at Whitby, at 'Worfolk', but this was to be the last of such occasions for him. Just before Christmas 1914 he was brought to a nursing home in Scarborough and then in January 1915 to Wrea Head at Scalby, the home of his widowed sister, Maria. It was there that he died on 9 February. Appropriately, his body was carried to the grave by men of his own Adult School at Scarborough.

Joshua had travelled all over the world but he always came back to Scarborough, the place he loved above all others. He had spent more than half a century studying everything about his native town—its history, its geology, its fauna and flora. His house on Ramshill was rich in paintings, photographs and books of and about Scarborough, and wide, thoughtful reading had made him an authority on the archaeology and history of the town and its vicinity. For instance, in 1908, he spoke to Scarborough's Philosophical and Archaeological Society on the title 'Prehistoric Man in the District'.

Joshua's guided tours of Scarborough castle were remembered by many with profit and pleasure. Naturally, he had made a special study of the history of Quakerism in the Scarborough area, and with unique authority he spoke and wrote about those courageous Friends, such as George Fox, John Whitehead and Richard Sellers, who had suffered for their faith. He would have been far too modest to have counted himself in their company.

26. Harry Smith

On Friday, 4 August 1944, a brief obituary notice appeared in the *Scarborough Mercury*: it announced the death on the previous day of Harry William Smith. On another page in the same issue under the rather ambiguous heading 'Hand That Laid Out Scarborough', an anonymous journalist explained that Mr Smith had been chief borough engineer for 36 years during which time he was mainly responsible for making Scarborough into a town of gardens. Here there were references to tree-planting on the slopes of Oliver's Mount and Woodland Ravine, to the Mere and the Floral Hall, but not to works normally associated with the borough engineer's department. Harry Smith might have been no more than the Corporation's head gardener had the reader not been aware that in fact he was the architect of twentieth-century Scarborough.

Harry William Smith was born in Birmingham in 1867, the younger son of Mr and Mrs George Fabian Smith. After 'apprenticeship' with Birmingham Corporation he moved on to Bournemouth where he became deputy borough engineer in 1892. No doubt his experience of and record with another high-class seaside resort counted in his favour when in 1896 he applied for the position of borough engineer and surveyor at Scarborough. However, still only 29-years-old and looking still younger, Harry was worried that the selection committee would think him too immature for the post; so he came up to Scarborough for the first time with a full beard to disguise his youthful appearance. Nevertheless, even a bearded Smith just scraped in by a committee majority of only one vote.

On 21 December 1896, a date of utmost significance in Scarborough's long history, Harry Smith was selected to succeed Joseph Petch as the town's chief engineer. The appointment was to take effect on 1 February 1897 at a salary of £300 a year with annual increments of £25 up to a maximum of £400 a year. Harry shaved off his beard and got down to work at once.

By 1897 Scarborough had reached a critical time in its development as a coastal holiday and health town. In June of that year the mayor had laid the first block of stone of what was to become the Marine Drive—

209

1,200 metres of promenade carriage-way and sea wall which would complete Scarborough's seafront by linking Sandside with the Royal Albert Drive, South and North Bays. But there had been much opposition to this boldly adventurous project: the Earl of Londesborough thought it would spoil the natural grandeur of the headland and North Cliff; the residents of South Cliff resented the benefits it would bring only to the North Side; and many ratepayers and councillors were appalled by estimates of costs which ranged from £62,000 to £85,000. If it had been known that instead of three it would take nearly eleven years to finish at a total cost of £124,700, the Marine Drive would never have been started.

Everyone underestimated the tremendous power of the North Sea, particularly when driven by storm-force winds against the exposed headland. Time and time again gales wrecked the newly-built sea wall and brought down boulders from the cliff face above. Expenses mounted; the original contractors went bankrupt and their successors took the borough council to court; and two resident engineers resigned in despair and defeat. At the beginning of 1905, after a tempest had demolished the North Pier and done serious damage to the Drive, Harry Smith was put in charge of further operations.

After yet another January storm in 1908, the Marine Drive was finally opened to the public the following April and officially inaugurated in August by one of Queen Victoria's sons, Arthur, Duke of Connaught. Harry Smith was present on both occasions, but it is unlikely that he was given much personal credit for the completion of what was then agreed to be Europe's finest seafront promenade and marine carriage-way.

By 1908 Smith was acknowledged, at least locally, as the most efficient and imaginative engineer the borough had ever employed. During the previous decade he had already begun, in the words of one of the town's leading councillors, 'to develop Scarborough majestically'.

Harry Smith's first design was that of a public shelter at the junction of Victoria Road and Westborough where Falsgrave meets Scarborough. After more than a hundred years of misuse, neglect and weathering, Smith's elegant but sturdy iron shelter has survived and was recently rewarded with well-earned renovation.

The conversion of St Nicholas House into Scarborough's Town Hall was Smith's earliest major undertaking. The house and its extensive grounds running down to Foreshore Road had been bought from the Woodall family by the Corporation in 1898 for £33,575. As a private residence it was spacious and grand, but quite inadequate for the borough's purposes and needs. Nevertheless, Smith kept the Woodalls' furnishings, fireplaces and wooden panelling and extended the building eastwards in a similar 'Elizabethan' style. Dining room, library and drawing room became Committee Room 1, Members' Retiring Room and Mayoress's Parlour, and to them were added a Council Chamber, Mayor's Parlour and Robing Room under a public gallery. Fred Plaxton, the master carpenter and founder of Plaxton's, the coach-building company, was commissioned for the Council Chamber's panelling. Scarborough's new Town Hall, a conspicuous improvement on its predecessor in Castle Road's Court House, was officially opened by Princess Henry of Battenberg in 1903. On the same day she also unveiled a statue of her mother, Queen Victoria, in St Nicholas Gardens.

St Nicholas Gardens, opened in 1899, were Harry Smith's first successful enterprise in converting a private into a public amenity. Woodall's grounds were laid out in terraces connected by steps and winding footpaths which minimised the steep gradient. Seats and shelters were placed along the pathways and at the foot of the slope, overlooking Foreshore Road, a stone balcony with seats and a central flight of steps were built for viewing and access.

As early as 1889 Scarborough Corporation had bought a bare, windswept, four-acre hill site overlooking the south side of Peasholm Gap. Though it was re-named Alexandra Field in honour of the Princess of Wales, no use had yet been found for it: part had become a children's playground, part a donkey-grazing close, and part allotments. However, during the winter of 1907-8, under Smith's direction and supervision, the whole area was transformed into two bowling greens, three tennis courts and, at the southern end, an open-air concert theatre. To provide shelter for players and spectators, as well as a variety of trees, shrubs and flowers, the northern and eastern sides were protected by high earth embankments. Alexandra Field had become Alexandra Gardens.

However, after the wet summer of 1909, the borough engineer proposed that a glass roof should be put over the apron stage and front seats of the theatre. In the teeth of 'strenuous opposition' from ratepayers and all three of the North Ward councillors, and at a cost of £3,000, the new roof was erected in three months. The Floral Hall, as the concert pavilion now became, opened in July 1910. Two years later, further extensions and additions were made to the building to increase covered seating for 1,500. Altogether the gardens and hall had cost the ratepayer less than £10,000, and at the end of the 1913 season receipts exceeded the annual costs of upkeep and loan charges.

Alexandra Gardens and the Floral Hall were jewels in

Scarborough's crown, but Peasholm Park was the brightest and best of all Smith's many creations. In 1911 the Duchy of Lancaster was pleased to sell to the Corporation a swampy area—part of the royal manor of Northstead—then occupied by allotments, fishermen's nets and pigs, and known as Tucker's Field. In the middle of it was a natural, barren mound, 43 feet high, called Peasholm Hill. By that time Smith's plans for the unpromising site were well advanced: as early as December 1910 about a hundred otherwise unemployed local men were set to work with picks, shovels and wheelbarrows digging out what was to be a natural lake fed by Peasholm Beck. Money ran out in February 1911 and the work was not resumed until the following winter. The lakeland park was finally opened by the mayoress in June 1912.

Smith's design of a water park and pleasure garden was the product of a landscape artist of imaginative genius. The wooden humpback bridge to the island, boathouse, shelter and landing stage were all constructed in a Japanese style and the whole effect was that of a willow-pattern plate. Yet the overall cost was minimal: even with the 20 rowing boats and Indian canoes for the lake, it came to little more than £2,000. Still, the Peasholm Park of 1912 was only the beginning. Though interrupted by the 1914-18 war and its austere financial aftermath, Smith's long-term vision was gradually implemented and augmented. Bare hillsides were eventually covered with trees and flower beds; an aviary for British and exotic birds was built on the lakeside; and it was soon followed by a large cafe, public shelter and lavatories. Finally, in 1929, the island that had once been Peasholm Hill was given a waterfall plunging into the lake and a pagoda to crown its summit.

By that time another of Smith's wonderful transformations had taken place: in 1924 Wilson's Wood, a ravine wilderness, was converted into The Glen, a woodland walk along the course of Peasholm Beck. The ravine was so deep and narrow that the bottom had to be raised for the footpath and bridges over the beck. John Woodall's old plantation of trees on Barrow Cliff was preserved and to them were added many more specimens of plants and shrubs, all labelled with their botanical names and places of origin.

After mayoress Mrs Good had opened Peasholm Park in June 1912 she received a bouquet of carnations from Harry Smith's daughter Margaret and then, with a numerous party of Town Hall dignitaries, she tried out one of the lake boats. Afterwards, she walked to North Bay promenade to untie another white ribbon and declare the opening of the country's first beach bungalows.

The development of Peasholm undercliff in 1911-12 was yet another of Smith's successful works. The land had been bought from the Crown at the same time as Tucker's Field, but the boulder-clay cliffs overlooking North Bay had first to be stabilised with drainage pipes, footpaths and reinforced terraces. Further support was provided by a concrete promenade buttressed by a stout sea wall. Then, behind and above the promenade were built 46 wooden beach bungalows and 40 bathing boxes, cold shower baths, lavatories and three public shelters. Previously, North-Bay bathers had only a few horse-drawn machines to change in; now, thanks to Smith's enterprise, they had facilities to surpass those of the South Bay foreshore. Within a few years most English seaside holiday resorts had copied his pioneer shore-line chalets.

Peasholm promenade, along with the Marine Drive, Alexandra Gardens and Peasholm Park, had taken the town far beyond its former northern limits; but simultaneously Harry Smith was also busy extending Scarborough southwards. In 1910 he persuaded his employers to purchase six acres of the undercliff between the South Cliff tramway and the Belvedere Rose Garden from the Cliff Bridge Company, then owners of the Spa. Two years later, the Corporation bought George Lord Beeforth's own Belvedere Rose Garden and his woodland beyond it, so that for the sum total of £10,500 the borough now owned all the undercliff south of the Cliff tramway as far as Holbeck.

Again, the precipitous clay slopes had to be drained, terraced with strong retaining walls and provided with stone steps and tarmacked footpaths. Beeforth's private Rose Garden was removed and replaced with Smith's public Italian Gardens which gave full scope to his unrivalled talent for landscape design. Furnished with teak seats, sheltered on the seaward side with larch poles and oak lattices, and surrounded by shrubs and rockeries, Smith's new rose beds were approached on two sides by flights of stone steps and flanked by pergola shelters. A graceful lead figure of Mercury stood on a pedestal in the middle of a circular lily pond. The borough engineer had one of his young assistants pose on the pedestal while he viewed him from all angles. The Italian Gardens were first opened to the public in the summer of 1914; as with Alexandra Gardens, Peasholm Park and The Glen, there was no admission charge.

Meanwhile, Smith had been working on his next major building project. Though the Corporation had obtained parliamentary permission to construct a bathing pool on the sea shore as early as 1900, it was not until after the purchase of the Esplanade undercliff that he had a perfect site for his plans. Work started in 1913, and despite the outbreak of war and the German bombardment of 1914, the finished pool was opened by the mayor, Alderman Christopher Graham, in July 1915.

Smith got his idea of an open-air, sea-water, tidal swimming pool from one he saw in Guernsey, but Scarborough's was the first of its kind in Britain. One hundred metres long and over fifty metres wide, the pool held nearly two million gallons of fresh salt water and cost about £5,000 to build. The outer concrete sea wall was low enough to allow the incoming high tide to flow into the pool and wide enough to serve as a promenade for bathers and a platform for spectators. On the landward side there was another promenade for the general public which also gave access to the changing areas. Here there were 76 'boxes for gentlemen' and 61 'for ladies', hot and cold showers, lavatories, and rooms for first-aid and pool attendants. Behind and above these Smith cut a series of terraces into the steep cliffside to support a cafe and rows of beach bungalows similar to those already in North Bay.

Scarborough's original sea-water, open-air swimming pool proved a major success. During the 1920s and 1930s Blackpool, Margate, Folkestone, Ramsgate and other resorts copied it. Until the 1960s, when bathing in the tepid, placid waters of the Mediterranean was preferred, the South Bay pool remained one of Scarborough's most popular and, for the Town Hall, most profitable, entertainments. Not least of the benefits of the South Bay pool was that it afforded effective and permanent buttressing to the base of a notoriously unstable undercliff. By the beginning of the twenty-first century, without it there would have been no South Cliff gardens and perhaps no Esplanade above them.

The South Bay pool was not the only one of Harry Smith's sea defence and cliff protection schemes. In the immediate post-war years there were serious undercliff movements in both North and South Bays. The Clarence Gardens, laid out between 1886 and 1890, were casualties of the landslip of the winter of 1921-2, and to save Queen's Parade it was urgently necessary to stabilise the undercliff below it. At the same time, in 1923, the Royal Albert Drive had to be buttressed to minimise further outward movement of the road and promenade. Similarly, on the South side, beyond the South Bay pool, the cliffs had to be shored up to protect the town's Holbeck Gardens.

Smith's concerns, however, were not only coastal defence: a long-term project he valued highly was the conversion of Scarborough Mere. This freshwater lake, once forty acres in extent covering much of Burton Dale, had by 1900 shrunk to a quarter of that area. Its only recreational use was as a skating rink for townspeople when severe winter weather iced over its shallow muddy waters. Nevertheless, the borough engineer saw its potential as another lakeland park and pleasure garden for visitors as well as residents; and he also saw how Scarborough's refuse could be put to practical use.

Slowly but surely, though interrupted by the 1914-18 war, the transformation took place. The Mere was widened, deepened, extended southwards and surrounded with shrubs and trees. Town rubbish was tipped between the water and the Scarborough-York railway line, covered with spoil excavated from the lake extension, and then planted with a screen of trees. The area of water was doubled in size to twenty acres. In 1913 the Council fitted out a small fleet of rowing boats and canoes and built a landing stage, boathouse and cafe on the northern shore. The Mere was stocked with coarse fish and anglers charged sixpence a day. The finishing touches to Scarborough Mere were not applied until 1923, but long before then Smith had the satisfaction of describing his creation as 'a sound venture financially', as well as a beautiful improvement of the principal approach to the town by road and rail.

The completion of the Mere in 1923 coincided with the unveiling of Scarborough's War Memorial. Senior borough councillors had almost come to blows with each other over what form the memorial should take and where it ought to be located. Sir Meredith Whittaker, proprietor of the *Evening News* and *Mercury* and mayor 1919-21, was a sturdy advocate of a 'Temple of Remembrance' designed by the native architect Sir Edwin Cooper. They wanted it to be put in Valley Gardens. In brave opposition to this proposal, Harry Smith submitted his own plan of a stone obelisk, nearly 23 metres high, to stand on the summit of Oliver's Mount, where it would be clearly visible from all parts of Scarborough. Fortunately, in the end, the War Memorial Committee wisely accepted Smith's submission.

Whittaker and Smith had disagreed about the War Memorial, but as far as the further development of Scarborough's North Side was concerned they were in perfect harmony. In 1925 the pre-war North Bay promenade was extended northwards as far as Peasholm Dale, and at its southern end, in Peasholm Gap, the Council opened its Corner Cafe. This was much more than a beachside tea house: with its ballroom for dances and concerts, bar and restaurant, the Corner became one of the Corporation's most lucrative investments in holiday catering and entertainment. At this time also more improvements were made to Peasholm Park and in 1930 a cliff tramway, Scarborough's fourth, was built to link Alexandra Gardens with North Bay promenades and the Corner Cafe.

Harry Smith's parting gift to Scarborough was Northstead Manor Gardens. During the 1920s the Corporation had acquired the remainder of the Northstead Manor estate from the Crown, but the area north of Peasholm Park was undeveloped, occupied only by a holiday camp, allotments and the North Cliff golf course straddling Burniston Road. However, between 1928 and 1932, under Smith's capable direction, the whole of the land between Burniston Road and the North Bay undercliff was totally transformed.

The first stage of Harry Smith's ambitious North Bay Pleasure Gardens was finished for the summer season of 1929. On the hill top between Mickledale and the North Bay promenade the Council opened ten tennis courts, an open-air roller-skating rink and a cafe. A year later, councillors agreed to Smith's remaining proposals for the site—a miniature railway and a boating lake with water chute surrounded by paths and gardens. As in the case of Peasholm Park 20 years earlier, local unemployed labourers were put to work excavating the lake and laying the North Bay railway.

What was known disparagingly by some sceptics as 'the Borough Engineer's Toy', the miniature diesel locomotive called *Neptune*, pulled the first open passenger coaches out of Peasholm station in May 1931. Such was the immediate appeal of Scarborough's new railway that ran nearly a mile from Peasholm to Scalby Mills, that in 1932 another exact scale model of the LNER's Gresley engines, named *Triton*, joined *Neptune*. In its first season, the North Bay railway had carried almost half a million passengers and made nearly £4,000 net profit. So much for the borough engineer's 'toy'!

Some dispute still survives about which Council officer was first responsible for testing the acoustics of Mickledale and appreciating that here was a natural amphitheatre. According to one account, the credit goes to George Horrocks, entertainments manager; according to another, it was Harry Smith himself who hit upon the idea of turning Mickledale into an open-air theatre. More to the point, it was the borough engineer who drew up the design plans for what became Britain's most famous, outdoor theatre with seating for 7,000. From its initial performance in July 1932 of 'Merrie England' every summer until 'Bohemian Girl' in 1939, Scarborough's Operatic and Dramatic Society staged a succession of musical operas to full audiences. Unhappily, Smith did not live to witness the resumption of performances after the war in 1945, but it is fortunate that he died long before the theatre went out of fashion in the 1960s and was finally abandoned by the Council in the 1980s.

The outdoor theatre had been opened by London's lord mayor and at the same time his wife was invited to do the same service for Harry Smith's new Glen or Northstead Bridge, the final piece in his strategy to bring Scarborough and the North Side into the age of the motor vehicle. The first piece had been the Valley Bridge, which had belonged to the Corporation since 1891 and been toll-free since 1919, but was too narrow and weak for two-way motor traffic. The work of widening and strengthening the Victorian bridge took three years. Most of the cost was borne by central government. It was therefore fitting that the opening ceremony in July 1928 was performed by Mrs Ashley, wife of the Minister of Transport.

The next stage, which involved cutting a dual carriageway from Valley Bridge northwards to Columbus Ravine and thence North Bay, encountered more local resistance than Harry Smith had faced since the Floral Hall. The borough engineer's formidable ally, Alderman Meredith Whittaker, had died in 1931, but by the date of Smith's retirement in October 1933, the new road called Northway had reached the head of Columbus Ravine, gateway to Peasholm Park and the North Side.

Such were some of the major achievements of Harry William Smith. During his 36 years as the borough's engineer and surveyor he had spent about a million pounds of ratepayers' money and increased the town's area of public pleasure grounds from 55 to 350 acres. What he had done to make Scarborough a paradise for visiting holiday-makers was unrivalled, yet what he had also done for its resident population was just as important.

Smith was mainly responsible for carrying out the borough's earliest slum clearance and house-building schemes. After the 1914-18 war the Council began to demolish the most unfit domestic properties in the old town and re-house their occupants on the new Edgehill estate off Seamer Road. By 1933 compulsory purchase orders were beginning to clear whole streets, such as Cross and Dumple, and replace them on the same site with modern homes. Outdoor pail closets, once so common in old Scarborough, gave way to indoor flush toilets. Five years later, commenting on the town's slum demolition and house-building record, the Emeritus Professor of Town Planning at London University wrote: 'Scarborough has done well.'

In addition to his principal responsibility for Northway and Columbus Ravine, Smith also carried out many other road-building and road-widening plans, such as Woodland Ravine, Aberdeen Walk, North Marine Road and Valley Road, which were designed to ease traffic movement through the town. During Smith's long career horses and carts gave way to trams and they in turn to motor coaches and cars. Though Peasholm Park, the Glen, Northstead Manor and South Cliff Gardens were his pre-eminent creations, other smaller gardens, such as West Square and Prince of Wales, and the Castle Dykes and Holms, owe their ordered lay-out to his designs. During his retirement he also designed the extensive grounds and gardens of Scarborough hospital which opened in 1936. Though no sportsman himself, Smith was concerned to provide outdoor facilities of every kind to meet the needs of residents as well as summer visitors. Golfers, tennis-players, roller-skaters and bowlers were all indebted to him. For example, Manor Road crown bowling green, Scarborough's oldest, dating from 1902, was the result of Smith's response to local requests for a full-size playing area. Finally, he also had a hand in the design of some of Scarborough's best buildings, such as the North Cliff Golf clubhouse, the sanatorium on Cross Lane, and the electricity showrooms in Westborough.

But Harry Smith's greatest affection was for trees and flowers. As he once said to one of his juniors: 'If you do nothing else, whenever you can, plant a tree. It will be there when you have gone.' In some cases, nearly a hundred years later, many of his trees are still standing—around the Mere, on the slopes of Oliver's Mount, in the Glen, along Woodland Ravine and down Columbus Ravine. As for his flowers, their descendants are still raised in the nurseries he planted in Manor Road next to his bowling green. Characteristically, in his will he left £50 to the Corporation of Scarborough 'either for planting bulbs on the roadsides and open spaces or in commencing planting of azaleas and rhododendrons along the roadway through Raincliff Woods.'

Harry Smith was a friendly, quiet, unpretentious man. To many he became a familiar figure—small, neat, quick-moving, usually wearing an open overcoat, one hand in trouser pocket, the other brandishing a walking-stick, and a hand-rolled cigarette dangling from his lips. At Council meetings he said little unless asked; as members droned on he sketched birds, flowers, butterflies and his favourite drawing subject, peacocks. His hobbies were building wireless sets, fresh-water fishing, and growing begonias in his own greenhouse. He offered a shilling to anyone who could find a weed in his lawn at Beverley Lodge, 41 Westbourne Grove. No one ever did.

On his retirement at the age of 65, Harry Smith was presented with a gift from his staff and private well-wishers of six Chippendale chairs and a cheque for £309. No formal appreciation of his service during the past 36 years was recorded in the minutes of the Council and no celebration of his achievement was organised by the Town Hall. Still, Harry Smith needed no blue plaque: he was a landscape artist of rare genius whose creativity had transformed Scarborough into a pleasure garden by the sea.

GLOSSARY

Alure	Walk or passage along the top of a castle wall
Attainder	A person condemned to death or outlawry for treason also forfeited his personal and real estate and his right to inherit or transmit property and title
Chapter	The governing body of a cathedral or religious house
Demesne	Land held directly and not sub-let to tenants
Fee-farm	Annual cash payment to the Crown in return for corporate privileges of a borough
Hauberk	Coat of chain mail
Mark	Medieval English money worth two-thirds of a pound, or 13 shillings and fourpence, about 66p.
Messuage	A dwelling-house with surrounding land
Solar	Literally, the sun room - the upper, private apartment in a medieval keep or hall
Stank/Stew	Fish pond
Tithe	Annual tax of one tenth of goods or produce levied by the parish church to pay for the upkeep of the building and its clergy
Warren	Small ground game such as rabbits and hares
Whin	Gorse or furze valued as fuel. Scarborough has a Whin Bank

BIBLIOGRAPHY

Chapter 1

Arnold M, 'The Legendary Origins of Scarborough' in Crouch D & Pearson T (eds), *Medieval Scarborough* (Leeds, 2001)
Baker J B, *The History of Scarbrough* (1882)
Binns A L, 'Anglo-Saxon and Viking Scarborough to 966' in Edwards M (ed.), *Scarborough 966-1966* (Scarborough, 1966)
Gordon E V, 'Scarborough and Flamborough', *Acta Philologica Scandinavica*, 1 (Copenhagen, 1925)
Hinderwell T, *The History and Antiquities of Scarborough* (York, 1811, Scarborough, 1832)
Smith A H, *The Place-Names of the West Riding of Yorkshire* (1910)
Page W (ed.), *Victoria County History of Yorkshire: North Riding*, II (1923)
Rowntree A (ed.), *The History of Scarborough* (1931)
Smith A H, *The Place-Names of the North Riding of Yorkshire* (Cambridge, 1969)

Chapter 2

Binns A L, 'Scarborough 1066' in Edwards M (ed.), *Scarborough 966-1066* (Scarborough, 1966)
Brooks F W, *The Battle of Stamford Bridge* (East Yorkshire Local History Society 6, 1956)
Faull M & Stinson M (eds), *Domesday Book: Yorkshire* (Chichester, 1986)
Hey D, *Yorkshire from AD 1000* (1986)
Lloyd A, *The Year of the Conqueror* (1966)
Magnusson M & Palsson H (trans.), *King Harald's Saga* (1966)
McLynn F, *1066: The Year of the Three Battles* (1998)

Chapter 3

Bond E A (ed.), *Chronicon Monasterii de Melsa* I (Rolls Series, 1866)
Brown R A, 'Royal Castle-building in England', *English Historical Review* 70 (July, 1955)
Clark J, 'Scarborough Castle', *The Archaeological Journal* 154 (1997)
Colvin H M (ed.), *The History of the King's Works* II (HMSO, 1963)

Dalton P, 'The Foundation and Development of Scarborough in the Twelfth Century' in Crouch D & Pearson T (eds), *Medieval Scarborough* (Leeds, 2001)
English B, *The Lords of Holderness 1086-1260* (Oxford, 1979)
Farrer W (ed.), *Early Yorkshire Charters* I (1914)
Howlett R (ed.), *Historia Rerum Anglicarum* in *Chronicles of the Reigns of Stephen, Henry II and Richard I*, I (1884)
Page W (ed.), *Victoria County History of Yorkshire, North Riding*, II (1923)
Pearson T, *Scarborough Castle* (Royal Commission on the Historical Monuments of England, Survey Report, 1999)
Rowntree A (ed.), *The History of Scarborough* (1931)

Chapter 4

Brown R A, 'Royal Castle-building in England 1154-1216', *English Historical Review* 70 (July 1955)
Clark J, 'Scarborough Castle', *The Archaeological Journal* 154 (1997)
Crouch D, 'Church Life in Medieval Scarborough' in Crouch D & Pearson T (eds), *Medieval Scarborough* (2001)
Holt J C, *The Northerners* (Oxford, 1961)
Rowntree A (ed.), *The History of Scarborough* (1931)
Rushton J H, 'Scarborough 1166-1366' in Edwards M (ed.), *Scarborough 966-1966* (Scarborough, 1966)
Talbot C H, 'Citeaux and Scarborough', *Studia Monastica* 2 (1960)

Chapter 5

Brown W (ed.), *Yorkshire Inquisitions*, 4 vols, Yorkshire Archaeological Society Record Series, 1892-1906
Calendar of Close Rolls
Calendar of Inquisitions Miscellaneous
Calendar of Patent Rolls
Childs W R, 'Mercantile Scarborough', in Crouch D & Pearson T (eds), *Medieval Scarborough* (2001)
English B (ed.), *Yorkshire Hundred and Quo Warranto Rolls*, Yorkshire Archaeological Society Record Series, CLI (1996)
Jeayes I H (ed.), *Copy Translations of Charters etc* (1912)
_____(cal.) *Description of the Documents contained in the White Vellum Book* (Scarborough, 1914)

Rushton J H, 'Scarborough 1166-1366', in Edwards M (ed.), *Scarborough 966-1966* (Scarborough, 1966)

Chapter 6

Binns J, 'Did Scarborough Burn?', in *Transactions of Scarborough Archaeological and Historical Society* 35 (1999)
Bond E A (ed.), *Chronica Monasterii de Melsa* II (1868)
Calendar of Close Rolls
Calendar of Fine Rolls
Calendar of Patent Rolls
Denholm-Young N (ed.), *Vita Edwardi Secundi* (1957)
Hamilton J S, *Piers Gaveston, Earl of Cornwall 1307—1312* (Detroit, Michigan, USA, 1988)
Jeffrey R W, *Thornton-le-Dale* (Wakefield, 1931)
Luard H R (ed.), *Flores Historiarum*, Rolls Series, iii (1890)
McKisack M, *The Fourteenth Century 1307-1399* (Oxford, 1959)
Stubbs W (ed.), *Chronicles of the Reigns of Edward I and Edward II*, Rolls Series, ii (1883)

Chapter 7

Calendar of Close Rolls
Calendar of Inquisitions Miscellaneous
Calendar of Patent Rolls
Childs W R, 'Mercantile Scarborough' in Crouch D & Pearson T (eds), *Medieval Scarborough* (2001)
Dobson R B (ed.), *The Peasants' Revolt of 1381* (1970)
_____ 'The Risings in York, Beverley and Scarborough 1380-1' in Hilton R H & Ashton T H (eds), *The English Rising of 1381* (Cambridge, 1984)
Hinderwell T, *The History and Antiquities of Scarborough* (Scarborough, 1832)
Jeayes I H (ed.), *Copy Translations of Charters etc* (1912)
_____ (cal.), *Description of the Documents in the White Vellum Book* (Scarborough, 1914)
Roskell J S et al (eds), *The House of Commons 1386—1421*, 4 vols (1992)
Rowntree A (ed.), *The History of Scarborough* (1931)

Thompson E (trans.), *Scarborough Wills*, 3 vols, Scarborough Central Library, 1931
York Probate Registers, Borthwick Institute of Historical Research, York

Chapter 8

Binns J, 'The Oldest Map of Scarborough', *Transactions of Scarborough Archaeological and Historical Society* 25 (1983)
Calendar of Patent Rolls
Chandler J (ed.), *John Leland's Itinerary. Travels in Tudor England* (Stroud, Glos., 1993)
Cottonian MSS, Aug. I, ii,1, British Library
Gillingham J (ed.), *Richard III, A Medieval Kingship* (1993)
Horrox R & Hammond P W (eds), *British Library Harleian Manuscript 433*, 4 vols (Upminster and London, 1979-83)
Jeayes I H (ed.), *Copy Translations of Charters etc* (1912)
_____ (cal.) *Description of the Documents in the White Vellum Book* (Scarborough, 1914)
Murray H, *Scarborough, York and Leeds. The Town Plans of John Cossins 1697- 1743* (York, 1997)
Richmond C F, 'English Naval Power in the Fifteenth Century', *History* 52 (1967)
Ross C, *Richard III* (1981)
Seward D, *Richard III, England's Black Legend* (1983)
Somerville R, *History of the Duchy of Lancaster 1265—1603*, i (1953)
Toulmin Smith L (ed.), *The Itinerary of John Leland*, i (1914)

Chapter 9

Bindoff S T (ed.), *The House of Commons 1509-1558*, 3 vols (1982)
Binns J, 'Scarborough and the Pilgrimage of Grace', *Transactions of Scarborough Archaeological and Historical Society* 33 (1997)
Brewer J S *et al* (eds), *Letters and Papers, Foreign and Domestic, of the Reign of Henry VIII*, 21 vols (1862-1932)
Dickens A G, *Lollards and Protestants in the Diocese of York, 1509-1558* (Oxford, 1959)
Dodds M H & R, *The Pilgrimage of Grace 1536-7 and the Exeter Conspiracy 1538,* 2 vols (Cambridge, 1915)
Hinderwell T, *The History and Antiquities of Scarborough* (Scarborough, 1832)

Hoyle R W, *The Pilgrimage of Grace and the Politics of the 1530s* (Oxford, 2001)
Jeayes I H (cal.), *Description of Documents in the White Vellum Book* (Scarborough, 1914)
Raine J et al (eds), *Testamenta Eboracensia*, 6 vols, Surtees Society (1836-1902)
Rowntree A (ed.), *The History of Scarborough* (1931)
York Probate Registers, Borthwick Institute of Historical Research, York

Chapter 10

Ashcroft M Y (ed.), *Scarborough Records 1600-1660*, 2 vols (Northallerton, 1991)
Baker J B, *The History of Scarbrough* (1882)
Binns J, 'Scarborough versus Seamer: An Elizabethan Tale of Market Forces', *Transactions of Scarborough Archaeological and Historical Society,* 34 (1998)
Calendar of Patent Rolls
Calendar of State Papers Domestic
Chapman J (trans.), Scarborough Records, 3 vols, Scarborough Central Library, 1909
Clay C T (ed.), *Yorkshire Deeds* VIII, Yorkshire Archaeological Society Record Series CII (1940)
Gooder A (ed.), *The Parliamentary Representation of the County of York 1258-1832*, II, Yorkshire Archaeological Society Record Series XCVI (1937)
Hasler P W (ed.), *The House of Commons 1558-1603*, 3 vols (1981)
Hinderwell T, *The History and Antiquities of Scarborough* (1832)
Rowntree A (ed.), *The History of Scarborough* (1931)
Salisbury (Cecil) Manuscripts, Historical Manuscripts Commission
Scarborough Corporation records, DC/SCB, North Yorkshire County Record Office, Northallerton

Chapter 11

Anon., 'Danby v. Sydenham: A Restoration Chancery Suit', *Yorkshire Archaeological Journal* XVII (1903)
Ashcroft M Y (ed.), *Scarborough Records 1600-1660*, 2 vols (Northallerton, 1991)

Binns J, *A Place of Great Importance: Scarborough in the Civil Wars* (Preston, 1996)
Cross C M, *The Puritan Earl* (1966)
Diary of Lady Margaret Hoby, MS Egerton 2614, British Library
Hackness estate documents, ZF, North Yorkshire County Record Office, Northallerton
Hasler P W (ed.), *The House of Commons 1558-1603*, 3 vols (1981)
Heal F, 'Reputation and Honour in Court and Country: Lady Elizabeth Russell and Sir Thomas Hoby', *Transactions of the Royal Historical Society* 6th series, VI (1996)
Historical Manuscripts Commission Reports: *De L'Isle MSS*, II, 77 (1934); *Salisbury (Cecil) MSS*, VI, VII, IX, X, XII, XIV, XV
Meads D M (ed.), *The Diary of Lady Margaret Hoby of Hackness 1599-1605* (1930)
Moody J (ed.), *The Private Life of an Elizabethan Lady* (Stroud, 1998)
Register of the Parish of Hackness, Yorkshire Parish Register Society (1926)
Slack P, 'Lady Margaret Hoby 1571-1633', Nicholls C S (ed.), *Missing Persons, Dictionary of National Biography* (Oxford, 1993)
Star Chamber records, STAC 5, Public Record Office
Walker J W (ed.), *Hackness Manuscripts and Accounts*, Yorkshire Archaeological Society Record Series XCV (1938)

Chapter 12

Ashcroft M Y (ed.), *Scarborough Records 1600-1660*, 2 vols (Northallerton. 1991)
Baker J B, *The History of Scarbrough* (1882)
Binns J, 'Mr and Mrs Farrer', *Transactions of Scarborough Archaeological and Historical Society* 26 (1988)
Clay J W (ed.), *Dugdale's Visitation of Yorkshire*, II (Exeter, 1907)
Foord S (ed.), The Scarborough Municipal Charities, unpub. typescript, Scarborough Central Library, Scarborough Room (1943)
Gent T, *History of Hull* (Hull, 1869)
Hinderwell T, *The History and Antiquities of Scarborough* (1832)
Jeayes I H (ed.), *Copy Translations of Charters etc* (1912)
_____ (cal.), *Description of Documents in the White Vellum Book* (Scarborough, 1914)
Norcliffe C B (ed.), Paver's Marriage Licences, V, *Yorkshire Archaeological Journal* X (1889)

Rowntree A (ed.), *The History of Scarborough* (1931)
Scarborough Corporation records, DC/SCB, North Yorkshire County Record Office, Northallerton
Scarborough St Mary's churchwardens' records 1607-1698, PE 165/241, East Riding County Record Office, Beverley
Scarborough St Mary's parish register, bishops' transcripts, 1602-1682, MIC 5582, Scarborough Central Library
Whittaker M, *The Book of Scarbrough Spaw* (Buckingham, 1984)
Wittie R, *Scarbrough Spaw* (York, 1660, 1667)

Chapter 13

Ashcroft M Y (ed.), *Scarborough Records 1600-1660*, 2 vols (Northallerton, 1991)
Binns J, *A Place of Great Importance. Scarborough in the Civil Wars* (Preston, 1996)
_____ (ed.), *The Memoirs and Memorials of Sir Hugh Cholmley of Whitby 1600-1657*, Yorkshire Archaeological Society Record Series, CLIII (2000)
Commons Journals
Historical Manuscripts Commission Reports:
Bouverie MSS (1887)
Lord Braye MSS (1877)
Portland MSS (1891)
Ormonde MSS (1903)
Newsbooks, I, *Oxford Royalist* i-iv (1971)
Scarborough Corporation records, DC/SCB, North Yorkshire County Record Office, Northallerton
Thomason Tracts, British Library

Chapter 14

Anderson R C (ed.), *The Journal of Edward Mountagu, first Earl of Sandwich 1659-65,* Navy Records Society LXIV (1929)
Ashcroft M Y (ed.), *Scarborough Records 1600—1660*, 2 vols (Northallerton, 1991)
Binns J, 'Sir John Lawson: Scarborough's Admiral of the Red', *Northern History* XXXII (1996)
Calendar of State Papers Domestic
Calendar of State Papers Venetian

Capp B S, *Cromwell's Navy. The Fleet and the English Revolution 1648-1660* (Oxford, 1989)
Commons Journals
Davies G, *The Restoration of Charles II* (Oxford, 1955)
Dictionary of National Biography
Firth C H, *The Last Years of the Protectorate 1656-58* (1909)
Gardiner S R, *The History of the Commonwealth and Protectorate 1649-1660*, 3 vols (1894—1903)
Gardiner S R & Atkinson C T (eds), *Letters and Papers Relating to the First Dutch War*, 6 vols, Navy Records Society (1899-1930)
Historical Manuscripts Commission:
Sixth Report (1877)
Heathcote MSS (1899)
Hodgkin MSS (1897)
Leyborne-Popham MSS (1899)
Latham R C & Matthews W (eds), *The Diary of Samuel Pepys*, vols i—vi (1983)
Letter Book of Sir Hugh Cholmley (1632—89), ZCG, North Yorkshire County Record Office, Northallerton
Mariner's Mirror
Scarborough Corporation records, DC/SCB, North Yorkshire County Record Office, Northallerton
Scrope R & Monkhouse T (eds), *Clarendon State Papers*, 3 vols (Oxford, 1786)
State Papers, SP 18 (Interregnum); SP 46 (Navy Papers 1649—60), Public Record Office
Thomason Tracts, British Library

Chapter 15

Ashcroft M Y (ed.), *Scarborough Records 1600-1660* 2 vols (Northallerton, 1991)
Ashley M, *John Wildman, Plotter and Postmaster* (1947)
Baker J B, *The History of Scarbrough* (1882)
Binns J, *The History of Scarborough* (Pickering, 2001)
Fletcher J S, *Yorkshiremen of the Restoration* (1921)
Hill C, *The World Turned Upside Down* (1972)
Hutton R, *The Restoration* (Oxford, 1985)
Penney N (ed.), *George Fox's Journal* (Cambridge, 1924)
Rowntree A (ed.), *The History of Scarborough* (1931)

Scarborough Corporation records, DC/SCB, North Yorkshire County Record Office, Northallerton
Scarborough St Mary's churchwardens' records 1607-1698, PE 165/241, East Riding County Record Office, Beverley
Thompson E (ed.), *Scarborough Wills*, 3 vols, Scarborough Room, Central Library, Scarborough

Chapter 16

Binns J, *A Place of Great Importance. Scarborough in the Civil Wars* (Preston, 1996)
____ *The History of Scarborough* (Pickering, 2001)
Clay J W (ed.), *Dugdale's Visitation of Yorkshire*, III (Exeter, 1917)
Corbin A, *The Lure of the Sea* (1995)
Hembry P, *The English Spa* 1560-1815 (1990)
Simpson W, *Hydrologica Chemica* (1669)
_____ *History of Scarbrough-Spaw* (1679)
Tunstall G, *Scarbrough Spaw Spagyrically Anatomised* (1670)
_____ *A New-Year's Gift for Dr Witty* (1672)
Whittaker M, *The Book of Scarbrough Spaw* (Buckingham. 1984)
Wittie R, *Scarbrough Spaw* (1660, 1667)
_____ *Pyrologia Mimica* (1669)
_____ *Scarbrough Spagyrical Anatomiser Dissected* (1672)

Chapter 17

Cliffe J T, *The Yorkshire Gentry from the Reformation to the Civil War* (1969)
Comber T (ed.), *A Book of Instructions, written by the Right Honourable Sir Christopher Wandesforde* (1777)
Fraser A, *The Weaker Vessel* (1984)
Jackson C (ed.), *The Autobiography of Mrs Alice Thornton of East Newton,* Surtees Society LXII (1875)
McCall H B, *Story of the Family of Wandesforde of Kirklington and Castlecomer* (1904)
Wedgwood C V, *Thomas Wentworth, First Earl of Strafford, 1593-1641: A Revaluation* (1961)

Chapter 18

Binns J, *The History of Scarborough* (Pickering, 2001)
Hinderwell T. *The History and Antiquities of Scarborough* (Scarborough, 1832)
London Daily Post, 16 Feb., 17 May 1738
Macky J, *A Journey Through England in Familiar Letters*, 2 vols (1714, 1722)
McIntyre S C, 'Towns as Health and Pleasure Resorts', D.Phil. unpub. thesis, Oxford Univ., 1973
Morris C (ed.), *The Journeys of Celia Fiennes* (1949)
Murray H, *Scarborough, York and Leeds. The Town Plans of John Cossins 1697-1743* (York, 1997)
Scarborough Collector, no.2 (1828)
Scarborough Corporation records, DC/SCB, North Yorkshire County Record Office, Northallerton
Schofield J, *An Historical and Descriptive Guide to Scarborough* (York, 1787)
Taylor J, *A Journey to Edenborough*, ed. Cowan W (Edinburgh, 1903)
Thomson G S (ed.), *Letters of a Grandmother 1732-1735* (1943)
Ward C & Chandler R, *A Journey from London to Scarborough in Several Letters from a Gentleman there* (1734, 1736)
Whittaker M, *The Book of Scarbrough Spaw* (Buckingham, 1984)
Withers letter, *Yorkshire Archaeological Journal* XII (1893)

Chapter 19

Bigland J, *A Topographical and Historical Description of the County of York* (1810)
Bottomley S, *A Sermon on the Death of Hinderwell* (Scarborough, 1825)
Cole J, *Thomas Hinderwell: Memoirs of his Life, Writings and Character* (Scarborough, 1826)
Dictionary of National Biography (WCS, 1891)
Evans B, Memoir of Mr Hinderwell, prefixed to the third edition of T Hinderwell, *The History and Antiquities of Scarborough* (Scarborough, 1832)
Hinderwell T, *The History and Antiquities of Scarborough* (York, 1798; London, 1811)
Hinderwell's last will: Public Record Office, PCC 578, St Albans (1825). PROB 11/1705 ff.219v.—220v.

St Mary's parish church, Scarborough, registers of baptism, marriage and burial (typescript copies, Scarborough Central Library)

Chapter 20

Annual Register 1802, 1803, 1837
Boyne W, *The Yorkshire Library* (Hull, 1869)
Bragg M, *The Maid of Buttermere* (1987)
Dictionary of National Biography
Hatfield J, *A New Scarborough Guide* (Scarborough, 1797)
Medley C, *Memorials of Scarborough* (1890)
Newspapers: *Carlisle Herald*
  Daily Advertiser
  Morning Post

Chapter 21

Bye J (ed.), The Works of Sir George Cayley, Scarborough Room, Scarborough Central Library
Fairlie G & Cayley E, *The Life of a Genius* (1965)
Gibbs-Smith C H, *Sir George Cayley's Aeronautics 1796-1855* (1962)
Nicholas C S (ed.), *The Dictionary of National Biography. Missing Persons* (1993)
Pritchard J L, *Sir George Cayley* (1961)
Proctor K H, 'Triumph of Reform in Scarborough', unpub. essay, n.d., Scarborough Room, Scarborough Central Library

Chapter 22

Clark M K, *A Gazetteer of Roman Remains in East Yorkshire* (Leeds, 1935)
Dictionary of National Biography
Hall I and Found J, *Cricket at Scarborough* (Derby, 1992)
Mosley C (ed.), *Burke's Peerage and Baronage*, ii (1999)
Roachsmith C, 'Lord Londesborough', *Collectania Antiqua*, V (1860)
Scarborough Evening News
Scarborough Gazette
Scarborough Mercury
Simpson G, 'Seamer Beacon and Scarborough Castle Hill', *Transactions of Scarborough Archaeological and Historical Society*, 33 (1997)

Spratt D A, *Linear Earthworks on the Tabular Hills, North East Yorkshire* (1989)
Taylor R V, *Biographia Leodiensis* (1865)

Chapter 23

Scarborough Evening News
Scarborough Mercury
Scarborough Poll Books, Scarborough Room, Scarborough Central Library
Scarborough Temperance Society records, Scarborough. Room, Scarborough Central Library
Whittaker T, *Life's Battles in Temperance Armour* (1884)
_____ *Brighter England and the Way To It* (1891)

Chapter 24

Blakey J W (ed.), *Some Scarborough Faces* (Scarborough, 1901)
Bradford S, *Sacheverell Sitwell: Splendours and Miseries* (1993)
Scarborough Evening News
Scarborough Mercury
Scarborough Post
Sitwell E, *Taken Care Of* (1965)
Sitwell O, *Before the Bombardment* (1926)
_____ *Autobiography*, 5 vols (1945-50)
The Sitwells (National Portrait Gallery, London, 1994)
Ziegler P, *Osbert Sitwell* (1998)

Chapter 25

Holford P I, *Regional Rowntrees*, Local History Archive Unit 10, Humberside College of Higher Education, Hull (1988)
Robson S E, *Joshua Rowntree* (1916)
Rowntree A (ed.), *The History of Scarborough* (1931)
Scarborough Evening News
Scarborough Mercury
Scarborough Post

Chapter 26

Foord S, 'Harry W Smith: Borough Engineer and Surveyor of Scarborough, 1897-1933', typescript, Scarborough Room, Central Library, 1970
Lord G W, *Scarborough's Floral Heritage* (Scarborough, 1984)
Newspapers: *Scarborough Evening News*
  Scarborough Mercury
Smith H W, 'Catering for the Wants of the Holiday Maker', paper delivered to the Institution of Municipal and County Engineers at Scarborough, 1915, Scarborough Room, Central Library